Harbor Hill, Gothic Room, Sir John Lavery, showing Louise Mackay, Clarence Mackay, and William Mackay, with dog, c. 1926 (Private Collection)

TO LET DOWN, SPACE INSIDE FOR LOCKERS

OPPOSITE FIREPLACE

DOOR TO BEDROOM

BAY INTO HALL

Harbor Hill, Clarence's sitting room, rendering by Davenport & Co *(Private Collection)*

TOWARDS FIREPLACE

Harbor Hill, Clarence's sitting room, rendering by Davenport & Co (Private Collection)

ABOVE AND OPPOSITE *Trinity Church, Roslyn, Long Island* (Jonathan Wallen)

Harbor Hill, Sir John Lavery, Main Hall, with Katherine O'Brien, Clarence and Katherine's granddaughter, c. 1926 (Private Collection)

Portrait of Katherine Mackay by Giovanni Boldini, c. 1905, Oil on canvas (Private Collection)

Study of Katherine Mackay for stained glass window, photo engraving, 1904 (Private Collection)

HARBOR HILL

HARBOR HILL

HARBOR HILL

PORTRAIT OF A HOUSE

RICHARD GUY WILSON

SOCIETY FOR THE PRESERVATION OF LONG ISLAND ANTIQUITIES

IN ASSOCIATION WITH

W. W. NORTON & COMPANY • NEW YORK AND LONDON

Copyright © 2008 by Society for the Preservation of Long Island Antiquities

For information about permission to reproduce selections from this book, write to
Permissions, W. W. Norton & Company, Inc., 500 Fifth Avenue, New York, NY 10110

For information about special discounts for bulk purchases, please contact
W. W. Norton Special Sales at specialsales@wwnorton.com or 800-233-4830

Manufacturing by Friesens
Book design by Jonathan D. Lippincott
Production manager: Leeann Graham

Library of Congress Cataloging-in-Publication Data

Wilson, Richard Guy, 1940-

Harbor Hill : portrait of a house / Richard Guy Wilson. — 1st ed.
    p. cm.
    Includes bibliographical references and index.

ISBN 978-0-393-73216-0 (hardcover)

1. Harbor Hill (Roslyn, N.Y.) 2. White, Stanford, 1853-1906.
3. MacKay, Katherine Duer, 1880-1930—Homes and haunts—New York
(State)—Roslyn. 4. MacKay, Clarence H. (Clarence Hungerford),
1874-1938—Homes and haunts—New York (State)—Roslyn. 5. Mansions—New
York (State)—Roslyn. 6. Lost architecture—New York (State)—Roslyn.
7. Roslyn (N.Y.)—Buildings, structures, etc. I. Title.

NA7615.H37W55 2008

728.809747'245—dc22

2007025479

W. W. Norton & Company, Inc., 500 Fifth Avenue, New York, N.Y. 10110
www.wwnorton.com

W. W. Norton & Company Ltd., Castle House, 75/76 Wells St., London W1T 3QT

1   3   5   7   9   0   8   6   4   2

FRONTISPIECE: *Harbor Hill, colored rendering* (Society for the Preservation of Long Island Antiquities)

To Abby

Contents

❦ ❦

Foreword

❧ ❧

Since the publication of *Long Island Country Houses and Their Architects, 1860–1940* a decade ago (also by W. W. Norton on the Society's behalf), we have often been asked what were the greatest country houses that are no longer extant. Heading the list are always Laurelton Hall, Louis Comfort Tiffany's treasure house in Oyster Bay that burned in 1957, and Harbor Hill, Katherine and Clarence Mackay's McKim, Mead & White masterpiece in Roslyn, which was razed for a housing development in 1947. Although the two rose at close to the same time, they could not have been more different! Laurelton Hall was cloaked in the mysticism of the genius who created it, while Harbor Hill, the castle on the hill of the American dream, was as Stanford White had promised his clients, an estate that with the exception of Biltmore, was without equal, an American ultimate.

Now Laurelton Hall has been revisited in a long-anticipated exhibition at the Metropolitan Museum (2006), and the Society has been pleased to facilitate this critical examination of Harbor Hill, ably undertaken by Richard Guy Wilson, Commonwealth Professor of Architectural History at the University of Virginia, advisor and commentator for the A&E program, "America's Castles," and writer on many aspects of American and modern architecture and art.

This project would not have been possible without the support of the Gerry Charitable Trust, whose founders, Roger and Peggy Gerry, were the late-twentieth-century restorers of historic Roslyn, and its chairman, Huyler C. Held, who can recall walking through the abandoned and vandalized Harbor Hill shortly before its destruction. Nancy Green of W. W. Norton recognized the possibilities in this topic when it was still only an outline and understood how this McKim, Mead & White commission presaged the sea change in taste for European design and masonry construction.

Robert B. MacKay, Ph.D., Director
Society for the Preservation of Long Island Antiquities
Cold Spring Harbor, New York

Acknowledgments

I owe a great debt of gratitude to many individuals and organizations that over the years have assisted my research, opening their doors to me and making helpful suggestions. This book builds on the prior research and scholarship of many individuals, all of whom I hope I have properly acknowledged in the notes. In addition I want to acknowledge the help of Beverly Royce Aulman, Mary Ellin Barrett, W. Bernard Carlson, Jean Mackie Chase, Reverend Margaret Peckham Clark, Wayne Craven, Patty Decourcy, Linda Emmet, Father Gerald Fogerty, Francis Girr, Grace Laundis, Michael Mackay, Jefferson Mansell, Richard Marshall, Pauline Metcalf, Paul Miller, Julie Nicoletta, Elizabeth Peters, Monsignor Thomas J. Shelley, Samuel G. White and Elizabeth White, Barbara Ferris Van Liew, and Chris Verplank.

Thank you, too, to the many students whom I have been lucky to teach over the years and to whose research and scholarship I am indebted. Among them special thanks are due to Lydia Brandt, Heather Massler, Martin Perschler, Elizabeth L O'Leary, Eleanor Pries, and John Tschirch.

Many museums, historic houses, architects' offices, and libraries helped me. I thank these individuals and institutions: Janet Parks, Avery Architectural Library, Columbia University; Myrna L. Sloam, Bryant Library; Kristine Paulus, The New-York Historical Society; Kathryn Totton and Rachel Dolbier, University of Nevada, Reno; Museum of the City of New York; and Nevada Historical Society.

I am especially indebted to Robert B. MacKay, director of the Society for the Preservation of Long Island Antiquities, Lynda Dunn, and the staff. Bob MacKay approached me many years ago concerning McKim, Mead & White's work on Long Island, and has helped greatly over the years.

To Huyler C. Held of the Gerry Foundation of Roslyn, thank you. Finally, I acknowledge Roger and Peggy Gerry, whom I never had the honor of knowing but whose legacy, I hope, is reflected in this book.

HARBOR HILL

Harbor Hill and Its World

❃ ❃

"It is Mr. Mackay's ambition to eclipse all others. The homes of the Vanderbilts, Astors, Whitneys and Goulds are to be nothing in comparison to the splendid place planned by Mr. Mackay."

—Peter Ross, *A History of Long Island*, 1902

IN APRIL 1900, a construction project under way on the North Shore of Long Island had people up and down the East Coast talking. Just twenty-four miles from Manhattan, it would be one of the biggest, most lavish houses they had ever seen. The work in progress, in the Wheatley Hills overlooking the village of Roslyn and Hempstead Harbor on Long Island Sound, would yield a mansion surpassing nearly every private house ever erected in the United States: Harbor Hill.

When Harbor Hill was complete, its sheer massiveness struck awe in approaching visitors. Seated on a terrace that measured 284 by 151 feet, the house was 266 feet wide and 103 feet deep, larger than the Parthenon in Athens. Its central façade, of Indiana blue limestone, stretched 146 feet; the middle of its three pavilions soared upward more than 100 feet. The

great doorway, beneath a huge broken scroll pediment, had at its center a garland-festooned shield bearing the initial "M."

Sited atop the highest point in the area, Harbor Hill stood 378 feet above sea level. Its rooftop offered panoramas to the east of rolling landscapes to the Dix Hills; to the north, across the Long Island Sound toward Westchester County and Connecticut; to the west, the looming towers of New York City; and to the south, beyond Freeport and across the breadth of Long Island, to the Atlantic Ocean sprawling toward Europe.

From the moment the site was purchased by John William Mackay (pronounced Mack'–ee) as a wedding present for his new daughter-in-law, through construction of the main house and afterwards, Harbor Hill and its occupants remained in the public eye. In particular, the cost of the project—designed by Stanford White of the firm of McKim, Mead & White—elicited comment. Rumors flew, especially about the ultimate expenses, which reputedly ran as high as six million dollars. In fact, completing the house, its grounds, and its outbuildings came to just a fraction of that amount, but the total still staggered all but the very richest of the rich. No one took a greater interest

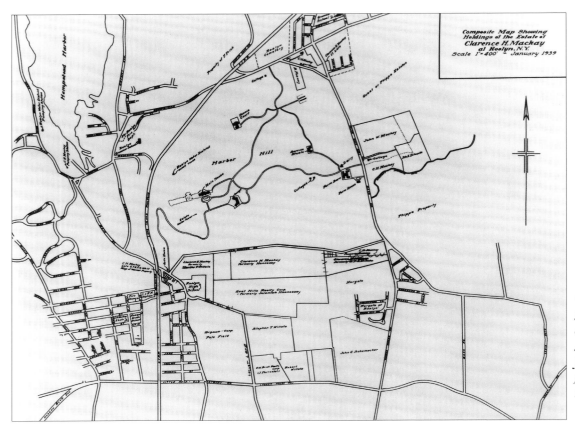

"Composite Map Showing Holdings of Clarence H. Mackay at Roslyn, N.Y.", January 1939 (Society for the Preservation of Long Island Antiquities)

Aerial view of house and stable, c. 1924 (Patterson, American Homes of Today, 1924)

North elevation of house (Museum of the City of New York, McKim, Mead & White Collection)

in this subject than the man paying the bills—John William's son, Clarence Mackay.

Early on in the construction of Harbor Hill the architect wrote to his client, "You must acknowledge that in the end, you will get a pretty fine chateau on the hill, and, with the exception of Biltmore, I do not think there will be an estate equal to it in the country."[1] In White's opinion, his mansion for the Mackays would compare favorably with Richard Morris Hunt's recently completed French Loire Valley chateau, built for George Washington Vanderbilt in Asheville, North Carolina. White was known for his hyperbole, but this prediction was accurate indeed. Harbor Hill became both a standard-setter for the Long Island Gold Coast and one of the most opulent structures ever built in the United States. When the house was completed in 1902, the costs all told came to some $830,000—roughly $20 million in today's dollars— and that was just the beginning.[2] A great deal more would be spent in the ensuing years, both on modifications to the house and on the extraordinary collection of art and antiquities the Mackays amassed.

From the start, Harbor Hill had detractors as well as admirers. Local newspapers publicized the complaints of local residents, who were now banished from what had been a favored picnic site. *House Beautiful* magazine derided Harbor Hill in an article titled, "The Poor Taste of the Rich."[3] *Architectural Record* called the mansion "grandiose and pretentious," pointing to it as an example of the sacrifice of taste for "'stunning' effect."[4] By and large, however, Harbor Hill drew awe and praise from architectural writers and critics. Even as late as 1938, newspapers extolled Harbor Hill as "one of the most beautiful, most spacious, most completely equipped country places in America."[5]

Likewise, the Clarence Mackays themselves lived with intense public scrutiny and judgment. The son of a penniless Irish immigrant who had transformed himself into one of America's wealthiest men, Clarence Mackay and his bride found themselves featured on society pages and in gossip columns throughout their conspicuous (and ultimately disastrous) marriage. Their way of life provided a wealth of material, for

Biltmore, Asheville, NC, Richard Morris Hunt, architect (Library of Congress photo)

"View from Hall Windows. Looking Over Hempstead Harbor, October 1901" (Private Collection)

stores now had unprecedented riches to display. The writer Henry James summed it up: "acquisition, if need be on the highest terms—may, during the years to come, bask here as in a climate it has never before enjoyed. There was money in the air, ever so much money—that was, grossly expressed, the sense of the whole intimation."[6] The period has been characterized variously as the Gilded Age, the Robber Baron era, and the Age of Excess. Revealing a certain self-satisfaction and a desired prominence in western history, some who enjoyed it most called it the American Renaissance.

Along with tremendous amounts of new money came a need to spend which would affect several generations to come.[7] John D. Rockefeller, Cornelius Vanderbilt, and John William Mackay made the initial fortunes, and while they did spend sizable sums, it was their children and in some cases their grandchildren who really caught the acquisition bug. One defined oneself during the Gilded Age by the objects, especially houses, with which one surrounded oneself for the world to see.

both adoring and damning social and cultural commentators and critics.

The Power of Ownership and the Country House

Harbor Hill reflected the confidence of a period of unprecedented American affluence and acquisitiveness. The agony of the Civil War and its aftermath had receded, and the country was enjoying a heady new atmosphere of robustness and self-certainty fueled by massive economic growth. People with fortunes made through canny investments in railroads, the telegraph, textiles, banks, oil fields, silver mines, and department

For the fabulously rich, "conspicuous consumption" (a term coined by University of Chicago economist Thorstein Veblen) provided the pattern for such self-presentation.[8] No symbol expressed more about a person than his house and what he purchased to go in it. Building a grand house that replicated an Italian palazzo or a French chateau, furnishing it with paneling and furniture that had graced an English mansion, and acquiring a Raphael painting and Boucher tapestries announced to all that the owner was cultured, cosmopolitan, and worldly. The upper classes in particular asserted in the objects they bought a right to the cultural legacy of the Old World. Clever entrepreneurs such as Stanford White and Bernard Berenson made a lucrative business of mining historical Europe to glorify their newly rich American patrons.

A powerful current of competition—the urge to outdo one's neighbors and peers—also drove much conspicuous consumption, and the Mackays displayed this competitive spirit in the most grandiose terms with the construction and decoration of Harbor Hill. As the historian Peter Ross wrote in 1902, "The house, which Mr. Mackay has said would be 'his little summer place,' will, as a matter of fact, probably be the most magnificent summer home in America. It is Mr. Mackay's ambition to eclipse all others. The homes of the Vanderbilts, Astors, Whitneys and Goulds are to be nothing in comparison to the splendid place planned by Mr. Mackay."[9]

Harbor Hill was built at what has been considered the apogee of the American country house era, which began in the 1880s and lasted approximately four decades. Behind the fascination with country houses, about which voluminous literature has accumulated, lies a longer history of American involvement with the country house.[10] What exactly constitutes the country house in America is a question marked by complexity and ambiguity. Even the terminology can be confusing. Harbor Hill has been identified variously as a country house, an estate, a place, or a seat, centered unquestionably on a mansion.[11] (The name itself, Harbor Hill, applies to the main house along with its outbuildings and the surrounding estate.)

In his *Dictionary of Architecture and Building* (1901–2), Russell Sturgis, the dean of American architectural writers at the turn of the century, defined the country house as "a residence so far away from a city or large village that it stands free among its outbuildings and dependencies, and is beyond the sidewalks and out of easy reach of the shops, etc., and has to be in a certain sense self-contained." Sturgis also noted that the country house could be considered under a number of reference entries including Castle;

View to south from third floor, overlooking approach drive (Museum of the City of New York, McKim, Mead & White Collection)

A cottage at Montauk, McKim, Mead & White, architects, c. 1882 (Society for the Preservation of Long Island Antiquities)

Chateau; Cottage; Country Seat; Manor House; Schloss; Seat; and Villa.[12]

The plethora of terms results from the different locations and uses of the buildings that came under the rubric of "country house." Country houses fell into at least three categories. A *country place* consisted of a mansion built on land ranging from just a few acres to a hundred acres. A country place always had a stable, and many included a small farming operation; most were reasonably accessible from an urban center. Long Island, northern New Jersey, Westchester County in New York State, and adjacent Connecticut counties—all convenient to New York City and endowed with either attractive shorelines or serene inland landscapes—were especially popular sites for country places. Indeed, all major American metropolises spawned country places—north of Chicago, the western shore of Lake Michigan; the peninsula south of San Francisco; Cape Ann north of Boston; the Berkshires of western Massachusetts; and the Main Line west of Philadelphia.

Then there was the *resort mansion* or *cottage*. Some of the most famous cottages were erected in Newport, Rhode Island; Palm Beach, Florida; and on the New Jersey Shore.[13] In size, numbers of rooms, and appointments, the resort mansion resembled the house of a large country place. But most resort mansions were built on relatively small lots, usually a few acres or less. They were used only at certain times of the year for periods of a few months or weeks, and for such purposes as sailing, enjoying the beach, holding parties, or just getting away from the city.

Associated with the resort mansion, though distinct in setting and land, were the *grand camps* such as those located in upstate New York's Adirondack Mountains. The grand camp served many of the same purposes as the resort mansion, and it was usually comparable in size, but it was sited in wilderness. The extensive land of the grand camps was seldom cultivated except occasionally for logging operations.[14]

A *country mansion* was located on substantial acreage in a rural location and included a full-scale farming operation. Perhaps the paramount example was Biltmore (built 1889–94); though smaller in most respects, Harbor Hill would be a close second in size and scope. Erected on 125,000 acres at the head of the Great Smoky Mountains, Biltmore was a great French chateauesque structure with 225 rooms, surrounded by extensive formal and informal gardens.[15] Its property encompassed outbuildings and farm land, a small village, and a church.

More than a cottage because of the extent of its grounds, Harbor Hill, like Biltmore, was to be a country house that could be lived in at any time of year. The Mackays' plan was to occupy Harbor Hill full-time throughout the spring and fall months. During the winter—the social season—they would reside primarily in New York City at their East Seventy-fifth Street residence, though they could celebrate Christmas at Harbor Hill. They would divide the hot summer months between Newport, Saratoga (in upstate New York), and Europe. But Harbor Hill was made habitable in any season, and inhabited it was—throughout the harshest months—by members of the staff.

Main hall—cross axis, north side (Museum of the City of New York, McKim, Mead & White Collection)

Drawing room with portrait of Katherine by Edmund Chartran (Barr Ferree American Estates and Gardens, New York: Munn, 1904)

Not considered part of the American country house tradition were those houses built on huge tracts of working land—for example, the King Ranch, founded in 1853 in south Texas and controlling 825,000 acres. What distinguished the Kings of Texas from the Vanderbilts in North Carolina and the Mackays in New York was the gulf between reality and fantasy. The Kings' wealth was actually derived from the land itself, from cattle and crops; the country properties of the Vanderbilts, the Mackays, and others of comparable means only gave the appearance of generating income. The Vanderbilts' money, in fact, came from the New York Central Railroad; the Mackays', from silver mining, communications, and investments. (When the leisure country house bug did bite the descendants of Richard King, between 1912 and 1915, they constructed at the Santa Gertrudis Ranch a mansion that, in both size and cost, rivaled the large houses of the East Coast.[16])

The English Ideal

Many affluent Americans at the turn of the twentieth century were Anglophiles. William Waldorf Astor became so enamored of England that he moved there permanently and purchased Cliveden, a grand mid-nineteenth-century country house in Buckinghamshire; then, in Kent, he bought Hever, a medieval castle that he remodeled and enlarged into one of the grandest of all country seats.[17] Rich Americans such as the Mackays looked to the English for the inspiration for their country houses. Clarence Mackay, though born in San Francisco, had—because of his mother's Anglophilia—also spent most of his formative years in England. He must have derived great satisfaction from reading that Harbor Hill seemed "to have flowered out of rural England to [sic] nearby soil."[18]

The appeal of the English country house lay in its history and its association with political power. Mark Girouard, the leading scholar of the form, defined them not merely as large houses in the country for the wealthy, but as "power houses—the houses of a ruling class."[19] They were dynastic seats representing breeding and lineage, and with them came economic and political power derived from ownership of large tracts of land. Land ownership yielded income from farming to supplement inheritance. It also garnered revenue, from rent-paying tenants. More importantly, having a large British country house on ample acreage also usually meant a seat in Parliament. The foundation of political power in Britain rested on ownership of country property, with the owners of the great country houses wielding great influence in running the Empire. In the late nineteenth and early twentieth centuries, however, industrial and commercial wealth shifted power from the countryside to urban centers, undercutting the influence of country landowners. By the 1930s, Britain's country house had sunk in status to mere weekend getaway.

Few turn-of-the-century American properties ever fit the English definition of the country house (although several of Richard King's descendants became important politicians). The social critic Herbert Croly explicitly noted Harbor Hill's English source and its distinctly American twist. Of the American builders of country houses, he remarked, "They are becoming, if you please, country gentlemen, though in a different sense from an English country gentleman. They do not derive their subsistence from the soil, and their estates are laid out solely for . . . pleasure."[20]

Affluent Britons had their own yearnings after distant places. In the 1870s and later, large country houses such as Waddeston Manor explicitly invoked French themes. On the Continent, traditions of the *chateau*, the *villa*, and the *Schloss* paralleled the country house in England both politically and socially. Thus, when Clarence and Katherine Mackay chose a stylistic model for the main house at Harbor Hill, their vision was of something from the French Renaissance, as admired by English eyes.

In fact, the spell that England's country houses cast over aspiring Americans dated to the early nineteenth century. It emerges in the longings of Washington Irving, who toured England in 1818 and reflected that the country house had "all the conveniences and elegances of polite life." Irving observed that the Englishman's "country seat abounds with every requisite, either for studios [sic] retirement, taste gratification, or rural exercise. Books, paintings, music, horses, dogs, and sporting implements . . . in the true spirit of hospitality it's [sic] provides the means of enjoyment."[21] More than sixty years later, on the eve of the American country house boom, Henry James exclaimed, "Of all the great things that the English have invented and made part of the credit of the national character, the most perfect, the most characteristic, the only one they have mastered completely in all its details so that it becomes a compendious illustration of their social genius and their manners, is the well-appointed, well-administered, well-filled country house."[22] Great country houses in England and elsewhere often acted as settings in James's fiction.

The American Stamp

The symbolism of the English country house, if not its function as a source of revenue and clout, had strong appeal in early America. It motivated the construction of southern plantations such as Mount Vernon in Virginia and northeastern versions such as the Livingston family estates in New York's Hudson River Valley. And in fact, property ownership did qualify a man to vote, and hence to hold public office, until the end of the nineteenth century. But the size and value of one's holdings did not translate directly into the extent of one's political influence. The powerful might own great properties, but the owners of huge tracts of land did not necessarily hold high offices.

A survey of American millionaires published in 1892 revealed a shift in how fortunes were made. Four thousand and four men and women were identified as having a net worth of more than one million dollars. Only 2.1 percent of this private wealth—that is, eighty-four persons' worth—derived from agriculture. Most of the big money came from trade, transportation, manufacturing, communication industries, and mineral industries. John Mackay (Clarence's father) qualified as one of America's millionaires because of the Big Bonanza in silver mining, banking, and the Commercial Cable Company.[23]

The numerous country houses at the turn of the century became a subject of great interest among American observers of America. Some writers sought to link the new phenomenon with great houses of the American past. Many of the country's founders, they noted, came from a tradition of large landholdings, in which a sizeable house was an emblem. On a scale with George Washington's Mount Vernon and Thomas Jefferson's Monticello were other early American country places such as the pre-Revolutionary Philipse Manor in Yonkers, New York, and slightly later Benjamin Chew's Cliveden in Germantown, Pennsylvania.

Indigenous American characteristics nourished the turn-of-the-century boom in great country houses. A strong and venerable American tradition reveres the idea of a life lived close to nature. Ultimately, the Arcadian impulse of locating true worth, value, and the good life in the countryside is as old as America itself.[24] The ideals of small towns and of tilling the soil were fundamental to Thomas Jefferson's political phi-

losophy. Even as the United States became an urban nation in the nineteenth and early twentieth centuries, the pastoral ideal persisted.

An architectural ethos grew out of "the good life in the countryside," which gave rise to mid-nineteenth-century pattern books, such as those of Andrew Jackson Downing. In *The Architecture of Country Houses* (1850), Downing stated that "the villa, or the country house proper . . . is the most refined home of America—the home of its most leisurely and educated class of citizen."[25] This sentiment would be repeated often throughout the nineteenth century, and well into the twentieth. Some idealists, such as the Transcendentalists, whose creed was articulated by the poet and essayist Ralph Waldo Emerson, tended to invest or locate spiritual values in nature. Nature thus became not an enemy to be conquered but a sanctuary for renewal to be cherished.

In considering the origins of the American country house, Harry W. Desmond and Herbert Croly's *Stately Homes in America, from the Colonial Times to the Present Day* (1903) offered some particularly astute observations. In their survey (of urban mansions as well as country houses), the authors argued that large mansions were a unique American building type. "They are as different in size and magnificence from the earlier types of American residence as the contemporary 'skyscraper' is from the old five-story brick office." Of the few antecedents that might be claimed as models for the new wealthy person's house, Desmond and Croly noted Mount Vernon and the White House, among others. They declared Harbor Hill one of the best of the recent examples.[26]

The American love affair with nature underwent many permutations, but all had in common one feature: the contrast of the country with the city, which was held to be the source of turmoil, corruption, ill health, and worse. But in fact, the turn-of-the-century country house could not have existed without the city. The industrial-commercial urban center provided not only the wealth to support the country house, but also its heart and circulatory system, in the form of transportation. The railroad, and later the motorcar, brought the goods, fine wines, and people.

Herbert Croly summed up the situation of the country house: "To the well-to-do American his estate is only one of the spoils of financial conquests. He may take a genuine interest in certain country spots; but beyond that in 'returning to the country' he is merely adapting himself to a tradition, which his common sense tells him is a good thing for himself and his children. The country means to him a country house within an hour or two of New York."[27] Harbor Hill fit this outline perfectly. Whether by train, automobile, ferry boat, or yacht, family members, friends, and business associates from New York could reach the Mackay's Harbor Hill haven on Long Island Sound within an hour.

Long Island: Millionaires' Playground, Architects' Boon

Most of Long Island was rural until the Civil War. Although the cities of Queens and Brooklyn clustered at its western end, the rest of the island was composed of farmland in the interior and fishing villages along the coasts. As early as 1834, the Long Island Railroad (LIRR) proposed construction of a line that, combined with a steam ferry from the North Shore to New London, Connecticut, would offer a relatively quick connection between New York City and Boston. But that scheme failed, and the LIRR instead built tracks to a number of small towns on the north and south shores to transport agricultural products and passengers. A few summer colonies grew up, but for the most part Long Island remained rural and thinly populated until the 1890s and

early 1900s. The great post-Civil War growth of wealth in the Northeast hastened the discovery of Long Island as an enticing getaway for city dwellers.

The South Shore, fronting on the Atlantic Ocean, was the first area to be developed intensely, starting in the 1870s. Large hotels, rustic cedar-shingled houses for middle-class vacationers, and clubs sprang up alongside the summer houses of the upper crust. An important example of the latter was Idle Hour (1878) at Oakdale, designed by Richard Morris Hunt in the

Idle Hour, for William K. and Alva Vanderbilt at Oakdale, NY, Richard Morris Hunt, architect, 1878 photo c. 1892 (Society for the Preservation of Long Island Antiquities)

Orchard, house for James L. Breese, Southampton, NY, McKim, Mead & White, architects, 1898–1907 (Society for the Preservation of Long Island Antiquities)

Stick style for William Kissam Vanderbilt and his wife Alva. Before long, McKim, Mead & White designed a house for the merchant John H. Cheever at Far Rockaway (1886), and almost immediately after that, the Argyle Hotel Casino (1888) at Babylon. At the tip of Long Island's south fork, McKim, Mead & White designed a group of houses and a clubhouse for a group of wealthy New Yorkers who made up the Montauk Point Association (1882). In the Southampton area, McKim, Mead & White designed the Shinnecock Hills Golf Club (1891–2), the first purpose-built golf clubhouse in the United States, as well as houses for art collector Samuel Parrish (1889) and artist William Merritt Chase (1890–2). Nearby, at Southampton, James L. Breese, a New York financier and photography enthusiast, had his friends at McKim, Mead & White add to his house a gigantic portico stylistically derived from Mount Vernon. A writer for *Country Life in America* saw Breese's house as an attempt to create an "American style of architecture" but noted that what was called the Colonial style "should be called 'Georgian,' because we got it from England during the reign of the Georges."[28]

On the North Shore, McKim and his partners designed a house for Anne Coleman Alden at Lloyd Harbor (1879), and another for Prescott Hall Butler at Saint James (1879). Five years later, Stanford White married a sister of Mrs. Butler and purchased nearby Box Hill, which doubled as a summer house and as a place for the architect's design experiments. In the 1870s and 1880s, McKim, Mead & White received the lion's share of architectural commissions on Long Island. The grounds around the new country houses became increasingly formal, with elaborate gardens and a row of orange trees in tubs that stood outside in the summer, and were sheltered in orangeries during

the winter. Many properties were adorned with classical-style ornaments, some of which served as settings for amateur dramas.

With the swing toward luxury and refinement in North Shore estates came increased size of both houses and acreage. Again, McKim, Mead & White played a leading role. The firm's works included Edwin Denison Morgan's Wheatley (1890–1900) in Roslyn on an estate adjacent to Harbor Hill. A monied Connecticut Yankee with a passion for sports, Morgan would one day become Clarence Mackay's competitor and ally. At 666 acres, Morgan's estate set a high bar for Mackay to surpass. The neighboring properties of Morgan and

Box Hill, the Stanford White house in St. James, McKim, Mead & White, architects, 1900 (Society for the Preservation of Long Island Antiquities)

Wheatley house for E. D. Morgan at Wheatley Hills, McKim, Mead & White, architects, 1890–1, 1895–1900 (Monograph of the Works of McKim, Mead & White, 1915, pl.149)

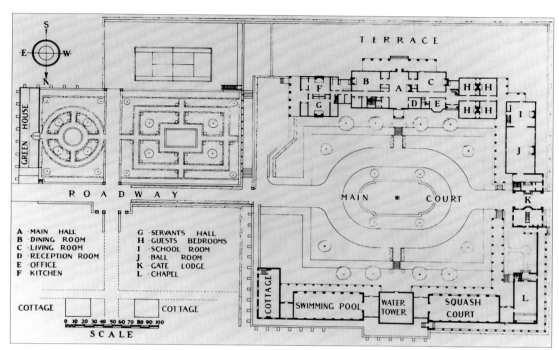

A · MAIN HALL
B · DINING ROOM
C · LIVING ROOM
D · RECEPTION ROOM
E · OFFICE
F · KITCHEN

G · SERVANTS HALL
H · GUESTS BEDROOMS
I · SCHOOL ROOM
J · BALL ROOM
K · GATE LODGE
L · CHAPEL

Wheatley, E. D. Morgan estate layout at Wheatley Hills, McKim, Mead & White, architects, 1890–1, 1895–1900 (Monograph of the Works of McKim, Mead & White, 1915, pl.147)

Roslyn, NY, c. 1875 (Roslyn Landmark Society)

Mackay would help to transform Roslyn from a working-class village into a colony of resident and visiting millionaires and other luminaries.

Initially called Hempstead Harbor, and first settled in 1643 by a handful of English colonists from Connecticut, Roslyn remained a small town throughout the eighteenth century. It consisted of only a few buildings and little industry, including one of the first paper mills in New York State. The town underwent some growth in the years leading up to the Civil War,

but essentially it still mainly served local fisherman and farmers with fields inland. Its main industry, a saw mill and lumberyard, belonged to the family of a man named Hicks. The first public figure to alight in the town was William Cullen Bryant, a poet and the editor of the *New York Evening Post*. Looking for a summer retreat, Bryant purchased an old house and forty acres near Hempstead Harbor in 1843—the year before the town was renamed Roslyn. Bryant spent part of every year in Roslyn until his death in 1878. Other than Bryant's house, Roslyn's only landmark was the Ward Memorial Clock Tower, a Richardsonian Romanesque structure in rough stone designed by the New York firm of Lamb and Rich and erected in 1895. By 1900, Roslyn's population stood at 1,378.[29]

Because of Bryant—and the LIRR, which pushed through to nearby Glen Cove in 1864—other people began to purchase houses or build new ones in the Roslyn area. The more affluent newcomers engaged some of the nation's most distinguished architects and landscape designers; Calvert Vaux, Jacob Wrey Mould, and Frederick Law Olmsted all worked in Roslyn.

Cedarmere, W. C. Bryant house, Roslyn, NY (Bryant Library Local History Collection, Roslyn, NY)

Ellen E. Ward Clock Tower, Roslyn, NY (Roslyn Landmark Society)

At the start of the new century, motorcars and new roads, improved train service, and construction of the Williamsburg Bridge linking Lower Manhattan to the island made travel to and around Long Island possible and relatively easy. Sporting activities attracted many people. Hunting clubs, horse breeding and racing (including Belmont Race Track), polo, fox hunting with hounds, sailing and yachting, tennis, golf (and, after 1910, even amateur aviation) became pastimes of the rich on Long Island. A 1916 directory listed sev-

enty-one sporting clubs east of the line between Jamaica and Flushing Bay.[30]

Much of Roslyn's appeal lay in its proximity to the American polo grounds and the Meadow Brook Club at Hempstead-Westbury. Polo, a game of the English elite, was brought to the United States in 1876 by James Gordon Bennett Jr., owner of the *New York Herald*. The large farms of the early Quaker settlers made perfect polo fields, and by the early twentieth century at least twenty polo clubs and many private playing fields had sprouted in Nassau County. Within easy reach of Manhattan, Long Island was the cradle of American polo, and the Meadow Brook Polo Club was the second oldest and most exclusive of all polo clubs.[31]

Of the 975 large country houses built on Long Island between the outbreak of the Civil War and World War II, eight date to the 1860s, fifteen to the 1870s, thirty-seven to the 1880s, one hundred thirty-one to the 1890s, and then, between 1900 and 1918, four hundred were built. Three hundred and four smaller country houses were built between World War I and 1930. Only eighty were constructed in the 1930s. The Long Island historian Robert B. MacKay (not related to John and Clarence Mackay) defines the phenomenon of Long Island's transformation as determined by economics and catalyzed by prosperity.[32]

At the beginning of the twentieth century, Harbor Hill's enormous size and opulence were to set a new standard for others to emulate, helping to transform the island into a field of country homes "with their mile long driveways . . . continuous for a hundred miles," as the *New York Herald* claimed in 1902. The reporter observed, "Long Island is rapidly being divided up into estates of immense acreage . . . beyond all precedence of American country life," creating a "density of the millionaire population."[33]

Main hall, view north side, prior to armor collection, c. Jan.1902 (Private Collection)

Upper stairway view (Desmond and Croly, Stately Homes in America New York: D. Appleton, 1903)

As the main house at Harbor Hill approached completion in 1902, McKim, Mead & White, with McKim in charge, designed a red brick country house in Roslyn for A. Cass Canfield, engineer and financier; White was designing a large country house (1900–2), and outbuildings (1906–10) for William Collins Whitney. A powerful businessman with major interests in the New York City street railways, Whitney was a New York City politician in the Democratic Party and Secretary of the Navy under President Grover Cleveland. (White also remodeled Whitney's Fifth Avenue house.[34]) Whitney vied with his neighbors Mackay and Morgan over who had the highest spot on Long Island, and Whitney went so far as to have White design him a 150-foot-tall water tower to

Cassleigh, A. Cass Canfield, McKim, Mead & White, architects, Roslyn, NY, 1902–3 (Society for the Preservation of Long Island Antiquities)

House for William Collins Whitney, McKim, Mead & White, architects, Westbury, NY, 1900–2, 1906–10 (Society for the Preservation of Long Island Antiquities)

press his claim; Mackay responded by adding a flag-pole to his roof.

Although Mackay, Whitney, and Morgan competed, they also cooperated to maintain the advantages they enjoyed. They sought to keep local taxes low and to prevent New York's masses from infiltrating Nassau County for recreation. They joined forces in developing utilities. When Morgan began to build, electricity and natural gas were unavailable; oil provided artificial lighting. But Morgan found the cost of oil too high, so he teamed up with Whitney and Mackay to establish an electric power company (which was later sold to the Long Island Lighting Company[35]). Common concerns made good neighbors.

The Harbor Hill Effect

Most of their notable neighbors in Roslyn had far-reaching reputations apart from their country houses; Harbor Hill made Katherine and Clarence Mackay celebrities. The Mackays were lauded as the authors of the estate's architectural grandeur, stunning art and furnishings, and gorgeous landscaping. The *New York Times*'s summary of grand houses proclaimed, "No country estate around New York surpasses that of Clarence H. Mackay's Harbor Hill."[36] The Mackay

name would be mentioned repeatedly to the notables entertained at Harbor Hill, the site of splendid balls for New York society as well as fund raisers for local charities and suffragette rallies.[37] And in the eyes of high-society watchers, Katherine Mackay was heralded for having solved the often vexing "servant question."[38] (See Chapter Six.)

The Mackays, in turn, saw a place for themselves in posterity, and had themselves and their environment recorded for all time. Through the photographer's lens observers saw not only Katherine, Clarence, and their children but also Harbor Hill and its conservatory, casino, indoor tennis courts and swimming pool, kitchens and cutting gardens, the dairy and dairyman's cottage, the dog kennels, the barns for prize Guernsey cattle, the poultry establishment, the winding drives, the bridges, and the lovingly preserved woods. They saw the gate lodge and the stables for thoroughbreds, draft horses, and polo ponies. And, too, they saw cozy retreats for conversation or tea, and deep in the wildest part "without suggestion of house," Katherine Mackay's "rustic cottage."[39] Astute observers detected the work of several designers: Stanford White's in the house and gate house; in other buildings that of the designers of Grand Central Station, Warren & Wetmore; and on much of the estate's six-hundred-plus acres that of Boston's Guy Lowell (see Chapter Four).

Even as Harbor Hill attained notoriety in reality, the house and its residents made their way into fiction.

Gate house (Private
Collection)

*Farm gardens, Harbor
Hill, c. 1906* (Bryant
Library Local History
Collections, Roslyn, NY)

Cow barns, distant view, with rear of Dairyman's Cottage, Warren & Wetmore, architects, photo by Thomas E. Marr (Avery Architectural and Fine Arts Library, Columbia University, McKim, Mead & White collection)

Main road, view from Lodge (Private Collection)

"Approach to the Stable of 'Harbor Hill,'" photo by Thomas E. Marr, in Croly, "The Layout of a Large Estate," Architectural Record, 16, no. 4 (October 1904)

Duck pond, photo c. 1902 (Bryant Library Local History Collections, Roslyn, NY)

Katherine Mackay, seated dressed with tiara for a ball, c. 1904, photograph by Davis & Samford (Private Collection)

A closer view of Harbor Hill (Private Collection)

South end of house and view of garden and house from end of garden (Museum of the City of New York, McKim, Mead & White Collection)

Close-up of entrance (Museum of the City of New York, McKim, Mead & White Collection)

Novelist Edith Wharton made Harbor Hill a backdrop for Lily Bart's downward spiral in *The House of Mirth* (1905), describing the view seaward and the ladies in "lace raiment and men in tennis flannels . . . dispersing themselves over the grounds in quest of the various distractions the place afforded: distractions ranging from tennis-courts to shooting-galleries, from bridge and whiskey, within doors to motors and steam-launches without."[40] In Wharton's *The Custom of the Country* (1913), Undine Spragg of fictitious Apex City follows a steep up-and-down social and romantic path modeled on the Mackays' quest for status. The grand parties held at Harbor Hill provided the prototypes for F. Scott Fitzgerald's depictions of Jay Gatsby's extravagant galas at his East Egg estate. Clarence Mackay, meanwhile, fit the role of Henry James' wealthy American businessman striding through English country houses, making a "proposition" to the owners to "sell their ancestors" to furnish his mansion.[41]

Such references in fiction help to illuminate the milieu of Harbor Hill and allow glimpses into the souls of the Mackays. Harbor Hill represents many themes, from conspicuous consumption, to religious zeal and rift, to social acceptance, rejection, and rebuff. While it stood for all that wealth could buy, Clarence Mackey's country house was ultimately a house of heartbreak. Harbor Hill would appear again and again on the pages of newspapers and magazines over decades, but gradually the people who inhabited the house faded from view. In time, the grand estate came to naught. Yet the lives lived there would continue to fascinate long after Harbor Hill disappeared, leaving hardly a trace.[42]

TWO

The Patrons

❁ ❁

"The best people are almost always Episcopalians. . . . Catholicism is the servant's religion."

—Mrs. Paran Stevens, in *Silver Platter*, p. 223

NEWSPAPERS ALWAYS REPORT important weddings, but the May 1898 marriage of Katherine Duer to Clarence Mackay was especially big news. The bride, an exceptionally photogenic debutante, had graced the society pages only recently. The groom, though hardly a heartthrob, was an extraordinarily good catch. Reporters were circumspect and did not dwell on the religious differences of the couple, nor did the couple's parents. John William and Louise Hungerford Mackay were delighted for their son, as their new daughter-in-law came from the top echelon of New York society. The Duers' status was everything to which the Mackays—especially Mrs. Mackay—aspired. And while the Duers were comfortable, they were not, as one social chronicler put it, "overburdened with this world's goods."[1] In short, the Mackays brought to the union the one thing the Duers did not have: enormous wealth.

Fittingly, the senior Mr. Mackay offered as a wedding present to his son's bride an estate with a grand house. Katherine Duer Mackay wasted no time in accepting her father-in-law's gift of property on Long Island and his promise to finance the building of an estate there. The Wheatley Hills near Roslyn were well known in the city for the impressive spreads of millionaires and other notables. John Mackay's gift to Katherine was about 190 acres overlooking Hempstead Bay. Within two years of the nuptials, in at least twenty separate transactions—some apparently handled by Katherine herself—a parcel of some 650 acres was assembled. That made the Mackay estate about double the size of the Principality of Monaco and one of the largest on Long Island. The total cost of the land came to more than $177,000.

Striking It Rich

The father of the groom, John William Mackay, was born in Dublin in 1831 to a desperately poor family; they left Ireland for New York City in 1840 during

Katherine Mackay dressed in black, c. 1902 (Private Collection)

Clarence Mackay, 1902 (University of Nevada, Reno)

the Potato Famine-induced wave of emigration.[2] The Mackays were part of the transformation of New York's Catholic population, which grew between 1814 and 1840 from fifteen thousand to two hundred thousand.[3] The death of John's father ended the boy's brief education, and he went to work for a shipbuilder. At age twenty, he headed west to seek his fortune. For a while he knocked around the California gold fields, but they were yielding few profits by that point. So, with his hopes pinned to silver instead of gold, he went to Nevada, where he acquired skills in timbering

and shoring up deep mines. In time, he amassed enough capital to try to develop his own mine.

After an initial failure, he began to see success at the Petaluma Mill, Gold Hill, in the Nevada Territory. With a partner, J. M. Walker, he joined forces with two San Francisco saloon keepers, James C. Flood and William S. O'Brien, and with James G. Fair—also from Dublin—who was enjoying good luck in what turned out to be the nation's hottest silver spot, Virginia City. Walker dropped out of the partnership early, but Mackay maintained the relationship with Fair. "Jim Fair's got strong guts," said Mackay. "I've placed my bet on him and I'm staying with it."[4] Competition was fierce at the Comstock Lode—the nation's fabled and probably richest deposit of silver named for the miner who claimed to have discovered it—and Mackay and Fair played a rough game.

Mackay, Fair, and their partners theorized that only the surface of the Comstock Lode had been mined and that, with deep shafts and new machinery, they could extract much more ore, both low- and high-

View of Virginia City, NV, c. 1870 (Library of Congress)

Louise Hungerford was born in New York City on December 21, 1843, to Catholic working-class parents who moved from tenement to tenement.[6] Louise's mother Mémé had emigrated from France, so Louise and her younger sister, Ada, grew up fluent in French. Mémé Hungerford worked as a seamstress who, Louise recalled, called at affluent households on Washington Square. Louise's father Daniel Hungerford, a barber, had served as a captain under General Winfield Scott in the war of 1848. Daniel Hungerford would later adopt the title of "Colonel." Embedded in Louise's memory was a myth that her father's family had been rich English lords, who became in time the Hungerfords of Farleigh Castle. Louise thus believed that she deserved a better life than her mother's. Ada followed Louise through most her life imbibing in the same theme of wanting more.

grade. John was determined. "In our time wealth is the only power," he observed to Maria Louise Hungerford Bryant, a slim, pretty, young widow whom he had met through the Fairs and who became Mrs. J. W. Mackay on November 25, 1867.[5]

Wanderlust and a quest for fortune drove Daniel Hungerford, and like John Mackay he departed in 1851 for the California gold fields. Three years later his family followed, crossing the Isthmus of Panama,

Portrait of Mrs. John W. (Louise Hungerford) Mackay (Morses' Palace of Art, San Francisco) (Private Collection)

John William Mackay, c. 1890 (Nevada Historical Society)

Downieville, CA (Sierra County), 1855 (The New York Historical Society)

Inside the Big Bonanza at 1800-foot level, James Fair on left and John William Mackay on right (Nevada Historical Society)

Visit of General U. S. Grant to Bonanza Mine, Virginia City, Nevada, October 28, 1879, left to right, John William Mackay, Mrs. M. G. Gillette, U. S. Grant, Jr., Mrs. U. S. Grant, General U. S. Grant, S. Yanada, Mrs. John G. Fair, Governor J. H. Kinkead, John G. Fair (Nevada Historical Society)

and found him in the gold camp of Downieville. There and elsewhere Hungerford cut hair and tried his hand at various enterprises, unsuccessfully. In Louise's mostly cheerless childhood a bright spot was a few months at a convent school in Benicia, California—until the money for school ran out.

At sixteen Louise married Edmund Bryant, a young Downieville doctor who was a distant relative of William Cullen Bryant. Their only surviving child (a second died at birth) was Eva, born in 1861. Edmund Bryant, too, had wanderlust, and the family moved to Virginia City. But Bryant began to drink and take drugs, and eventually disappeared. When Louise finally found him, very sick, in the mining camp of Poverty Hill, her ministrations were useless; in June 1866 he died. Destitute, Louise returned to Virginia City, where she and Eva, who was troubled by a congenitally lame leg which caused her to limp, lived in a single room. Louise trimmed bonnets and did piecework for Rosener's Dry Goods Store. She augmented her small income by teaching French at Saint Mary's convent school.

One of the women Louise sewed for was Theresa Fair. The daughter of a hotel keeper named Rooney, Theresa had married James Fair, John Mackay's business partner and superintendent of the Ophir Mine. After a year-long courtship, John and Louise married. John built a two-story cottage with a picket fence on one of the hillside streets, and Louise began to assume the demeanor of a lady. She would not allow her seamstress to sit with the family at dinner; after all, the woman was just "hired help."[8]

Mackay and Fair prospered due to complex maneuvers preventing other prospectors from taking control of a series of mines. In 1873 they struck the "Big Bonanza" at their Virginia Consolidated mine, and Mackay, who owned two-fifths of the mine's shares, became a multi-millionaire overnight. Although the exact value of Mackay's new riches in silver is not known, the worth of the ore extracted over the next six years has been estimated at between $150 million and more than twice that sum. Mackay and his partners became known as the "Comstock Quartet," or "the Irish Big Four."

John Mackay recognized that the silver bonanza

John Mackay house at corner of Howard and Taylor streets, burned 1875
(Nevada Historical Society)

St. Mary's Catholic Church, Virginia City, NV, c. 1870 (Library of Congress)

could not last, and as early as 1874 he began to diversify his investments with real estate and railroads. He, Flood, and Fair founded the Bank of Nevada, headquartered in San Francisco. So when the value of Virginia Consolidated plummeted from $160 million in 1875 to $1.7 million in 1881, the partners were still in clover.

Although Mackay maintained ties with the region and boasted of his roughneck origins, his interests increasingly lay elsewhere. His first house burned down in 1875 during one of the fires that ravaged Virginia City. Mackay built a new and larger house which still stands in Virginia City; however, he only lived there during business trips and neither Louise nor the children ever occupied it. A generous supporter of St. Mary's Catholic parish, John Mackay rebuilt the church after the fire. He donated wood for the reconstruction, and gave the crew two hundred pounds of flour, wine and brandy, and one hundred and fifteen pounds of beef. Louise, in contrast, was not noted for munificence; one of the nuns remarked, "Mrs. Mackay gave not so freely." She did, however, donate six acres of land on which the Daughters of Charity constructed Virginia City's first medical facility, which was diplomatically named St. Mary Louise Hospital.[9]

Already Louise Mackay was the acknowledged queen of Virginia City society. But she set her sights higher as the couple began spending time in San Francisco.

The Steep Ascent

After a trip to Europe to seek medical advice for Louise's daughter Eva, the Mackays settled in San Francisco in 1870. Both their children were born there—John William ("Willie") on the twelfth of August that first year, and four years later, on April 17, Clarence ("Clarie").

Their first house in San Francisco was a large three-story wooden structure on O'Farrell Street. Its double width among the standard, narrower houses attracted attention and brought Louise good press. One observer noted that the house gave a "balanced grandeur to the whole neighborhood . . . it trailed clouds of glory."[10] Louise filled it with fashionable French Empire furnishings. O'Farrell Street was in a prosperous neighborhood but not up to the social heights of Nob Hill, where John Mackay's partners, Flood and Fair, constructed large, ornate homes.[11] The O'Farrell Street house was modest by comparison and very likely a source of Louise's continuing restlessness.[12]

Louise observed San Francisco society closely. While the wealth in most cases was relatively recent, already there were barriers between old money and new. New wealth commanded no respect. Thus, even as John's riches increased, the top rank of San Francisco society remained unattainable. So Louise shifted her sights—to New York City and real high society.

"Rude shock" best describes her New York adventure of 1876. The circle in which Louise sought acceptance was a close-knit tribe linked by personal and family connections. The tribal rules became ever more exclusive when a dandy named Samuel Ward McAllister drew up lists of the city's "best families." Ironically, McAllister, a native of Savannah, Georgia, had made some of his fortune in the California Gold Rush, but that fact was conveniently overlooked. A short, plump man with a goatee, McAllister delighted in enumerating who was socially acceptable—the elite who should be invited to balls and grand dinners. In the 1870s he organized a set of loose groups known as the "Patriarchs" and the "Family Circle Dancing Class" and began winnowing his lists down to what he would eventually call "the New York Four Hundred." Caroline Astor, who virtually governed New York society for almost half a century, urged McAllister on in this effort to create an American aristocracy. Although McAllister did not coin the term "Four Hundred" until 1892, the criteria were in place in the 1870s, and the Mackays were not on the list.[13]

Entrance into New York society entailed not only an invitation to the occasional dinner party, but acceptance into a highly structured preparatory process: one had to be invited to call and to leave a calling card; and only sometimes might one be received. Attending the Academy of Music on East Fourteenth Street or the new Metropolitan Opera House on West Thirty-ninth Street on certain preordained nights was part of the ritual. Monday, for example, was Mrs. Astor's night. For those evenings seats were virtually unobtainable and what tickets there were cost the moon. "Coming out"—presentation to society at elaborate parties for ceremonious inspection by prospective suitors and the tribal elders—was essential for girls of the upper class when they reached age sixteen.

For an outsider to break into this society called for determination, a great deal of money, and connections. As one grand dame of New York society wrote a half century later, "Social distinction in America, at present, is a citadel set upon an eminence which can be scaled by any one of three routes—birth, wealth, or, less frequently, achievement." But, the lady claimed, "A half century ago a single trail led to that envied height. . . . the sanctioned pathway of birth and breeding." Mrs. John King Van Rensselaer, who had married into a family whose New York lineage could be traced back to the early seventeenth century, remarked with detectable regret that, "Society once connoted, first of all, family" and "breeding." But by the 1920s, the word meant "fortune" and "self-advertisement."[14] Mrs. Van Rensselaer may have overemphasized the patrician lineage notion, but she was clear about the problems of "getting in." To do so, arrivistes such as the Vanderbilts built themselves chateaus on Fifth Avenue and gave balls to entice Mrs. Astor and her set to come calling.

Mrs. Van Rensselaer set down her observations of the newly rich from points west descending on the city with hopes of acceptance into society's highest stratum. "The West was yielding up tremendous riches," she wrote. "Steel barons, coal lords, dukes of wheat and beef, of mines and railways had sprung up from obscurity. Absolute in their own territory, they longed for fresh worlds to conquer. Newspaper accounts of the affairs of New York society . . . thrilled the newly rich of the West. In a great glittering caravan the multimillionaires of the midlands moved up against the city and by wealth and sheer weight of numbers broke through the archaic barriers."[15]

The barricades were definitely up for Louise and John Mackay. They took a suite at New York's fashionable Everett House on Fourth Avenue at Seventeenth Street, and Louise sent out cards to the wives of John's business acquaintances, to no avail. An attempt to call on a resident of Washington Square (where her mother had once worked as a seamstress) was rejected. One society matron, Mrs. Paran Stevens, explained to Louise that, while new wealth—especially "bonanza money"—raised eyebrows, being Catholic and Irish was fatal. "The best people are almost always Episcopalians," she said. "Catholicism is the servant's religion." Mrs. Stevens suggested the Mackays remake themselves as Scotch-Irish, and for a fee, she arranged for Louise to be included in the forthcoming book *Queens of American Society*.[16]

Despite Mrs. Stevens's intervention, both Louise and John overheard someone say, at a party to which they were finally invited, "A washerwoman or boarding house keeper or whatever she may be all right in her place, but her place is hardly with us." And a newspaper report headlined "NEVADA'S CROESUS IN NEW YORK" described John as "courteous, kind, and . . . generally well liked," but mentioned his wife only in passing, unnamed.[17] Years later, the illustrator Charles Dana Gibson portrayed the social climbers' plight: inside, a grand ball filled with beautiful people in an opulent place, while outside, hacking through the wall with a pickax, is a miner's wife; the miner cowers in the background.[18]

The Mackays Take Europe

The Mackays gave up on New York, packed up their two boys, and fled to Paris. Louise's parents (the Hungerfords), her sister Ada, and her daughter Eva, whom John had adopted, were part of the retinue. An ample house was required.

John purchased a large, neo-Renaissance palace with an enormous garden near the Place de l'Etoile. For its decoration John told Louise, "The sky's the limit, my darling. I want your house to be the finest in Paris."[19] Louise set about procuring tapestries and commissioning murals emulating Pompeian frescoes. She visited fashionable cafés and gathering places to make inroads into international society, while John shuttled between Europe, New York, San Francisco, and Virginia City to attend to business.

Sometimes the traveling tycoon still got into scrapes. John had always prided himself on his fitness and loved to box; as a younger man he boxed nightly in Virginia City, taking on all comers at Bill Davis's gym. Now a multimillionaire, husband, and father of two, he still liked a good fight. In 1879, he was baited into a brawl with a "somewhat notorious" coal dealer. The *New York Times* headlined its account "THE BONANZA KING FIGHTING."[20] In 1891 John attacked a man in San Francisco suspected of circulating rumors about Louise; news stories about the assault carried headlines such as "MIL-

C. D. Gibson, "The Social Push—Almost In" from Life XLI, no. 1053 (1 January 1903), pp. 10–11.

LIONAIRES AT FISTICUFFS" and "MACKAY ON HIS MUSCLE."[21]

Mostly, though, John kept his eye on his business. Always seeking new investment opportunities, he teamed up with James Gordon Bennett Jr., to found the Commercial Cable Company in 1883. Bennett, notorious for outrageous and often inebriated behavior, was at the time battling Jay Gould and the Western Union company over the cost of telegrams. A monopoly, Western Union was charging seventy-five cents a word. Mackay and Bennett proceeded to undercut Gould by laying two marine cables to Europe and charging twenty-five cents a word. Gould reportedly remarked, "There is no beating John Mackay. If he needs another million or two he goes to his silver mine and digs it up."[22]

But how to deliver the cables? Mackay's solution: purchase the Postal Telegraph Company for a mere $1 million, enabling access to many cities and the new technology of sending multiple signals over one wire. He then strung telegraph lines across the continent, and by 1902, John Mackay's company was laying the first trans-Pacific cable.

Besides his continued involvement with mines in California, Nevada, Idaho, and Alaska, and his communications empire, John Mackay had extensive land holdings in California and Nevada, served as a vice-president of the great Spreckels Sugar Company, and was named a director of the Canadian Pacific and Southern Pacific railroads. His wealth—especially the money that went to Louise, her spending habits, and her quest for social acceptance—earned for the Mackays the title "bonanza king and queen." Although his riches made Mackay a political power, he twice declined the Republican nomination for Senator from Nevada. Jim Fair did become a Nevada senator, and the partners hosted politicians such as ex-President Ulysses S. Grant and in 1879 took them on tours of the mines.

In 1877, through a stroke of genius, Louise's father, Colonel Hungerford, invited the traveling former president to stay at the Mackays' Paris mansion during a world tour he was making. Louise wanted the Arc de Triomphe draped in the stars and stripes, which did not happen, but she did have some of the furniture at home covered in red, white, and blue silk. A single stroke, a huge ball held at their house, lasting until four in the morning, put the Mackays at the head of the social pack. Other parties followed. The international press noted the Mackays' presence in Moscow at the coronation of Czar Alexander III. In 1879, at a grand ceremony in Rome, the vivacious Ada married the Italian Count Joseph Telfener; King Umberto I of Italy was present, as was a special representative of the new Pope, Leo XIII.

Silver trumpeted the prominence of the Mackays. In 1877, John commissioned from the venerable New York firm of Tiffany & Co. a silver service for twenty-

Candelabra, Mackay silver, by Tiffany & Co. (W. M. Keck Earth Science and Mineral Engineering Museum, University of Nevada, Reno)

Tureen, Mackay silver, by Tiffany & Co. (W. M. Keck Earth Science and Mineral Engineering Museum, University of Nevada, Reno)

Louise Mackay, Meissonier portrait, Peter A. Juley & Sons, New York, 1880 (Private Collection)

and assumed ancestry. A Hungerford coat of arms was designed especially for the service, as was her monogram, MLM. At last, all 1,250 pieces were packed into nine boxes and shipped to Paris to be displayed in Tiffany's pavilion at the 1878 International Exposition. Some admired the "magnificent service manufactured for the Bonanza King, Mr. J. M. Mackay." But others decried it as "a monument to the wealth of the owner" and an "accumulation of coin and cunning."[23]

In addition to jewelry (including a necklace said to have cost three hundred thousand dollars), John commissioned portraits. Louise disliked the first, painted in 1880 by Jean-Louis-Ernest Meissonier, because it made her look dour and old. Moreover, the artist had apparently substituted another woman's hands for Louise's; the allusion to the maliciously circulated fiction about Mrs. Mackay's washerwoman past infuriated her—and was reported on in the

four. He had a half ton of bullion shipped to the Tiffany workshops, and for nearly two years, reportedly, two-hundred men worked at fashioning the pieces designed by Edward C. Moore, Tiffany's main designer, assisted by Charles Grosjean: knives, forks, and spoons, butter dishes, crumb trays, mustard spoons, candelabras, candle snuffers, a syrup jug, a celery vase. Some pieces were patterned with floral elements similar to the work of William Morris and the Aesthetic Movement. Others were classical in inspiration. A water pitcher hinted at Art Nouveau, mixing cattails, lilies, lotuses, and abstract Persian elements. Irish shamrocks and Scottish thistles adorned other pieces, reflecting Louise's actual

press. (In fact, the rumor dogged Louise throughout her life; years after the Meissonier portrait, a Parisian art dealer doing business with her son Clarence gossiped that his client "was the son of a woman who did laundry for miners"[24]). The next, and more flattering, portrait, by Alexandre Cabanel, depicted Louise with lace and décolletage and made her look far younger than she was, and very pretty. Léon Bonnat, in turn, painted Louise in an imperial robe that had belonged to Empress Eugénie of France, the wife of Napoleon III. One newspaper described how, in this portrait, the garment hung "from her shoulders . . . in light transparent folds over her bosom."[25]

Although John spent the better part of each year in the United States on business, he and Louise remained a devoted couple. While John admired his wife and her social aspirations and successes (and it was rumored that John was seeking a papal title as the Count of Mackay[26]), his style was to regale dinner companions about his real life and humble beginnings—about the cow and pigs in the one-room house and the rough-and-tumble years of the Comstock Lode. He refused to learn French and drank a slug of bourbon instead of French wines; he instructed every chef Louise engaged in how to prepare corned beef and cabbage.[27]

Louise's daughter Eva achieved her own social success. Plagued by her limp and emotionally insecure, Eva often felt outshone by her mother and Aunt Ada. But in Paris Eva cultivated her natural gifts, including a fine voice: she took singing lessons from composer Charles Gounod. In 1885 she married Don Ferdinand Colonna, Prince of Galatro and heir to the Neapolitan branch of Italy's noble house of Colonna. Though a smaller affair than Ada's wedding, Eva's nuptials, held at the papacy's Paris diplomatic mission (*Nunciature*), were very grand. The match was said to be "a genuine love affair—love at first sight." Alas, the marriage was doomed. Ferdinand gambled heavily, philandered, and otherwise mistreated Eva.[28] The marriage was annulled in 1895.

With their social position on the Continent well in hand, the Mackays were ready to launch a siege of London society. John proposed that Louise move to London, and she was willing to give it a try. Willie and Clarie, now fifteen and eleven, were enrolled in the Jesuit Beaumont College at Old Windsor. Louise took mansions in Piccadilly, then Buckingham Gate, and finally purchased a large house in Carlton House Terrace. Built in 1832, the terrace was the work of Sir John Nash; the Mackay house had belonged to the third Duke of Leinster and had been purchased in the 1880s by C. H. Sanford, an American millionaire who renovated it, reportedly spending twenty thousand pounds on the marble entrance hall alone. The house boasted a paneled dining room, several drawing rooms, and a fifty-foot-long ballroom overlooking St. James's Park. At the end of Regent Street, adjacent to the Pall Mall, and with the great Duke of York column looming overhead, the house stood at the nexus of London society.

The arrival of a flood of invitations to dinners and balls signaled immediate and total social success. Louise was presented to the Prince and Princess of Wales, who cordially asked after the Mackay children. Louise and John, in turn, invited the young royals to a dinner and musicale, and within a year Louise was presented to Queen Victoria at Buckingham Palace. Louise soon took a house at Cowes, where the queen's yacht *Osborne* was moored; during the summer she dined on board with the prince and princess. Other royal and aristocratic engagements followed. In short, the Mackays had made it in Europe. They were at "the top of the heap."[29]

Although unkind gossip continued to circulate, the Mackays' next American visit brought the long-sought success at home. They visited Bar Harbor, Maine, where the Boston elite summered, and Newport, Rhode Island, where the Astors, Vanderbilts, and others in their set occupied new, palatial mansions. In late August they attended a Newport "domino party" at Wakehurst, the Elizabethan-style mansion of sportsman and politician James J. Van Alen, and their presence was reported in the local newspaper.[30] They returned to London, and that November, the Mackay name finally made it into the New York *Social Register*.[31]

Carlton House Terrace, London, John Nash, 1827–32 (Author)

Louise Mackay in court dress at 6 Carlton House Terrace, London (Private Collection)

Crisis dimmed the glow of social attainment and brought Louise back to the United States in 1894. A crazed speculator in the San Francisco office of Commercial Cable shot John Mackay. Louise crossed the Atlantic with Willie and Clarie and headed west from Jersey City in a private rail car, the *Corsair*. The "race of death" caught the press's attention, and their trip was followed with avid interest. On her arrival in San Francisco, Louise gave an interview. Her sons were described as "resplendent [with] English topcoats," turned-up collars, and London accents—very different from their hardscrabble father.[32] A sturdy constitution pulled John through, and soon he was back on his feet and in business.

Often present during the Mackays' Paris and London years were Teresa Fair (divorced in 1883 from "Slippery Jim" for his many infidelities after negotiating a very large settlement) and her daughters,

James Fair, c. 1875 (University of Nevada, Reno)

Mrs. James Fair, c. 1875 (University of Nevada, Reno)

Tessie (Fair) Oelrichs (Preservation Society of Newport County)

The Fair house, Charles W. Kenitzer, architect, San Francisco, California, c. 1875 (California Historical Society, FN-00487A)

Rosecliff, Oelrichs house, McKim, Mead & White architects, Newport, RI (Monograph of the Work of McKim, Mead & White, 1915–20)

Theresa (Tessie) and Virginia (Birdie). Despite the old Mackay–Fair partnership, John and Louise stood by Theresa. John, Louise, and Theresa shared a hope that Birdie and Willie would become romantically attached; the Mackays took it badly that Birdie instead married W. K. Vanderbilt Jr. Tessie married Herman Oelrichs of the German steamship line in 1890. (Seven years later, Tessie commissioned Stanford White to design her summer cottage in Newport. Rosecliff [1897–1900], modeled after the Grand Trianon at Versailles, set a standard that the newlywed Katherine Duer Mackay would soon match with Harbor Hill.[33])

Clarie

Clarence returned to the United States in 1894. He emerged from his British schooling a considerable athlete, proficient in various racquet sports, and with a keen interest in horseracing. With the prospect of sharing with his elder brother some responsibility for the Mackay empire looming, he set about learning the ropes of the Commercial Cable Company. Both Commercial Cable and Postal Telegraph had headquarters in New York City, in buildings that were under construction in Lower Manhattan near where the New York Stock Exchange was soon to have its seat.

Clarie, who stood about five feet, six inches tall, was always a careful and stylish dresser. He sported a red mustache, and pursued the life of a well-heeled gentleman. He took rooms at the Belgravia at 611 Fifth Avenue and faithfully attended Mass on Sundays at St. Leo's on East Twenty-eighth Street. He was invited to join the usual men's clubs—the Metropolitan Club, the Union Club, the Country and Lawyers Club, the New York Yacht Club, several gun clubs, as well as the Racquet and Tennis Club. He also had an interest in the arts and joined the Metropolitan Museum of Art, but did not seek invitations to the artier clubs such as the Century Club, the Players Club, and the University Club.

Postal Telegraph Building, by Harding & Gouch, New York, 1897, in "The Work of George Edward Harding & Gouch," Architectural Record, 7 (July–September 1897)

Tragedy catapulted Clarie overnight to the position of heir apparent. On October 18, 1895, Willie was thrown from a horse while riding outside Paris. He died instantly. His father was in San Francisco and his mother was in Paris trying to sell their house. Amid sorrow, the Paris house was reopened so Willie's body could come home. A funeral service was held in the church of Saint-Ferdinand des Ternes on the rue d'Armaillé. A few months later the body was transported across the Atlantic on the steamship *La Touraine*; a mortuary chapel draped in black was erected on board. The *New York Times* reported in a front page story that *immortelles* (everlasting dried flowers) stood over the coffin and "candles were kept burning in the chapel throughout the voyage."[34] A requiem mass was celebrated at St. Leo's. Then, at the Green-Wood Cemetery in Brooklyn, Willie's body was placed in a temporary tomb to await a permanent mausoleum.

Mackay tomb, Green-Wood Cemetery, John R. Lowe, architect, Brooklyn, NY, 1896–1900 (Author)

By tradition, Green-Wood was a Protestant cemetery, but the Mackays succeeded in having the site consecrated to enable the celebration of Catholic mass.[35] They purchased one of the highest sites and commissioned John R. Lowe and the Muldoon Monument Company of Louisville, Kentucky, to design and build one of the largest mausoleums at Green-Wood, which was equipped with vaults for another twenty-three Mackays. The cost was rumored to be three hundred thousand dollars.[36]

Although both sons "had been born when the hard times were over," Willie, unlike Clarie, had inherited some of his father's toughness and had been groomed to head the family and take over the business. Now Clarie faced the daunting prospect of doing so in Willie's place. He tended to nervousness and often spoke too loudly.[37] Clarie would have to acquire *savoir faire* to bear the Mackay mantle. But as his business acumen grew, Clarie became one of New York's most desirable bachelors.

Katherine

Katherine Duer, born May 9, 1879, personified "high" and "old" New York society. Her family name appeared in the New York *Social Register* when it began publication.[38] That the name Duer was not among the top 319 that Ward McAllister gave to the newspapers when Katherine was thirteen may have been an oversight, since few New York families had comparable pedigrees. Indeed, the Duers had been part of New York's social establishment long before the Astors or the Vanderbilts were ever heard of. Relatives of the Kings, the Van Rensselaers, the Gracies, and the Van Burens, the Duers were among the families that Louise Mackay had wanted so badly to meet back in 1876.[39] The reason for their omission from McAllister's list may well have been that, though established, they were not very rich.

Katherine's father, William Alexander Duer, was descended from Colonel William A. Duer, who came to New York from England in 1747 to serve as secretary to the colonial governor, Lord Clive. He married Lady Katherine Alexander, daughter of Lord Sterling, who became known as "the celebrated Lady Kitty Duer of Colonial days." Lady Kitty's lineage on the maternal side traced back to the de Peysters and Livingstons—early Dutch, or "Knickerbocker," settlers of New York. Katherine's paternal lineage went back to a fourteenth-century king, Robert II of Scotland.

Katherine Mackay with tiara, signed "Katherine, Sept. 1900" (Private Collection)

Colonel Duer served in the Revolutionary militia, as a delegate to the Continental Congress of 1777, and as Assistant Secretary of the Treasury. Succeeding generations served as justices on the Supreme Court, president of Columbia University, and in other distinguished posts. Katherine's father, William Duer, a lawyer with the prestigious law firm of Deyo, Duer, and Bauerdorf, was known for his wit. This served the Duers well, for they entertained vigorously. They were said to be the first family "to have liveried servants, and the number of wines served at the table was a matter of comment."[40]

Katherine's mother, *née* Ellin Travers, also brought good breeding to the family. Her family's church, Richard Upjohn's Trinity Episcopal at the head of Wall Street, was the old establishment church for wealthy New Yorkers. Its congregation included many of McAllister's "Four Hundred."

An only child, Katherine Alexander Duer was named for Lady Kitty. She used this nickname occasionally, but most people found Kitty too informal for the majestic Katherine. Her childhood was typical for a girl of her status—private tutors and summers either abroad or in rented houses in Newport. She came out in 1895. Admired for her beauty, her stature, and her manner, which could sometimes be called imperious, Katherine was described with awe by one popular chronicler: "She was gorgeous to gaze upon—tall, incredibly slender, with tresses as black as the night; she possessed an ivory-like skin and a smile that captivated everyone."[41] A writer for a New York scandal

Consuelo Vanderbilt, c. 1896 (Library of Congress)

Katherine Mackay dressed for a costume party with a wig, c. 1905 (Private Collection)

sheet described Katherine Duer as "a delightful extravagant young woman . . . [a] perfect specimen of willful, wistful beauty."[42] Louise Mackay too perceived Katherine's willfulness, but found it less than charming. She saw Katherine as having been raised by parents who "had spoiled her and denied her nothing, so that she had never been aware of any need for money."[43]

Katherine was a bridesmaid when, in 1895, her childhood friend Consuelo Vanderbilt married Charles Spencer-Churchill, the Duke of Marlborough. The wedding was one of the great society events of the 1890s. Years later, when Consuelo was a divorcée, she reminisced: "Katherine was very handsome, with a straight nose, and a shock of dark hair that swept back over a low, well-shaped forehead. Her dark eyes flashed with ardor and the love of life. She wanted to dominate us all; she was one of those who assumed it to be her right. She was always the queen in the games we played."[44]

A Perfect Match

In the summer of 1896, while on a ship bound for Europe, Katherine met Clarence Mackay on his way to visit his mother in Paris. Clarence was smitten. "She's as beautiful as her name," he proclaimed. Katherine made social calls and was called upon in England; Clarence booked return passage on her ship. He proposed at sea, and she accepted. The announcement of their engagement appeared in February 1897.[45]

In preparation for Katherine's marriage to Clarence, the Mackays commissioned a portrait from the French painter Edmund Chartran. One newspaper noted that "beauty has made her a leading belle both in London and New York," and that the portrait "bids fair" to be more successful than the portraits of the young Consuelo Vanderbilt, Duchess of Marlborough by Carlos Duran and of Mrs. Harry Payne Whitney by Raimundo De Madrazo y Garreta, which had been cel-

ebrated the previous season. The reporter, noting Katherine's full-length likeness, remarked, "There is a joyous atmosphere and feeling of youth and summer in the canvas, which the brunette beauty and tall graceful figure of the fair sitter seem to naturally accord."[46] (Katherine stood about five feet, eight inches; there are very few photos of her and the shorter Clarence standing together.)

Designed to discourage mixed marriages, standard procedure when a Catholic married out of the faith was for a priest to officiate at a simple service in a Catholic rectory. The Most Reverend Michael A. Corrigan, Archbishop of the Catholic Archdiocese of New York, was a conservative in Church matters and outspoken in his opposition to any acquiescence to Protestants. Hence, his blessing on the event of Katherine and Clarence's union—in the home of well-known Episcopalians—spoke volumes about the influence of the Mackay wealth.[47] The site chosen for the nuptials was neither a Catholic nor an Episcopalian church. The marriage would be solemnized in the Duers' house—by Catholic clergymen.

As the day approached, Katherine appeared in magazines and newspapers.[48] Already there was gossip, to which the *New York Times* responded that the "absurd story . . . that the bride had neglected to invite some of her blood relatives in favor of the members of the very rich set . . . was disproved."[49] A Chicago gossip columnist claimed, "This marriage will be a great thing for . . . [Louise] Mackay, as it will introduce her to the society of the Duchess of Marlborough from which she has been barred in London." The writer added waspishly that the marriage would also "make her way smooth in New York's exclusive circles."[50]

The Duers' living room at 17 West Twenty-first Street was decorated for the occasion as "a grotto of white lilies and apple blossoms." Estimates of the cost of Katherine's gown put it at more than ten thousand dollars (not counting the jewels). The guest list, kept to a relatively modest one hundred and fifty because the Duers' house was not large, glittered with New York high society names: Burden; King; Van Rensse-

Katherine Mackay dressed for Hyde Ball, oil portrait by John White Alexander
(Private Collection)

laer; Cutting; Gerry; Whitney; Webb; Fish; Stevens; Travers; Sloane. Countess Telfener, Clarence's aunt Ada, attended, as did his half-sister, Princess Colonna. Archbishop Corrigan himself officiated, with the assistance of his secretary, the Reverend James N. Connolly. Father Thomas J. Ducey of St. Leo's was present as well.

A wedding breakfast followed the ceremony, and at about three o'clock in the afternoon, the new couple left in a shower of rice and congratulations for a honeymoon in a cottage at Westbury, Long Island. At the bride's instruction, the flowers were sent to the Working Girls Club. A newspaper writer summed it up: "It was remarkable because it came as the finale of what seems like a fairy tale, a tale that brims with romance, the career of the Mackays."[51]

While the couple set up house in the city and in a rented cottage at Wheatley, Katherine deliberated about which architect would be best suited to designing the Long Island mansion that would be built with the Mackays' money.

THREE

Stanford White and McKim, Mead & White

❧ ❧

"His talent was a decorative, festive talent, nourished upon the pageantry of the Cinquecento."

—John Jay Chapman, "McKim, Mead & White: Especially Concerning the Influence of Stanford White on American Architecture," *Vanity Fair* 13, no. 1 (September 1919), 102.

KATHERINE'S DECISION, with Clarence's approval, to select Stanford White to design Harbor Hill was virtually a given, considering the stellar reputation of McKim, Mead & White at the time. White and his firm would have been well known to Clarence and Katherine, through the Mackays' business contacts and friends. White and his firm were quite simply the leading architectural firm of the turn-of-the-century; they had created city, country, and resort houses for many of leading socialites and the wealthy of New York and elsewhere, along with major commercial and public buildings. Their only possible competition as far as palaces for the wealthy would have been Richard Morris Hunt, who started the intense house-building competition back in the 1870s and early 1880s, with his work for the Vanderbilts.

Hunt, however, had died in 1895, and while his sons carried on, McKim, Mead & White now dominated the building of the rich man's house, and American architecture in general.

The firm was composed of three very different personalities, which explains to some degree its success. Charles McKim and Stanford White were the main designers. William Mead acted as the administrator and office manager; he made sure that steps did not rise too steeply, that drains were at the lower end of bathtubs, and, as he once explained, kept his partners from "making damn fools of themselves."[1]

Charles Follen McKim was nominally the senior partner of the firm. His name appeared first not for alphabetical reasons, but because he founded the firm, and was its style setter and guiding light. He was born in 1847 in rural Pennsylvania, the son of a leading abolitionist, James Miller McKim, and a Quaker mother. In 1865, his father and Frederick Law Olmsted founded the leading liberal magazine *The Nation*. McKim attended Harvard from 1866 to 1867, studying engineering. There he made friends who would later become clients, such as Prescott Hall Butler of Smithtown, New York. An interest in architecture led

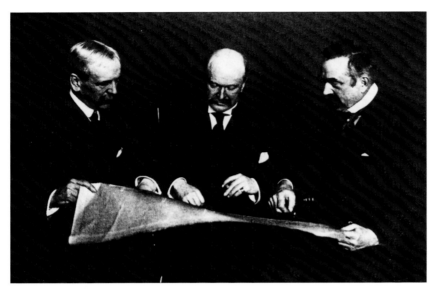

Portrait of firm of McKim, Mead & White, 1906 (Author)

was derived from the classicism of Greece and Rome as reinterpreted by architects from the Renaissance onwards. He also traveled widely and spent the summer of 1869 in England viewing country houses. Of the three partners, McKim was the only one with formal architectural training.

McKim returned to New York in 1870 and joined the office of H. H. Richardson, where he worked on numerous designs, including Trinity Church in Boston, as assistant designer. He began to separate from Richardson in 1872, although he occasionally still supervised projects. McKim and Richardson together edited *The New York Sketch Book of Architecture* (1874–6), an important journal.

In 1877 McKim entered into partnership with his brother-in-law William Bigelow, and William Mead. McKim had married Annie Bigelow of New York and Newport, Rhode Island (her parents had a large house at Newport) but they were divorced in 1879. Stanford White, an old friend of McKim's from the Richardson office, joined the firm in September 1879, when Bigelow left because of the divorce. By that point, McKim, Mead & Bigelow, with McKim as the main designer, had done several houses for wealthy New Yorkers at Elberon on the New Jersey shore, Lenox in the Berkshires of western Massachusetts, and Newport. In the summer of 1879 James Gordon Bennett, Jr., the owner of the *New York Herald* and later a partner of John Mackay in the cable business, commissioned McKim to do the Newport Casino.

McKim to spend the summer of 1867 in the New York office of Russell Sturgis. The first American school of architecture was just being founded at MIT that year, but McKim elected to go abroad and study at the leading school of architecture and fine arts, the École des Beaux-Arts. He stayed at the school for three years, absorbing the Beaux-Arts methodology, which

Portrait of Charles McKim, c. 1896–7 (Library of Congress)

In 1885 McKim married Julia Appleton, a member of a socially prominent and wealthy Boston family; however, she died only 18 months later. McKim immersed himself in public and professional activities, serving as president of the American Institute of Architects, and as a member of the McMillan Commission for Washington, D.C., which replanned the Mall.

He also founded in 1894 the American School of Architecture in Rome, which became the American Academy in Rome. Always very socially active, McKim belonged to many New York clubs—the buildings of which his firm designed—where he met prospective clients. McKim counted among his personal friends prominent socialites such as the Vanderbilts along with powerful political figures like Theodore Roosevelt, for whom he remodeled the White House. He also made suggestions for Sagamore Hill, Roosevelt's home on Long Island. McKim died at Smithtown Long Island in 1909. He never remarried and had one daughter from his first marriage.

William R. Mead was a native of Brattleboro, Vermont, where his father was a lawyer. One of Mead's brothers, Larkin Mead, became a prominent sculptor, and his sister Elinor married William Dean Howells. William graduated from Amherst College and then apprenticed with an engineer. After that, he apprenticed for two years in the office of Russell Sturgis. In 1871 Mead spent time in Europe, briefly attending classes at the Academia delle Belle Arti in Florence. Like his partners, Mead was active in New York society and belonged to several clubs. However, his wife Olga Kilenyi, a Hungarian sculptress whom he married in 1884, suffered from depression in the 1890s, and Mead thus somewhat restricted his social activities. He died in 1928 while on a visit to Rome. They had no children.

Stanford White has become the best-known figure of the firm, partially for his architecture, but also because of his glamorous lifestyle and his liaisons with chorus girls, and especially because of his dramatic murder in 1906.[2] He was born in New York City in 1853 and grew up there and on nearby family farms. His mother, Alexina Mease White, wrote poetry and his father, Richard Grant White, was a well-known, although impoverished, literary critic whose complaints about his penurious position may have inspired Stanford's later craving for fortune and riches. His father also had a series of mistresses, which may have influenced Stanford's later behavior. White exhibited a talent for sketching and watercolors at an early age, but his family could not afford to send him to school. John La Farge, a family friend, warned White of the likely poverty of an artist's life (La Farge went through a considerable family inheritance very quickly) and suggested he try architecture.

White joined H. H. Richardson's firm as an office boy in 1870, at the same time that McKim became the lead designer. White's talent for drawing quickly became evident, and he progressed to preparing many of the presentation sketches and drawings, eventually becoming the office expert in ornamentation. He—along with McKim—became a close friend of Augustus Saint-Gaudens, with whom he collaborated on sculptural projects. In 1878 White left Richardson's firm to travel and study abroad, primarily in France and England. McKim joined White (and Saint-Gaudens) for a tour of Loire Valley chateaus during the summer of 1878. Presumably they discussed White becoming a partner, for he joined the firm immediately upon returning to New York in September 1879.

In New York White became known about town for his appearance—tall, bright red hair, loud cloth-

Portrait of Stanford White, c. 1886 (Library of Congress)

Hyde Ball, New York, January 31, 1905, left to right: Mrs. Sidney Smith, P. A. Clark, Mrs. James Burden, Stanford White, James Henry Smith, Norman De R. Whitehouse, in chair Mrs. Stuyvesant Fish, on floor Sidney Smith (Bryon Collection, Museum of the City of New York)

ing—his energy, and his love of the high life. His marriage in 1884 to Bessie Smith of Smithtown did not diminish his activities; he was known as a consummate partygoer, often showing up at three parties a night as well as the opera. He also frequently contributed the decorations for elaborate parties. Photographs of White illustrate his style. About 6'2" in height, his bright red hair was close cut in the German manner, and he had a red mustache. Photographs show him colorfully dressed: a dark blue coat; a purple vest with white piping; a chartreuse silk shirt; and a florid orange tie. McKim described his partner's appearance at a Yale–Princeton football game in 1893: "White wore an enormous buttonhole bouquet of blue violets and perhaps the brightest blue necktie ever seen, a blue handkerchief, blue trousers—and probably a blue

shirt—and the air of a Wilbur Bacon. He might have been mistaken for the Yale mascot."[3]

In the later 1890s and early 1900s White's activities grew even more frantic; he seemed to be everyplace and with everyone. His financial situation grew precarious, as he had built an elaborate house at Gramercy Park and expanded his Long Island house at Smithtown, only to see a warehouse fire consume a large collection of European antiquities and *objets d'art* that he had purchased for resale to clients. A series of bad investments compounded the problem and he was forced to sell his portion of the partnership, becoming a salaried employee.

In addition to having financial problems, White was a serial adulterer. Within a group composed of his artist friends and a few clients White became well known for his exploits with the "girls." These young women, frequently showgirls in late adolescence or their early twenties, were a constant preoccupation of White's. He also employed prostitutes when he was not involved in a liaison. His sexual exploits seem to have been confined to showgirls and prostitutes; no evidence exists that he preyed upon or had affairs with the wives or daughters of clients. Indeed, White was known for his gallantry towards women and he was welcomed at major parties and society events.[4]

On June 25, 1906 White was murdered by Harry K. Thaw on the roof garden of Madison Square Garden (which White had designed in 1889). White's affair with Thaw's wife, Evelyn Nesbit (which started in 1900), and her taunts to him about White's sexual prowess, provoked Thaw to shoot White during an intermission. Thaw's violent revenge and the ensuing trials provoked an avalanche of "yellow press" scandal-mongering and an unending series of articles, books, and movies, which ensured White a lasting notoriety.[5]

In addition to the three partners, numerous other individuals employed by the office contributed to the firm's designs. The size of the office varied from just a few employees in the late 1870s to well over 100 around 1900. The office records of the period from 1877 to 1914 list 573 employees. Some were just draftsmen and specification writers; others reached the point of being actual collaborators with the partners. McKim, Mead & White was an important training office, and many significant architects passed through the drafting room. John Carrère and Thomas Hastings joined the office after returning from study at the École des Beaux-Arts in 1883. They would later rent space from the firm before moving out on their own. Other significant office men included Edward Palmer York and Philip Sawyer, and Francis L. V. Hoppin and Terrence A. Koen, who set up respective partnerships. Through the office passed many architects who would become important in San Francisco or Portland, as well as some who acquired national reputations, such as Cass Gilbert, Henry Bacon, Edward Tilton, William Boring, Egerton Swartwout, Harrie T. Lindeberg, and many more.

The office employed numerous individuals who spent their entire careers with the firm and became

"A Bud," portrait of Evelyn Nesbit (Library of Congress)

Charles Dana Gibson, "The Eternal Question," portrait of Evelyn Nesbit, c. 1902
(Author's Collection)

important and well-regarded in their own right. Shortly before White's murder in 1906, the partnership was expanded to include William Mitchell Kendall, who had joined in 1882, Bert L. Fenner, who had joined in 1891, and William S. Richardson, who had arrived in 1895. Richardson, for example, became the lead designer for the Mackay School of Mines at the University of Nevada, along with White's former assistant, F. J. Adams.

Early in the firm's career they were located at 57 Broadway; the quarters were three small cubicles with room for one chair and a large drafting room. One draftsman remembered: "I attributed a large part of the firm's unique success to the fact that they [the members of the firm] were always in the drafting room."[6] One consequence was that at first the designs produced by the office were genuine collaborations; however, as the firm grew each of the partners took on more specific duties. As the firm moved uptown—first in 1891 to the old Herter Mansion at 1 West 20th Street, and then in 1894 to the Mohawk Building at 160 Fifth Avenue—roles became more defined, with offices for different functions, from bookkeeping, to specification writing, to drafting. The partner's offices grew in size and became more isolated from the drafting room. The result was an "office style," in which for some projects the partner in charge may have only verbally suggested to the draftsman what to do, and approved of the final design. There were also projects of special importance, such as the Mackay house, which demanded the attention of the partner-in-charge.

Within the firm McKim appears to have been the leader in setting stylistic directions. Regarding design decisions, one office man recalled: "Sometimes one, sometimes another; but if anyone more than the others it would be that of Charles Follen McKim."[7] Lawrence Grant White (Stanford's son) claimed: "McKim was a calm deliberate scholar . . . [with] a strong will, so that he usually carried his point in an argument. Each building he produced was an architectural event. He built decidedly in the grand manner even to the point of austerity; and his work has a no-

ble, intellectual quality, a sober perfection."[8] McKim's intellectual interests were revealed in his assistance to Edith Wharton with her manuscript for *The Decoration of Houses*. Edith knew McKim and White and had assisted in fundraising for the American School of Architecture in Rome. In her autobiography (published in 1934) Wharton characterized McKim and White as "men of exceptional intelligence," who "stirred the stagnant air of Old New York . . . [with] the dust of new ideas."[9] She approached McKim about reviewing the manuscript she had assembled with some help from Ogden Codman Jr. McKim expressed some reservations about the assertion that the Italian villa was unsuitable for northern climates, but he fully agreed that France had a "present superiority" in architecture. He concurred with Edith and Ogden that originality lay not with a "willful rejection of what have been accepted as the necessary laws of the various forms of art . . . but in using them to express new . . . conceptions." He more explicitly stated the prospect as follows: "The designer should not be too slavish, whether in the composition of a building or a room, in his adherence to the letter of tradition. By conscientious study of the best examples of classical periods, including those of antiquity, it is possible to conceive a perfect result suggestive of a particular period . . . but inspired by the study of them all."[10]

The only designer at the firm educated in architecture, McKim was known for his cerebral design methods, and his habit of poring over pattern books for the correct motif. Trained in the Beaux-Arts system that put a premium on memory of plans, orders and details, one draftsman recalled: "He liked to sit down at the draftsman's table, usually in his hat and immaculate shirt sleeves, and design out loud . . . the room reverberated with architectural terms . . . Cyma Recta; Cyma Reversa; Fillet above; Fillet below; Dentils; Modillions: and so on."[11]

Stanford White possessed an equal ability to assemble architectural fragments, but whereas McKim tended towards an academic respectability, White could be more innovative. An office man remembered of White: "In directing his draughtsman he expressed his thought always with a pencil rather than by discussion. After covering often times, yards of tracing paper with alternative suggestions for work under consideration, he would eliminate all but two or three of the most pleasing and turn the matter over to his draughtsman to do 'something' which he would either reject at sight or, if this 'something' was found favorable, used it as the basis of future study."[12]

His design methods could be frenetic, as a draftsman recalled from working with White: "He would tear into your alcove, perhaps push you off your stool with his body while he reached for pencil and tracing paper and in five minutes make a dozen sketches or some arrangement of detail or plan, slam his hand down on one of them—perhaps two or three of them if they were close together—say 'Do that!' and tear off again. You had to guess what and which he meant."[13]

White's talents with drawing and watercolors earned him his position at the firm; when Mead questioned the wisdom of offering a position to White, McKim supposedly replied in 1879: "White has not had much training in architecture, . . . but he can draw like a house a-fire!"[14] Early in the career of the firm, White often made presentation sketches for clients. Of these, H. van Buren Magonigle, a draftsman and architect, remembered: "He used pastel on colored paper as a rule and rubbed it in or scrubbed it out with anything that came handy—usually his own silk handkerchief . . . These pastels had a curious charm and . . . made you think of the Morte D' Arthur and enchanted dream land forests."[15] But time grew increasingly precious, and the later sketches of White are fleeting scrawls done at top speed. His own hand became practically impossible to read; one friend complained: "Frankly I could not make out one word of Mr. Stanford White's letter."[16] Clients on occasion became upset, as exemplified by Whitelaw Reed, who tried unsuccessfully to get White to answer letters. After several polite requests, he wrote, "I must ask you dictate an immediate reply—*and see that it gets mailed.*" J. P. Morgan claimed of White, "He is always crazy."[17]

Mead was the quietest member of the firm. His office nickname was "dummy," reflecting his quiet demeanor in comparison to his more voluble and colorful partners. White's son noted "*Vogue la Galere* (The ship sails on) was the motto of the firm; and if McKim was the hull and White the sails of the ship, Mead was both rudder and anchor."[18] The divergences of the partners caused Saint-Gaudens to once draw a cartoon showing Mead flying kites pulling in opposite directions—one labeled McKim, the other White. Mead did assist with many designs and had a talent with plans and functional layouts that often eluded his partners. He ran the office, oversaw the production of the drawings and specifications, ran interference with contractors, and saw that the bills got paid. He looked over his partners' drawings and suggested corrections. A note to White indicates his role: "Dear Stanny, I see that, in the main stairway of the Payne Whitney house, from the saloon floor to the first bedroom the risers are seven and a half inches and treads ten and a half inches. A tenant house couldn't be worse."[19]

Mead's oversight of White's work indicates the significant role that construction played in the life of every architect and their office. The position of general contractor had not yet been invented, and in complex projects such as Harbor Hill, the architect was in charge of designing all details, choosing heating systems, setting up the plumbing, doing the engineering, writing the specifications, obtaining the competing bids, and coordinating the construction schedule. In lavish houses such as Harbor Hill, the architect designed the interiors, or worked closely with a firm such as Allard or Davenport in their production.

The architectural achievements of McKim, Mead & White were significant; they helped define the cultural epoch of the end of the nineteenth century and beginning of the twentieth, and the American Renaissance. The firm gave the United States a national architectural image that drew upon earlier traditions and remained viable into the 1940s. The initial work of McKim in the 1870s and then the firm in the early 1880s has received a number of labels. Much of their important work was in the realm of seaside and country resort houses, which has been called the Shingle Style because of the wooden shingles that covered much of the buildings' exterior surface.[20] The style was the result of a melding of the American wooden house tradition with the English Queen Anne style, as well as early American Colonial architectural details such as saltbox shapes, broad roofs, additive forms, and classical details such as pediments and widow's walks. McKim published photographs of early American buildings and furniture in 1874, and in 1877 McKim, Mead, Bigelow, and White made what Mead called "our 'celebrated' trip" along the Boston North Shore, during which they "made sketches and measured drawings of many of the important Colonial houses." He asserted, "these must represent some of the earliest records of the Colonial period."[21] The resultant houses, such as the Alden house (1879–80) at Lloyd's Neck, or the Isaac Bell Jr. house at Newport (1881–3) designed for James Gordon Bennett's brother in-law, were frequently called "modernized colonial" because of the employment of forms and details that owed a debt to early American buildings. Although the firm did numerous town houses and some commercial buildings, it was with the seaside resorts that they made their initial reputation.

Beginning in about 1883, the firm's work begins to demonstrate a new eclecticism that might be called scientific or academic, in contrast to the earlier synthetic eclecticism, as exemplified by the Shingle Style. With synthetic eclecticism, forms and details, while based upon historical precedent, were applied freely, with little concern for historical accuracy. Scientific eclecticism treated historical forms and details with a greater degree of accuracy and also tended towards a single type of reference, such as eighteenth-century Georgian mansions, or French chateaus. In resort houses the new approach can be seen in the H. A. C. Taylor (1883–85) project in Newport, which explicitly drew upon eighteenth-century Georgian prototypes.

Probably the breakthrough building for the firm

was the Henry Villard house (1882–6) on Madison Avenue in New York. Assisted by an office draftsman, Joseph Morrell Wells, the partners (all three participated in the design) used Italian Renaissance prototypes, specifically the Palazzo Cancelleria in Rome, which was thought to have been designed by Bramante. The Cancelleria was readily available to the designers through photographs and scale drawings in books such as Paul-Marie Letarouilly's *Edifices de Rome Moderne* (1840–57). This was typical of many source and pattern books that architects purchased while studying or traveling in France (the firm's office had a huge library of such books). Although the firm had done city houses prior to the Villard commission, none were as explicit in their adherence to historical detail, or had such lavishly decorated interiors. A number of the partners' artist friends, such as Augustus Saint-Gaudens, John La Farge, D. Maitland Armstrong, George Maynard, Frederic MacMonnies, and others, contributed to the interior. Fragments of European buildings were incorporated for the interior. The Villard house was McKim, Mead & White's contribution to the extravagant robber baron houses of the period, which had until then been primarily designed by Richard Morris Hunt and his protégées, such as George B. Post.

Although the Shingle Style and the synthetic eclectic approach would continue to be employed by the firm for many years (as exemplified by the William Merritt Chase house at Shinnecock), the new direction for which the firm became known was more explicit in its recall of grand architectural traditions. McKim was the partner in charge of the Boston Public Library (1887–95), which took the form of a large Italian Renaissance palazzo. Lavishly decorated on the interior with murals by Pierre Puvis de Chavannes, Edwin Austin Abbey, and John Singer Sargent, the building announced a new civic monumentalism that perfectly captured the spirit of the American Renaissance. As noted earlier, White was the partner in charge of Madison Square Garden in New York, which was a privately funded project that took up an entire city block and contained spaces for theaters, exhibitions, gardens, and apartments. Appropriately more decorated and colorful than McKim's sober library, White's use of the Spanish Renaissance as a source for Madison Square Garden was apparent.

This academic classicism or scientific eclecticism dominated the firm's work. The scale of projects grew, an example being the Loire Valley chateau in Great Barrington, Massachusetts they did for the widow of one of the California "big four," Mrs. Mark Hopkins (1884–6). For a son of California Gold Rush wealth, Ogden Mills Jr., they created a giant columned country house at Staatsburg on the Hudson River. French eighteenth-century sources provided the motifs for the Fred Vanderbilt house (1895–9) at nearby Hyde Park. The firm adopted the English Georgian style for a giant country house and estate they designed for one of the Vanderbilt daughters and her husband, Hamilton McKown Twombly, in Madison, New Jersey (1890–1900). In Rhode Island they designed the new statehouse (1891–1904), which, with its full-bore classicism and great dome, invoked the U.S. Capitol and became a model for a number of state capitols built over the course of the next forty years. McKim designed the new Morningside Heights campus of Columbia University, and White was responsible for a Bronx campus for New York University. In both cases giant domed libraries dominated a classical ensemble. At the University of Virginia, White was in charge of restoring Thomas Jefferson's Rotunda (destroyed in a fire) and making additions to the historic campus. Equally important was the partners' work at the civic monument scale, with bases for statues by Saint-Gaudens, MacMonnies and Daniel Chester French. They also worked with landscape architects on parks and designed significant monuments such as the Washington Square Arch in Manhattan, and Grand Army Plaza in Brooklyn.

The firm designed most of the interiors of their buildings. With office and commercial structures the attention was generally focused on the lobby or, in the case of banks, the main banking room, such as at the Bowery Savings Bank (1895) in New York, but houses usually meant a more complete approach. By the mid-1890s most of McKim's attentions were focused on public and commercial buildings, and his involvement with interiors dropped off. White, on the other hand, loved to do interiors of houses, and one of his major strengths was the care with which he created them. White was able to combine elements from different styles and periods, creating a mélange that was impressive, lavish, and perfectly suited to the aspirations of his clients. To do this White developed a coterie of art and antique suppliers both in the United States and abroad. In the mid-1880s he began making shopping trips to Europe, where he would purchase old paneling and ceilings, antique chests and sofas, architectural fragments of destroyed buildings, church fittings such as choir stalls, stained glass windows, pieces of sculpture, mantels, rugs, draperies, ironwork, pictures, and other items and ship them back to New York. Sometimes the items were for specific projects, but in many cases they were warehoused and when needed sold to a client. His connections with European dealers and his knowledge made him the architect of choice—for those that could afford him.[22]

Although McKim and White approached design from different perspectives, attempts to distinguish the primary architect of any given project is difficult. While it is popular to claim a single hand in the firm's work—more often than not that of Stanford White—it is difficult to determine who was primarily responsible for many finished projects. It is generally held that McKim's designs tend to be more sober, academic, and less ornamented, while White's buildings display a more relaxed attitude toward historical sources, are more ornamented, and are more colorful. McKim's work, such as the Pennsylvania Railroad Station (1905–8), is seen as tending towards the grand and monumental, while White's designs, such as Rosecliff (1897–1900) (designed for Tessie Fair Oelrichs) have a carefree quality; his source was the Grand Trianon of Versailles (with a second floor added), or the Garden City Hotel (1893–5; rebuilt 1899–1901).

Garden City Hotel of 1893–5, McKim, Mead & White, architects, burned and rebuilt 1899–1901 (Society for the Preservation of Long Island Antiquities)

Harbor Hill, view of house, distant, with trees bare (Private Collection)

However, the highly ornamented University Club (1896–1900) was designed by McKim, while the much more sober Metropolitan Club (1891–4) was done by White. Harbor Hill, which is a Stanford White project, evokes on the exterior a sober, restrained quality. White here clearly tried to invoke grandeur rather than frivolity. The firm really was based on a partnership, and the partners did discuss their work with each other and make modifications based on such discussions.

The success of McKim, Mead & White was due to the talent of the three partners and their interaction with each other and their office staff. They were fortunate in that they attracted wealthy clients who knew what to expect: expensive, impressive, and in some cases, memorable buildings.

FOUR

Designing and Building Harbor Hill

꽃꽃

"We are not yet hampered by national traditions and may take only as much of any one style as happens to please us."

—Guy Lowell in *American Gardens*, 1902

GRUMBLING COULD BE HEARD when the Mackays took over their Long Island property in 1899. The Roslyn newspaper reported that they had preempted a favorite picnic spot with a venerable tower. "Mrs. Mackay has been trying to close the road to the tower which people have been using for many years . . . [and] is about to remove the old observatory . . . at the end of the road. . . . The people have regarded the hill as a sort of park for so long that the assertion of an individual right in it seems to anger them." The writer continued, "People are being excluded from Harbor Hill woods. . . . When the property was in the possession of Walter R. Willets of this village, he generously allowed poor persons to gather the fallen wood for their winter fires. This winter they will be shut out." Local indignation was not placated when the new owners paid to dig up the Old Zion African Methodist Episcopal cemetery on their

land and relocate it. The newspaper was clear about who was to blame: Mrs. Mackay alone was responsible for the assault on what had been a pleasant, quiet village on the Sound.[1]

Untroubled, Katherine pondered which architect would best realize the baronial house of her dreams. Stanford White was clearly the man for the job, and Clarence apparently concurred. White and his firm had certainly done well with various commissions in Newport, notably his house for Jim Fair's daughter, Tessie Fair Oelrichs. Rosecliff was under construction, and was going to be a palace.

Mrs. Mackay Plans Her Dream House

Wherever she might be on a given day—at home in Manhattan, visiting in Newport, with her in-laws in London, or in temporary lodgings on their Rosyln property—Katherine was planning Harbor Hill. More than one hundred notes and letters, most written in purple ink on pink or orchid-colored note cards ("Without mauve, life would be a blank for her," one

Perspective rendering of Harbor Hill (Museum of the City of New York, McKim, Mead & White Collection)

Katherine watcher remarked[2]), chronicle how Katherine apprised White of her wishes. Although she was just twenty and White, with a long and distinguished roster of achievements, was forty-six, Katherine did not hesitate to wield the client's authority.

She had only just written to White in mid-July 1899 for design advice when a torrent of prints and photographs arrived. From Newport she promptly replied, "I have decided to begin on those plans at once so will you express me as soon as you get this, some books about and drawings of Louis XIV Chateaux. Their severe style preferred. Also of halls Henri II (French), staircases Henry II. Should you be coming to Newport the end of the week, I should be glad as I really want to begin at once. On enclosed sheet you will find my idea of the ground floor. Up-

stairs will have to be explained to you verbally. Hope you will give this your immediate attention."[3]

With books from McKim, Mead & White's working library in hand, Katherine wrote again three days later. Already she had spotted the model for her house and had clear ideas of how to adapt it to suit her. "I do mean a very severe house. The style of the full front view of the Maisons-Laffite comes nearest to what I

Elevation of Ancien Hôtel de Montescot à Chartres, plate from Claude Sauvageot's Palais, Chateaux, Hôtels et Maisons de France du XVe au XVIIIe Siecle, 1867

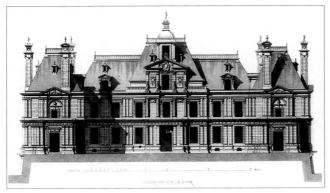

Elevation of Maisons-Lafitte, 1642, also known as the Chateau de Maisons-sur-Seine, plate from Claude Sauvageot's Palais, Chateaux, Hôtels et Maisons de France du XVe au XVIIIe Siecle, 1867

mean. And, even that has the windows too ornate to suite [*sic*] ·us." Commissioned by a nobleman in the court of Louis XIV and completed in 1642, the Maisons-Lafitte was the work of architect François Mansart. The pinnacle of French Renaissance design, it served as a model for other French palaces. (Also called the Château de Maisons-sur-Seine, the Maisons-Lafitte still stands in suburban Paris in the forest of Saint Germain.)

Among White's books was Claude Sauvageot's 1867 work, *Palais, Châteaux, Hôtels et Maisons de France du XVe au XVIIIe Siecle* (Palaces, Castles, Hotels and Houses from the 15th to the 18th Century). With scale drawings of facades and details and perspective views, the Sauvageot was an invaluable source that documented the Maisons-Lafitte precisely. White certainly relied on it for Harbor Hill—eliminating, as Katherine specified, much of the ornamentation.

Many of Katherine's affluent predecessors and contemporaries may have looked to English models for their mansions, but her choice of a French prototype was also in keeping with current vogue. Edith Wharton and Ogden Codman's new book, *The Decoration of Houses* (1898), exalted French classicism as most suitable to modern America, asserting that "modern domestic life really began" with Louis XIV.[4] The connotation of French royalty and imperial taste of course attracted Katherine. And Rosecliff (1897–1900), modeled after the Grand Trianon at Versailles, attested to Stanford White's skill with French prototypes.

Whatever the influences, Harbor Hill's emulation of the Maisons-Lafitte conveyed a distinct message: here is a new American aristocracy that rules by divine right of money.

Katherine's early letters make clear that she and her architect—always addressed courteously as "Dear Mr. White"—saw eye to eye. White's initial drawings met with immediate general approval. Katherine was ready to go into detail, down to minutiae. She ex-

North elevation (Monograph of the Works of McKim, Mead & White, 1915, pl.169)

East elevation (Monograph of the Works of McKim, Mead & White, 1915, pl.169)

pressed her wishes mostly as demands and orders, however, rarely as requests:

> The plan where the sides project is what I meant, I have made notes on it to give you points. . . . I want my floor (over the ground floor) on the north side over the library my suite. Consisting of a dressing bathroom combined opening to a bedroom which opens into a sitting room which is to be the corner room facing water view—next to my bathroom I wish another room as large as it for dresses. Also; over the hall facing the water a suite for Clairie the same as mine his study opening into my boudoir. I wish an antechamber to my suite. I don't want my rooms to open to the hall excepting a door in my bathroom. . . . The other side of the hall facing my suite I wish three simple rooms with one bathroom: a linen closet, large and next to that in the south corner a bedroom; good size for my maid—no rooms over the front door as I wish their windows to light the hall. The floor above this to be arranged with the hall left as my hall. The rooms as follows: 2 suites of 2 large bedrooms (re: bath & dressing room combined per suite) and on the south side 6 bedrooms with 3 bathrooms, every 2 rooms a bathroom—on this floor an attick for trunks—no division. . . . The servants' quarters over wing. On the ground floor of the wing, a large pantry opening on one side into a servants' hall and kitchen though no laundry. Where you see B small room for polishing and cleaning silver. Over this floor 15 servants' rooms with washroom with tub—Also could you put off the smoking room a dressing room for Men. No bath. . . .

> I hope this is all clear. Show me the plans after you get to Newport. That is time enough. I do not want a single shutter on the house. All must be inside—and I want the rooms of my suite to have folding doors, so I can have lots of room.

> —Hoping we will understand each other.[5]

In a later message she stipulated, "I also want [*sic*] estimate of fitting out wine cellar and plan showing exact place of wine cellar, laundry wood and coal place." This communiqué, from London, concluded, "Hoping you will rush this."[6]

Sometimes Katherine acknowledged her imperious manner, coyly signing a note, "the Tyrant." Or she would inject a coquettish note; when conflict over the gate lodge arose between Stanford White and the Mackays' chosen landscape designer, Guy Lowell, she wrote to White, "Whatever *you* decide about its placement is my decision also."[7] But another missive closed, "This is *imperative*." Rarely but occasionally Clarence entered her correspondence, especially to add pressure, as in, "Clary now says that until the four green columns in the hall are in place, he will not move in to the house . . . ! See to all these things, *please*."[8]

Katherine Mackay was an important client, but White could be elusive. He tended to take on too much, both professionally and socially, and at times Katherine had difficulty getting his attention. On August 7, 1899, she cabled: "Bring plans when you come and see me either Wednesday or Thursday afternoon at 6:30 o'clock please telegraph which day you are coming." Two days later, having had no reply, she wired again: "Please come and see me at ten o'clock promptly on Thursday morning."[9] And then: "I will call at your office at 4 o'clock this afternoon. Will you be there & able to give me half an hour of your *undivided* attention.[10] She could also wheedle: "Can't you arrange to come here Monday. . . . ? It's a long time since I have seen you. Telegraph your answers & please see to all these things which I have tried to convey as clearly & laconically as possible from my mind to yours."[11] Then, after some weeks, Katherine demanded, "Will you take the 5:30 from town on Friday next and dine & spend the night with us? There are several questions I wish to see you about. . . ." (Below her signature she added an afterthought: "What an appetite a new house has! Oh for $250,000 to spend here!"[12])

This time, at least, White slipped past her, first accepting but then declining, with the blame shifted to his long-suffering wife, Bessie. "You will think me a fraud of the first water," he wrote back, "but I forgot entirely that I had promised my wife to go out of town on Friday, to the Webbs, up in the Adirondacks."[13]

Amid the verbal parrying, White successfully produced what Katherine wanted. By August 20, 1899, with his draftsmen's help, he sent her a preliminary scheme. Her response was favorable. "Your very satisfactory letter received yesterday morning. You have placed the house exactly as I meant and I think it is indeed a fine site." She directed him to proceed with de-

Drawing of exterior details (*Monograph of the Works of McKim, Mead & White, 1915, pl. 170*)

tailed drawings, and to begin thinking about the entrance lodge and larger estate, including the other buildings.[14]

Speed was critical to Katherine, as she was eager to start entertaining and impressing her peers. On November 7, 1899, she cabled White to send tracings of the new plans to her chosen interior designers, Allard & Sons and A. H. Davenport & Company; his accompanying letter was to say, "these are the final plans," meaning they should suffice for designing the interior.[15] (This turned out to be a mistake; the interior designers wound up bidding on incomplete plans; see Chapter Five.) More changes followed, and in December 1899 White instructed his assistant, William Symmes Richardson (later a full partner in the firm), that should he, White, be late for an appointment, Richardson must "send by messenger the perspective of the house, the two perspectives of the lodge, and also of the gates which are somewhere on Ives's table but I cannot find." He also wanted a set of blueprints of the latest plans, which Katherine had seen, as "they contain changes from the ones she has, she wishes them."[16]

Katherine's barrage of instructions and reminders to White continued. "Remember to make the ceiling of the Saloon 2 or 3 feet lower so as to allow for my bath to be 3 feet deep," Katherine cabled in October 1899.[17] And from another letter:

I want a bell outside by anteroom which rings in the maid's room.

I want in my bath room: A telephone to my maids room.

A telephone to the nursery
A telephone to the Servant's hall
A telephone to the Linen closet
A bell to butler's pantry
A bell to maid's room.

In my bed room:
A bell to my maid's room.

In my boudoir:
one bell to butler's pantry.[18]

Angle of main facade showing service wing (Museum of the City of New York, McKim, Mead & White Collection)

Photo of west loggia end—elevation, c. Jan. 1902 (Private Collection)

While Katherine planned her dream house and saw it start to rise on its foundation, Clarence mostly played the role of good-humored but vigilant husband. A businessman, he added up the builders' charges and compared them to White's estimates; when the two came close enough, he paid without complaint. When he brought excesses to White's attention, the architect responded with some trimming—for instance, he reduced the size of the gate lodge so it could be built for about $20,000 instead of the original $30,000.[19]

Occasionally Clarence attempted to rein in his wife's excesses, but at other times he served as her agent. For example, he pressed White on the design of the estate's perimeter. "Please let me know when the rough model of the fence will be finished as the Mrs. is very anxious to go down and see it."[20] But Katherine ruled, as Clarence made clear in a letter about the terrace. "I should like to have you come down and talk it over with my wife. She doesn't get up before eight o'clock, so arrange to take a 9:30 train from New York. Telegraph her the day previous to coming, which I trust will be very soon."[21]

The rapport between Clarence and White was very much man to man. Clarence addressed his correspondence, "Dear Stan," and his tone had none of Katherine's hauteur. Though respectful, he was willing to question, prefacing one gentlemanly challenge, "Please understand that I am writing this purely in a business way."[22] He could be jocular: "Very sorry to hear that you got a crack on the head, but by the tone of your letter I think that you must be quite your old self again, for it is written in your usual quick and snappy style." He thanked White for "the kind congratulations about my horse winning. Only wish you had been on him."[23]

Aesthetics as well as money engaged Clarence in the building of Harbor Hill. When White proposed to enlarge a fireplace, Clarence replied, "As it is absolutely in accordance with [the] Louis XIV design of the room, I think we had better not have it enlarged."[24]

Although his father's gift to Katherine was generous, and his inheritance would ultimately leave Clarence exceedingly rich, he saw his wealth as finite and other men as far richer than he. His response to the purchase of a fireplace that White proposed was characteristic: "I will tell you right here that I would not think of paying such an absurd price as 100,000 francs for any mantelpiece, unless I had the income of a Carnegie or a Rockefeller!" Or about a certain moose head: "You seem to forget the main point, viz: the price."[25]

And problems eventually did arise over the extras—things that had been overlooked during planning, such as the terraces and balustrades to surround the house. To persuade Clarence to accept his proposal, White wagered, "that the cost of this extra terrace wall will be more than covered (when all your contracts are let) by the saving I will have made on the final estimate on the cost of the house."[26] This was fantasy, of course, or a bit of guile on the architect's part. As costs mounted, Clarence's temper began to show: "I . . . accept the Johnson estimate of $2790, for regulating the temperature in the house. I do hope that this is the last of these fancy tricks of yours. There is always something turning up, which adds extra and extra to the cost."[27]

Nonetheless, the bond between Clarence and Stanford White strengthened over time. They traveled together in Canada to fish for salmon, and White asked for Clarence's support for getting his young colleague, John Russell Pope ("Bobo"), into the Union Club.[28]

Current Vogue and Stanford White's Free Hand

Katherine Mackay's unequivocal choice of the Maisons-Lafitte as the model for Harbor Hill greatly simplified Stanford White's job. While the seventeenth-century French palace was unlike other McKim, Mead & White commissions, at least White was spared having to assemble a mélange of styles from examples spanning all recorded history, as indecisive clients some-times required. The problem was widely recognized. A popular novelist, the American Winston Churchill (not the British statesman of the same name) parodied such hodgepodges. In Churchill's 1898 novel *The Celebrity*, an industrialist explains the sources for his mansion: "Take, for instance, that minaret business on the west; I picked it up from a mosque in Algiers. The oriel just this side is whole cloth from Haddon Hall [a twelfth-century manor house in Derbyshire], and the galleried porch next to it from a Florentine Villa. The conical capped tower I got from a French château, and some of the features on the south from a Buddhist temple in Japan."[29]

The wide-ranging eclecticism of the 1870s and '80s persisted, albeit moderated, through the '90s, but certain limitations did apply. In most cases the accept-able styles for rich Americans' country houses were those descended from classical antiquity. East Asia, al-though it fascinated eighteenth-century European monarchs such as Frederick the Great of Prussia and Queen Sophia Albertina of Sweden, was simply be-yond the pale for American millionaires.[30] Artists could adopt Asian motifs—as for instance, Louis Com-fort Tiffany did for his house, Laurelton Hall, which went up at almost the same time as Harbor Hill—but for practical people not given to artists' flights of fancy, elements from the Far East were beyond consid-eration. A few American country houses had prece-dents in Germany, Spain, and Scandinavia, but the main sources in 1900 were England, France, Italy, and America's own colonial heritage.

Academically-trained American architects favored the Italian Renaissance. Richard Morris Hunt adopted one of Genoa's great urban palaces for The Breakers, Cornelius Vanderbilt II's house in Newport (it was criticized as overblown and inappropriate).[31] More common were villas modeled after those of Italian Re-naissance architects such as Andrea Palladio and Se-bastiano Serlio—houses with temple-like colonnaded porticos and decorated pediments. Charles McKim thought well enough of quoting the Italian Renais-

sance, and did so in designing E. D. Morgan's Beacon Rock (1889) in Newport.[32] In the late 1890s the painter-architect Charles Adams Platt designed sev-eral small country houses following Italian models. But by 1900, the Italian villa seemed too obscure and small to suit an American magnate.

French architectural and interior design elements began appearing in large American houses as early as the 1850s. Hunt found favor among rich Americans with houses invoking the early Renaissance chateaus of the Loire Valley in his designs for houses such as William K. and Alva Vanderbilt's mansion at 660 Fifth Avenue (1878–82) and Ogden Goelet's Ochre Court (1888–92), both in Manhattan, and in Asheville, at Biltmore. And the McKim firm's Hopkins-Searles Castle (1884–6) in Great Barrington, Massachusetts, for Mary Frances Hopkins, follows the French exam-ple. But by the 1890s the newly popular idioms, though still French, were more academic and came from the eighteenth century. Hunt's Marble House (1888–92) in Newport, also for the W. K. Vanderbilts, offers an example, as does Stanford White's Rosecliff for the Oelrichs. (A contributing factor was the cult of Marie Antoinette that sprang up in this period; Amer-icans prized anything said to be connected to Louis XVI's queen—chairs, grillwork, tapestries, and any-thing else that passed as royal and French.)

As Katherine stipulated, White's design modified many features of the French model. He did away with the pilasters with which Mansart articulated the Maisons-Lafitte's façade; at the corners, he replaced pi-lasters with subtle quoins. He also changed the fenes-tration patterns and the proportions of the hyphens and the wings. At the main pavilion, he greatly sim-plified the complex pediment and windows above the cornice. Elsewhere, too, White's touch was subtle. To emphasize the house's large size he planned a belt course, a deep entablature, and balustrades over the entrance pavilion; the perfectly balanced service and piazza wings enhanced the effect. The chimney stacks atop the Maisons-Lafitte's end pavilions were replaced by White's dormer windows. Instead of separating the

Marble House, for William K. and Alva Vanderbilt, Richard Morris Hunt, architect, Newport, RI, 1888–92 (Preservation Society of Newport County)

Laurelton Hall, Louis Comfort Tiffany house, Oyster Bay, NY, 1902–5 (Library of Congress)

roof of the central block from the wings, White merged them. As a result Harbor Hill would give a more compact and more vertical impression than the Maisons-Lafitte. White also gave the exterior of Harbor Hill a particulated appearance, enabling the viewer on the outside to "read" the interior.

The restraint with which White decorated the exterior was closer to Charles McKim's work than to most of his own. Following Katherine's order for severity, ornament was confined to the area of the doorway, dormer window pediments, and some ironwork on the roof crest. In fact, White borrowed the entrance ornamentation not from the Maisons-Lafitte

but from the Ancien Hôtel de Montescot at Chartres (also in the Sauvageot book). Huge strapped columns supporting an elaborate pediment framed the doorway. Over the tall windows, flanking the door, he placed garland panels with repeated Venus heads.

In designing the interior, especially the ground floor, White followed Katherine's orders only partly, departing freely not only from the Maisons-Lafitte but also from his client's ideas. The floor plan of Harbor Hill owes little to Mansart. Instead, it is a reinterpretation of sixteenth- and seventeenth-century English country houses. To surround the two-stories-high main hall, White planned four corner pavilions to accommodate the stairwell, a billiard room, the stone room, and the dining room. The wing that stretched eastward housed service rooms; the one to the west included a conservatory and a piazza.

White followed Katherine's orders for the second floor more closely. His plans gave Katherine the antechamber she wanted for her boudoir. Her dresses would have a room of their own—measuring 26 by 14 feet, per her specifications—a bit smaller than her sumptuous bath.[33] Clarence got his portion of space, and the head butler also was placed on the second floor. Guest rooms would take up most of the rest of the second floor and part of the third.

The third floor housed ten guest rooms, three servants' rooms, a nursery for the children who would be born, a large room for the maids' sewing, plus substantial storage for trunks and a large dress closet for Katherine.

In planning service space, both Katherine and White subscribed to the ideas of a reform movement concerning servants' accommodations that had begun in the 1880s. Writers such as Amelia Barr and Mary Elizabeth Carter, who helped explain to Americans the way to treat servants, advocated decent housing and a modicum of privacy for house staff. Servants' bedrooms should have windows to the outside and doors and bureaus that locked.[34] Harbor Hill's service spaces, distributed over three floors, occupied nearly as much square footage as did the public areas.

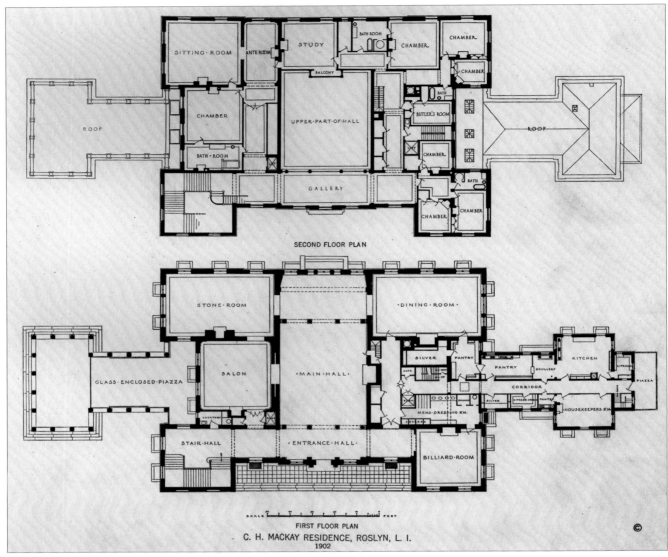

SECOND FLOOR PLAN

FIRST FLOOR PLAN
C. H. MACKAY RESIDENCE, ROSLYN, L. I.
1902

First and second floor plans (Monograph of the Works of McKim, Mead & White, 1915, pl.169)

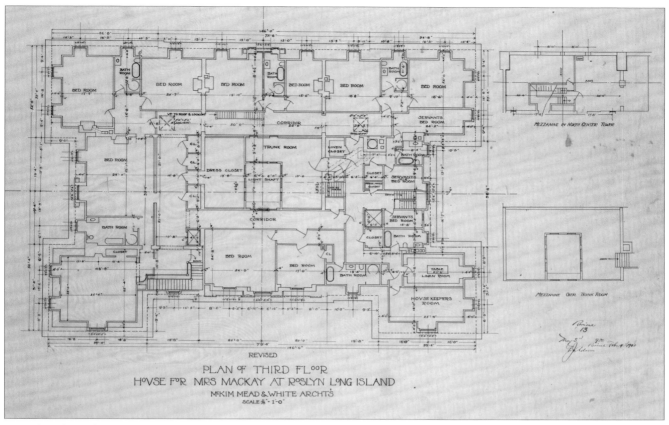

Plan, third floor, ink on linen (The New-York Historical Society, Cd. 78462)

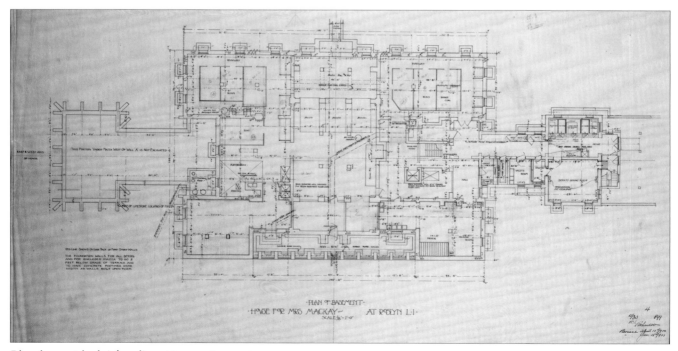

Plan, basement level, ink on linen (The New-York Historical Society, Cd. 78461)

The ground floor of the service wing contained the kitchen (which was unusual in not being "below stairs"), scullery, pantries, silver vault, a dining room for the higher-ranking ("upper") staff, and a house-keeper's room. Several back stairways and a servants' smoking piazza were located at the ground floor.

While the exterior in some ways mirrored the interior, it also hid certain features. Some window openings, such as those outside the ground floor of the hall, framed blank spaces, and no windows were planned for the corresponding portions of interior walls. White arrayed the house around the dominant 36-foot-high interior hall. Elsewhere ceiling heights reflected the function of each space and the status of expected occupants. The ground-floor public rooms surrounding the great hallway rose 20 feet high. The family's and guests' rooms on the second floor had 16-foot ceilings, while the third-floor rooms had 12-foot ceilings. In the service wing, ceilings measured just 10 feet high. The exterior windows indicated some of the different interior floor height.

The mansion's enormous basement was equipped to accommodate ambitious social plans. It housed four walk-in ice boxes; a meat-chopping area; a root cellar; storerooms for food and cleaning supplies; a wine cellar, rooms for washing, hanging, and ironing laundry; and a great cedar vault intended to serve as a linen closet. Maintaining Harbor Hill called for a carpentry shop, a workroom for a resident electrician and house painters, a plumber's room, a second servants' dining room, a heating plant consisting of three boilers in a sunken pit with a railing, plus a coal cellar.

At first water was a problem. Land was therefore purchased in Roslyn proper, and a well dug and outfitted with a steam pump. Pipes were laid up the hill to a 60-foot-tall water tower that stood 410 feet above sea level; this provided adequate water and water pressure for the house and outbuildings. (Later, a small reservoir was added, and the water pumped up to the tower.)

Heating approximately 60,000 square feet of interior space was a major undertaking, for which New

Water tower (Bryant Library Local History Collection, Roslyn, NY)

York's J. S. Haley steam fitting and engineering company was engaged. Haley calculated, "For the three months, when the house is wholly occupied, on mild days the consumption will be about one ton of coal in twenty four hours, and in severe cold weather it will probably come up to as high as four tons in twenty-four hours. The probable average of two tons for each twenty-four hours for the three months will be one-hundred and eighty tons. For the other three months when partially occupied by the servants, about three tons a week ought to be enough to keep the servants quarters warm and the rooms the water is in from freezing, will be around forty tons or a total of two hundred and twenty tons for the year." Along with the massive set of boilers and furnaces, Haley provided the piping, radiators, circulation fans, and duct work. Harbor Hill would therefore need a boiler man on duty around the clock; the plan for "below stairs" provided a room for this worker as well.[35]

The Mansion Materializes

Katherine Mackay would have had her Long Island palace appear overnight, but constructing the mansion and the roads to and around it took from late 1899 through much of 1902. The project required the skills and muscle of numerous artisans and laborers as well as supervisors—probably more than one thousand all told. A legacy of records, including contracts, bills, and payments, provides a picture of who was responsible for what in constructing Harbor Hill, and how much their services and materials cost the Mackays.

As was customary, supervising and coordinating construction fell to the architect's office. Thus, besides writing specifications for construction and mechanical systems and overseeing the work, the McKim firm solicited bids and presented them to their clients. White's annual office salary was around $28,000.[36] Most day-to-day particulars in the McKim office were delegated to the staff. William Symmes Richardson assisted White with most of the designs and worked on the early Harbor Hill drawings. White's main assistant during the construction was Frederick J. Adams, who joined the firm as a draftsman in 1896 and became one of White's righthand men; Adams, in turn, had his own assistants.

The basic structure of the house White designed was load-bearing masonry faced with blue Indiana limestone. The walls supported horizontal I-section iron beams that varied in thickness from eight to twenty-four inches to support different loads and spans. The I-beams were laid in a horizontal pattern that, in turn, supported the edges of low, saucer-shaped Guastavino vaulting. A recent invention of the Spanish-born architect Rafael Guastavino that had been used to good effect in the Boston Public Library and other McKim, Mead & White buildings, Guastavino

vaults were also employed in some stations of the the New York subway system, then under construction. Handsome as well as practical, the ancient Catalan technique using high-fired bricks won favor for both its strength and its resistance to fire.[37] The Guastavino firm's bill for work at Harbor Hill came to $25,647.07.

Structural iron for the floors and roof was supplied by Milliken Brothers Civil Engineers and Contractors in Iron and Steel Construction, headquartered on Lower Broadway near many architects' offices, with a manufacturing plant in Brooklyn. The iron for Harbor Hill was rolled in Brooklyn and shipped directly to Roslyn, where Milliken workmen erected it.

The masonry, laid by the W. A. & F. E. Conover Company, came largely from the old Forty-second Street reservoir in Manhattan. The water supply was being drained, the structure dismantled, and the great hole it left filled for the New York Public Library on Fifth Avenue and adjacent Bryant Park. More than 166,000 tons of stone were shipped from midtown Manhattan to Roslyn. Conover's share of the final cost of the entire job came to $117,006.76.

William Hyers, Conover's foreman, was paid six dollars a day. He supervised the masonry work of many individuals such as Hy Fitzpatrick, John Curran, and James Kennedy, who came out from Manhattan to Brooklyn by ferry or on foot over the bridge, then traveled by train to Roslyn, where they were lodged for the week; they were reimbursed for their carfare and board. Workers from Brooklyn or Queens also roomed for the week in Roslyn, where lodgings and board cost between fifty cents and a dollar per man per day.

Most so-called city laborers were paid two dollars a day, though they had no real trades, while "country laborers"—the men with picks and shovels—received just one dollar. (The average annual income of a working American at the time was $490.[38]) Laborers with slightly more than minimal skills got 33 cents an hour for a ten-hour day. At Harbor Hill, some workers earned more than the average, with others earning the average.

Master masons received 60 cents an hour, and a

basic carpenter received $2.75 per day. The master electrician, E. H. Pietach of the E. Nielson Company, earned $4.25 per day, while his two assistants got $3.50, and their "helper," $1.50 per day. When Harry Perine, of Perine Bath-Room Speciality Company, sent men to polish the bathroom fixtures, he received 40 cents an hour for each worker plus the cost of the polish. The watchman earned $2 a day.[39]

In a key position during the construction, the architect's on-site captain was Leland S. Sudlow, who had been with the McKim firm since 1891 (and worked there until he died in 1917). Sudlow was seasoned in dealing with contractors and coordinating the work of different trades. Over the course of the Harbor Hill project, his pay rose from $75 to $100 a month.

White followed the progress of the job largely through Sudlow and Adams. Sudlow kept him informed by memo, such as, "Write to Guastavino about the roof of the kitchen" or, referring to some delay in the framing, "For some reason Guastavino will not instruct his foreman to go ahead with this."[40] White visited the job site periodically and returned to the office with hastily scrawled notes, which a secretary deciphered and typed.[41]

In the rush to get architect's drawings out for contractors' bids, some details got overlooked. Milliken discovered that the subcontractors doing the furring and lathing had drawings that did not match the architect's originals; the subcontractor's set "did not show any cornice work," and, in fact, full-size drawings arrived three months later "showing sections of cornices in different rooms."[42] Several phone calls later, Milliken decided, rather than argue, to order the "furring man to get out the furring and lathing as called for on these drawings, the cost of which amounted to quite an item." A month later, still more drawings arrived "showing a lot of extra cornice furring and lathing." The problem was that, "We have already furnished more material than called for, and the work has also cost us considerably more than allowed."[43]

Sometimes the different contractors on the job were at odds. Milliken reported, for instance, that Guastavino's workmen were removing some of the tie rods between the iron beams and turning the arches in an opposite direction. "This may be all right and it may not," wrote Milliken, continuing, "We very much fear that any such procedure on the job may lead to trouble sooner or later." Sudlow had to intervene with Guastavino and order them to follow the original plans.[44]

There were, also, the inevitable "changes." Redesigned skylights and roofs, for example, required different construction members from those first specified.[45] And some instructions were missing altogether, as with construction drawings showing plates "of considerable heavier section than we estimated on, as you did not specify any thickness."[46]

Katherine pushed the builders hard, and her demands inspired respect bordering on fear. That she did not fully understand the complexity of construction was evident from the start, when she ordered that the servants' wing be built first. The farmhouse in which she and Clarie were living had space for only six servants and none at all for her dresses and the linens. Immediate construction of the mansion's servants' wing, Katherine proposed, would solve that problem.[47] Katherine did not understand that building the house as a series of separate units would only prolong the construction process; eventually she accepted White's suggestion for how to proceed. With work fully under way, she often complained that it seemed not to be proceeding; White's office took the blame. "Those plans for terraces have not yet been delivered to Conover. . . . I insist on their being in Conover's office by 4:30 today."[48] And when she thought the project ought to be nearing completion: "Will you please see that your men finish the mantelpieces in the hall and the ones in the dining room at once. . . . I want to know cost & exact times within which it can be done as the latest date is Friday Nov. 8th on that date I wish all workmen out of the house for good."[49] Construction progressed this way, from one round of problems, resolutions, complaints, and placations to the next, as the autumn of 1901 advanced.

Katherine and daughter Ellin on garden terrace, c. 1905 (Private Collection)

Katherine and Clarence with daughter Katherine in carriage, c. 1906
(Bryant Library Local History Collection, Roslyn, NY)

As overseer of the job, Leland Sudlow kept an eye on the calendar. While he was diplomatic with clients, whom he shielded from design and construction conflicts and his own exasperation, he could be tough with the builders. In the McKim office, Frederick Adams often got to hear Sudlow's stifled annoyance, as in this relayed instruction: "Mrs. Mackay wishes the mezz-trunk room made into four servant's bedrooms—she wished this at once, so I made the enclosed sketch."[50] And a bit later: "Speak to Mr. White about heating the outside of Mrs. Mck's bath tub."[51] And then: "Mrs. Mackay stated positively to day that she intends living in the house by Nov. 16th."[52]

To Katherine, at least, the mansion was ready for occupancy not when all the workmen were ready to vacate with their equipment, and not when all the furnishings and decorations had been acquired or fabricated and placed, but when she said so. From the start,

her heart had been set on a November 1901 move-in date; despite the many fits and starts of construction, this remained fixed. With a great deal of building still to be done—not to mention decoration and correction of errors already detected—the Mackays took up residence at Harbor Hill in November 1901.

They were by now a family of three. Their first child, another Katherine, had arrived on February 5, 1900. The baby was installed, along with her nurse, in Harbor Hill's third-floor nursery in late 1901. Two more children would be born: Ellin on March 22, 1903 at Harbor Hill, and John William on January 29, 1907 at the Mackays' New York house.

With J. S. Haley's boilers stoked and running at full capacity, an inaugural dinner party and concert were held on December 26. Guests were primarily relatives and "a few others" and were brought from New York by "special train and . . . met at the station by the Mackay's several coaches and fours."[53]

But Harbor Hill's impression on those first guests can only have been partial. That winter the mansion stood amid largely untamed terrain.

Taming "a Howling Wilderness"

The design and siting of the house had been settled before the time came to plan the surrounding estate.

The land was to be divided into three portions: the immediate environs of the house, with formal gardens and terraces; the farm; and the remainder, to be treated as a park. Stanford White designed a portion of the outdoor elements, including the surrounding terraces—fifty feet deep on the entrance side and adorned with stone lions—and those at the gate house, plus the gate lodge, the boundary wall, and the water tower.[54] But he had opinions about work that would be done by others' hands.

In 1900 he wrote to Clarence his feelings about the impression Harbor Hill should make on an approaching visitor, "Now you cannot come up to this great house by a road shaped like an ell and past your kitchen. You have to have a fine and dignified approach to the house, and I feel very certain that the plan I send you with this will give you the fine and dignified approach. . . ."[55]

For the configuration and development of the estate grounds beyond the house itself, the Mackays turned to landscape architect Guy Lowell. Scion of a venerable family of writers, educators, and businessmen, Lowell personified the Boston Brahmin. After attending Harvard College, he studied architecture at the Massachusetts Institute of Technology, from which he graduated in 1894. He studied further in London at the Royal Botanic Gardens, Kew, and then in Paris at the École des Beaux-Arts. Having received there yet another diploma in 1899, Lowell went to work for France's leading landscape architect, Edouard-François André. Returning to Boston, he accepted a lectureship in landscape design at MIT, set up a practice, and compiled materials for his first book, *American Gardens* (1902), which included the garden at Stanford White's Long Island house Box Hill, at Saint James.[56]

His Boston lineage made Lowell socially acceptable to the Mackays. A society columnist for the *New York Times* noted that Lowell and his wife were dinner guests at Harbor Hill.[57] From the Harbor Hill association, Lowell hoped other commissions on Long Island's stylish North Shore would follow (which they did, including the elite Piping Rock Country Club in nearby

Portrait of Guy Lowell (Author)

Locust Valley). He must have been stimulating company, for the cultivated young designer was just then formulating his philosophy of landscape architecture:

> Our gardens need not, when adapted to this country, follow any recognized style. In the first place we are not yet hampered by national traditions and may take only as much of any one style as happens to please us; secondly, American vegetation is very different from that of other countries. In spite of the fact that the same flowers sometimes grow in the American garden as in those abroad, they seem to grow differently—less formally, perhaps—and we, as a nation, prefer a freedom which to the English or the French gardener would almost seem like untidiness.[58]

The drive that Lowell designed must surely have met with Stanford White's requirement of "fine and dignified." The approach from the south curved gracefully as it wound up the hillside. A mile long and six-

Gate house, rendering by McKim, Mead & White (Museum of the City of New York, McKim, Mead & White Collection)

teen feet wide, it was lined with maple trees and imported lindens. Close to the summit, it turned perpendicular to the house and was intersected by a bell mouth (a large circular turning space). At the junction, a carriage or car could either turn toward the house or continue toward the stables, which stood near the main hilltop along with a carriage house. To create the axial, or head-on, approach to the house, a gully had to be filled in. When completed, the drive set the Mackays back roughly $150,000.

The academic Bostonian and the free-spirited New Yorker did knock heads about the placement of the main gate lodge, which White's plan had located at the intersection of two major roads. White's design for the gate house echoed the high-roofed pavilions of the main house, with quarters for the gate-keeper on either side and Doric columns framing the entrance. A massive iron gate was to swing inward to admit the privileged. Lowell objected to the lodge's placement in a letter to Clarence, but Katherine intervened, forwarding Lowell's letter to White with a note that asserted her allegiance: "Please read enclosed and whatever your opinion . . . it is

View south taken from main door (Author)

"The Bell-Mouth at 'Harbor Hill,'" photo by Thomas E. Marr, in Croly, "The Layout of a Large Estate," Architectural Record, 16, no. 4 (October 1904), 536.

needless to tell you I shall abide by your opinion."[59] White seems to have responded with a quote of the potential cost of moving the gate lodge, to which Katherine replied: "I am glad to say that your figure and my request have persuaded Clairie not to consider the possibility of moving the lodge from where you [placed] it. When you go to Roslyn tomorrow, see if Lowell has staked it out exactly according to your ideas and remember that whatever *you* decide about it's position is my decision also."[60]

Lowell conceded the placement of the gate house as the starting point for a network of roadways. He wished to respect the terrain and preserve as much as possible of the woodlands. His design involved some clearing, but it spared most of the native trees and underbrush. Lowell insisted on native plants and trees for both the park and the formal gardens. Accordingly, laurel, dogwood, and rhododendron were

View of drive, photograph by Underwood & Underwood (Bryant Library Local History Collection, Roslyn, NY)

planted, and some large maple and linden trees were transplanted. Through the woods and across farmlands and low hills there opened seemingly boundless vistas to the Sound. Ten miles of bridle paths just wide

Entrance gates to road to stable, c. Jan. 1902 (Private Collection)

View of woodland paths showing planting, photograph by Underwood & Underwood (Bryant Library Local History Collection, Roslyn, NY)

"The Farm Road, October 1901" (Private Collection)

enough for a carriage, with stone bridges, snaked through the park. Streams enhanced the bucolic mood, and several ponds, such as Mirror Pond, were created as sites amenable to contemplation.

Like most large estates, Harbor Hill had a model farm composed of seventy acres that included a series of cutting and vegetable gardens. The farm and the other outbuildings were set along the northern portion of the estate, well out of olfactory and audible range of the house. In no formal order, the farm buildings were situated solely as picturesque objects in the landscape.

Exterior of the main façade (Museum of the City of New York, McKim, Mead & White Collection)

Construction photograph, main house with scaffolding (The New-York Historical Society)

Construction photograph, gate house (The New-York Historical Society)

Execution of Lowell's design for the grounds fell to assorted local laborers under the supervision of Isaac Hicks, owner of a nursery in nearby Jericho. Hicks also oversaw the planting of shrubs and extensive flowerbeds, and supervised construction of the roads and ponds.

Design critic Herbert Croly summed up Guy Lowell's Harbor Hill plan: "To make a park—not a French park, after the model of Fontainebleau, but a park which shall keep its native American character."[61] Lowell strove for a "simplicity and propriety of effect," tempering only somewhat the "original wildness." A

French association struck the architecture connoisseur Barr Ferree, who thought of the grounds surrounding another Mansart princely estate, Chantilly. Barr Ferree focused on Chantilly's tranquility. "This resemblance," he wrote, was "in its quiet woodiness and perfect calm; for Harbor Hill had none of the cultivated wealth of Chantilly, with its trimmed walls of foliage and it [*sic*] many works of art."[62] Peter Ross, a local writer with a conservationist bent, approved of Lowell's approach and applauded his client's wish "transform the howling wilderness into a luxurious abode. . . . [Mr. Mackay] has personally conducted many of the plans. He is jealous of his wild woodland effect and is spending tens of thousand of dollars in saving the trees."[63]

Deep in the woods Katherine had her hideaway constructed—what she called her *Hameau* after a woodland sanctuary of Marie Antoinette's at Versailles. There she entertained close friends and wrote. Other rustic pavilions were scenically placed around the property.

When Lowell's plan for the estate was fully executed, Barr Ferree reported that a ride through the grounds attested to the designer's success: "In an instant the spirited black horses were whizzing us through the cool woods, down steep inclines, then up again to higher grades. There was barely room for the carriage to pass between the trees, and the grades were so steep I wondered the carriage brakes held. It was a veritable 'scenic railway,' with all the excitement of the ups and downs, but with real scenery, wild and beautiful. It was without suggestion of house, save it was Mrs. Mackay's rustic cottage, deep in the woods, but placed just where the look is across the country's finest."[64]

By the time Harbor Hill's outbuildings reached the top of the agenda, the workload at McKim, Mead & White was so heavy that the firm eschewed all but primary buildings, leaving stables and other secondary structures for other architects. The firm of Warren & Wetmore was commissioned to design many of Harbor Hill's outbuildings. The rationale for choosing Warren & Wetmore was probably social: Whitney Warren was a fixture on the New York social scene and had been a guest at Katherine and Clarence's wedding.

Cow barns, Warren & Wetmore, architects, photo by Thomas E. Marr (Avery Architectural and Fine Arts Library, Columbia University, McKim, Mead & White collection)

He had studied architecture at Columbia University and the École des Beaux-Arts. Stanford White called Warren "one of de gang." Some people saw similarities between Warren and White, "not so bad . . . but pretty nearly."[65] White had recently helped Warren to obtain the commission for the New York Yacht Club, and in general supported Warren's work.[66]

Warren & Wetmore's assignment at Harbor Hill included the huge farm barn done in brick, which Ferree found "simple and unpretentious"—unlike the main stable, done in an exuberant chateauesque style. A large structure, its 45-foot-long central section supported a belfry plus wings 70 feet long terminating in twin rotundas each 32 feet in diameter and capped with conical roofs. The second floor housed the stable head, with a living room, dining room, three bedrooms, a pantry, a large laundry, and a large kitchen to provide meals for the farm staff. Each wing held a sitting room plus housing for six to eight stable workers. A separate stable for polo ponies was dominated by broad roofs with many dormers and ventilator stacks.

Warren & Wetmore's extensive dog kennels, built in the Stick Style with the framing members placed on the clapboards, was an innovative structure that generated particular interest. Planned to house a pack of hunting hounds, the kennels were arranged in a semi-circle with the runs converging at one end. Rooms were provided for handling the dogs. At either end were cottages for a staff of four dog handlers.

Other outbuildings included small houses for the families of house staff members (over time, more cottages were added), a chicken farm with poultry yards and an incubator house, and a large Normandy-style

The stables, Warren & Wetmore, architects (Avery Architectual Library, Columbia University)

Dairyman's cottage, Warren & Wetmore, architects, photo by Thomas E. Marr (Avery Architectural and Fine Arts Library, Columbia University, McKim, Mead & White collection)

Conservatory and service gardens, photo by Thomas E. Marr, in Croly, "The Layout of a Large Estate," Architectural Record, 16, no. 4 (October 1904), 536.

Polo pony stables, Warren & Wetmore, architects, photo by Thomas E. Marr (Avery Architectural and Fine Arts Library, Columbia University, McKim, Mead & White collection)

Dog kennels, Warren & Wetmore, architects, photo by Thomas E. Marr (Avery Architectural and Fine Arts Library, Columbia University, McKim, Mead & White collection)

"The Farm Entrance, Showing Dairy," October 1901 (Private Collection)

dairy barn for Harbor Hill's prize cattle. The dairyman's family lived in an ample two-story medieval-style cottage with a jerkinhead roof.

In contrast to Lowell's bucolic park, the Mackays favored formality for the gardens adjacent to the house. Trees in various shapes grew in tubs on the terraces during the warmer months. A large formal garden opened to the west off the conservatory and piazza and spilled 1,000 feet down the hillside. Stanford White originally designed the large garden, and he offered the Mackays at least two different plans. The plan that was executed featured terraces of broad green swaths bordered with twenty-one copies of ancient Greek and Roman statuary and modern reinventions in various states of dress and undress terminating with a goddess at the end. A fountain with a triton figure at the center stood on the middle terrace; White acquired it and other statuary in Paris through the noted art dealer, Joseph Duveen, and resold it to Clarence Mackay.[67]

With resources to realize ever-evolving visions, the Mackays never hesitated to initiate changes and additions. In 1910, Katherine decided to have the Italianate McKim, Mead & White garden transformed into the French palace garden she really wanted. Guy Lowell either could not or would not design a French-style garden, so the Mackays hired a young French garden specialist, Jacques Greber. A newly minted École des Beaux-Arts medalist, Greber eventually developed a substantial trans-Atlantic practice.

At Harbor Hill he translated what had been a succession of green carpets extending westward from the mansion into *parterres de broderie*. Intricate flower beds similar to elegant French marquetry on cabinets lined the

"Harbor Hill, taken October 1901 to show planting done." (Private Collection)

Horse tamer statues, distant view (Bryant Library Local History Collection, Roslyn, NY)

Horse tamer statue, Harbor Hill (Bryant Library Local History Collection, Roslyn, NY)

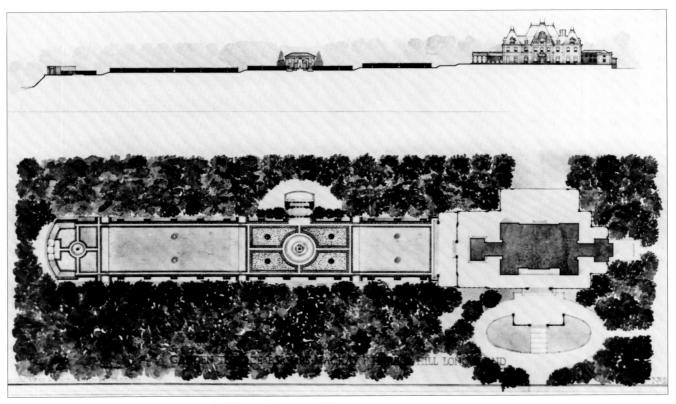

Plan No. 2 for south garden, McKim, Mead & White, architects, c. 1901 (The New-York Historical Society)

View of south garden, by McKim, Mead & White, architects, from house, third floor looking west, photo c. 1902 (Museum of the City of New York, McKim, Mead & White Collection)

View of south garden, at mid-level showing central fountain garden, McKim, Mead & White, architects, photo c. 1902 (Museum of the City of New York, McKim, Mead & White Collection)

Aerial view of house and south garden by Jacques Greber, 1910 (Town & Country, June 1, 1923)

central axis and surrounded the fountains. With White's western garden completely regraded, he created two intricate terraced *parterres*; the third and lowest level he transformed into a fan-shaped greensward terminating at a low balustrade where copies of Louis XIV's 40-foot-tall horse tamers were installed. These 25-ton replicas in pink granite were carved by Franz Plumelet, whom Clarence paid $25,000. Many of the statues from the original garden were moved to the sides.

At the center of the second terrace Greber installed a new, circular, "Versailles" fountain sculpted by his father, Henri. North of it a semi-circular exedra—a freestanding niche describing an 80-foot arc—provided garden seating. Around this stood a 15-foot rose trellis interrupted by niches for more statues that looked onto *parterres de broderies* and two small fountains. South of this axis was a smaller exedra, more water, and more ornamental flowerbeds. Stairs led to the woods below. Intricate patterns evocative of French marquetry lined the central axis and surrounded the fountains. Greber's garden at Harbor Hill was an immediate sensation that set off a fad for *parterres de broderies*, which appeared on Long Island at the Walter E. Maynard estate in Jericho, and in Newport at the Berwin Elms mansion.

Ever Upward

Accounts of Harbor Hill differ widely concerning when construction concluded; some put the end date at 1902, others not until 1905. In fact, initial construction and remodeling flowed together, and the latter

"*View of Hempstead Harbor from North Terrace, showing completed north vista,*" *May 1902* (*Private Collection*)

"*Steam Roller used on grounds,*" *1902* (*Bryant Library Local History Collection, Roslyn, NY*)

began almost before the first round of paint was dry. The Mackays' association with Stanford White and the main builders continued through the years following Katherine's preemptive 1901 occupancy, and plans for fundamental changes appeared on drawing boards when the first guests had hardly departed.

The costs of new ideas and plans became Clarence's recurring nightmare. In January 1903 he wrote Stanford White, "Before accepting any estimates, I wish you would have a detailed drawing made and accepted by Fisher [a stone cutter], so that there

can be no misunderstanding about extras. I have a horror of 'extras,' and the word 'extra' keeps ringing in my ears day and night; so I want to take all the precautions I can." Clarence seemed to sense that he sounded petulant and added, "I can see you laugh!"[69] However, then he put his foot down. "I want to bring to your attention now that never mind what is ordered for the house, either by the housekeeper or anybody else, I will not be responsible for it unless it is O.K.'d by me, and a letter written to that effect."[70]

The architect's audacity knew no bounds, and at times he seemed to toy with his clients. Regarding a remodeling of the library (see Chapter Five), White informed Clarence that the new estimates were "in certain ways very satisfactory. That is, *without changing* the room *to any great extent*. I have cut down the estimate from $40,000 to $25,995 *for the room complete in every respect*, with the exception of the moveable portieres and curtains, the movable candelabra, and the fireplace fixtures."[71] In the spirit of camaraderie that had grown between the two, Clarence accompanied a check to White with a note that read, "I hope you will pay your bills with it and not blow it on suppers, etc.," adding at the bottom, "to say nothing of flower pots."[72]

As always, White had an ally in Katherine. Despite Clarence's concerns about costs and his wife's fleeting satisfaction—in one letter she wrote, "I don't want another thing at all"—Katherine always wanted *things*. Her directions concerning the remodeling of the library illustrate why controlling costs was a pipedream: "Will you treat my library in the following two ways: First; Renaissance. Plaster ceiling to look like old marble. Marble windows and door trim, marble mantel pieces. Walls covered with that red stuff from Baumgarten's. The two best tapestries hung on the two panels where the bookcases now are. Second, Louis XV: French walnut, unfinished, no gold, large French mantelpiece tapestries framed in panels.

Tapestry curtains to [*sic*] all windows. Please make me two colored drawings of these, very carefully and think about it, as I want the room fine when I do it."[73]

Katherine and White congratulated themselves on their successful collaboration. In 1903, she wrote, "You and I have certainly continued friends through these two years of building, and I want to tell you I am perfectly satisfied with the results of your work and thank you for the personal interest you have shown."[74] The admiration was mutual, and it continued. Several years later, White described to his wife Bessie Katherine's appearance at the Hyde Ball—though he identified her as Theodora, empress of the Eastern Roman Empire. She "looked beautiful. . . . in a gown of spun silver and gold all encrusted with turquoise, and with a great turquoise and silver crown on her head. . . . As far as I could make out, she had absolutely nothing but her dress on. Her train was at least ten feet long and was carried by two little bare-armed and bare legged negroes with gorgeous gold dresses."[75]

In one respect, Clarence matched Katherine in extravagance. In 1906, he had Warren & Wetmore add to the great house a multistoried tennis court build-

Clarence Mackay's Palatial Country Place Given a Christmas House-Warming

CLARENCE MACKAY'S PALATIAL COUNTRY PLACE WHICH RECEIVED ITS HOUSEWARMING YESTERDAY.

"Clarence Mackay's Palatial Country Place Given a Christmas House-Warming" (Boston Post, Dec. 26, 1901)

Casino, exterior, Warren & Wetmore, architects, photo by Thomas E. Marr (Avery Architectural and Fine Arts Library, Columbia University, McKim, Mead & White collection)

Casino, Warren & Wetmore, architects, under construction, photo by Thomas E. Marr, Feb. 13, 1907 (Avery Architectural and Fine Arts Library, Columbia University, McKim, Mead & White collection)

Casino, interior, Warren & Wetmore, architects, photo by Thomas E. Marr (Avery Architectural and Fine Arts Library, Columbia University, McKim, Mead & White collection)

ing, called the Casino, with a 140-foot facade. The Casino suited Clarence's passion for sports. Its exterior was French-style half-timber over brick, with Doric-columned porches. On the ground level its ceilings were Guastavino tile vaults. Within its 46-foot-high walls, it housed tennis courts, a gymnasium, a swimming pool, a squash court, a shooting gallery, a billiard room, a sitting room, and dressing rooms. Several outdoor lawn tennis courts were situated beside the Casino, and tall potted half-ball trees in tubs sat on the stone terraces around it. Besides sporting facilities, the Casino was provided with a sitting room furnished with divans; on its parquet floor lay a giant polar bear skin with bared teeth. The cost of the Casino was estimated at $200,000.

The opening of the Casino in June 1907 was a formal "stag affair." Approximately ninety guests arrived by automobile and carriage and in two private railroad cars. After a two-hour lunch, the men roamed the building and praised the tennis courts; one of them told his host he "wouldn't have a ghost of a show, Mr. Mackay being an expert at the game." The group left at 6:30 feeling very satisfied and privileged to have been included "among the chosen few . . . [to] inspect the finest club house on private grounds in this country."[76]

The design of Harbor Hill and its grounds and outbuildings was a mammoth task. It involved the talents of not just architects and designers, but also many other individuals, some known, many only names in account books. The estate stood ready to become the center of life for the Mackays, their children, and their staff. Already the subject of intense speculation, Harbor Hill would receive even more attention, as people from all walks of life visited it either in person or vicariously. It was a dream come true representing all that money could buy—but what would life there be like?

FIVE

Overnight Renaissance Palace

❧ ❧

"In the past, dominant nations had always plundered works of art from their predecessors. . . . America was taking a leading place among nations and had, therefore, the right to obtain art wherever she could."

—Stanford White in Lawrence G. White, *Sketches and Designs by Stanford White*, 1920

A S WITH THE DESIGN and construction of Harbor Hill, Katherine Mackay wielded primary authority over decorating the interior. To supplement the work of McKim, Mead & White, Katherine selected interior design firms in New York and Boston and oversaw their subcontracts with the McKim firm. In April 1900 she apprised Stanford White, "I have given Davenport the order of that estimates of decoration of the hall & dining room after your designs. . . . I have ordered the decoration of the library from Allard."[1]

Although both Allard & Sons and the A. H. Davenport Company were noted experts, they did not begin their assignments with a blank slate or a free hand. Stanford White specified many elements in the

main public rooms and in Katherine's and Clarence's apartments. As with Guy Lowell's design for the grounds, any plan for the interior that did not originate with White himself was carried out under the architect's supervision and was subject to his approval. He directed the subcontracted decorators via designs either by his own hand or by his assistant, Frederick Adams. Allard's contract explicitly stated, "We hereby agree to execute all these rooms as per sketches submitted" and stipulated colors, grades of materials, and other elements. For Katherine's private rooms, the contract specified, "All the hardware . . . of Louis XV design, French make and finished in gilt bronze."

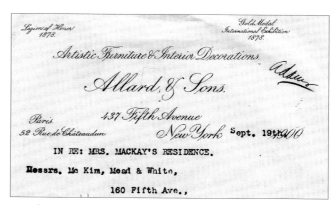

Letterhead of Allard & Sons (Private Collection)

"The contract included the following:" All the work complete for these rooms executed in the most artistic and workman like manner, and to the entire satisfaction of Mrs. Mackay."[2]

The authority of Stanford White offered a compensating liberty, however. As Royal Cortissoz, then art critic for the *New York Herald Tribune* put it, "It [is] an axiom of Stanford White's that the work of any period would go with the work of any other period—if both were of superlative quality."[3]

The Doyens of Decor

The American vogue for French household décor had a long history. As early as the 1780s, Thomas Jefferson had fine furniture brought from France for Monticello. By the early nineteenth century, French cabinetmakers were established in New York, and by mid-century, Marcotte, Alexander Roux, and other transplanted French cabinetmakers were importing French decorative arts. English design had a following, but to most cosmopolitan Americans the world leader in decorative arts was France.

Céléstin Allard (1807–1854), the founder of the Allard firm, grew up in France's centuries-old tradition of fine furniture-making. Production was a collaboration of artisans in diverse trades: the *ébéniste*, the cabinetmaker who fashioned a piece's basic frame; the *doreur*, who applied the gilding; the *marquetiste*, who did the inlay work (i.e., marquetry); the *antiquaire*, who dealt in old furniture, paneling, and parts; the *tapissier*, the upholsterer and also a dealer in fine fabrics and tapestries; and the *meubler*, who made suites of multiple, coordinated pieces. It was Céléstin Allard, who, in the 1850s, conceived the idea of producing a complete ensemble for an entire room, including its cabinets, drapery, rugs, and wall panels, as opposed to merely producing individual pieces.

By the early 1800s most Parisian custom cabinetmaking was based in the Twelfth Arrondissement, where Allard's workshops occupied a large building. The lower three floors provided work space, and the top floor was the family's living quarters. In 1878, when Céléstin's son Jules (1832–1907) took over the firm and renamed it Jules Allard et fils, it gradually expanded to three workshops situated in a chic townhouse, in the suburbs, and in a chateau.

Architects liked the efficiency of Allard et fils's integrated approach. Through several important commissions for the noted French architect Gabriel-Hippolyte Destailleur, the Allard firm came to the attention of Richard Morris Hunt. Early in the 1860s and 1870s Allard supplied stock to the New York City design firms of Marcotte and Herter Brothers. Allard's display at the 1878 Paris International Exhibition won the firm a gold medal and world renown. Around 1880, Allard furnished rooms in the adjacent Fifth Avenue mansions of two Vanderbilt brothers.

Setting up shop close to the clients made good business sense. To supply the growing American market for lavish, French-inspired interiors, Allard opened an office in New York in 1885 at 436 Fifth Avenue, with letterhead inscribed, "Artistic Furniture & Interior Decorations." Although other firms such as Marcotte and Herter had been providing entire interiors, Allard seemed more up-to-date by the 1880s and hence captured a new American market. As the firm's fame grew, Allard became the decorator of choice for mansions in Newport and New York, as well as Paris, London, and Vienna. Although the firm worked mainly in private houses, it also produced hotel ballrooms and a few public commissions, contributing in Paris to the opera house and the city hall and in New York to Richard Morris Hunt's Metropolitan Museum, Charles McKim's University Club, and some of the city's poshest hotels, such as the Plaza, the St. Regis, and the Waldorf-Astoria.[4] In other words, New York's most prominent architects found Allard's work compatible with their own.

The Allard firm's approach also fit perfectly with the spirit of the American Renaissance. Allard's designers drew elements from highly developed European sources, accurately copying their precedents. They had a particular talent for adapting historical fragments to new settings, and such fragments were easily obtained. With some twenty thousand Parisian houses demolished in the 1850s and '60s for the city's reconfiguration by Georges-Eugène Haussmann, the firm could purchase whole interiors, stockpile them, and reuse their parts as needed.

The distinction between old and new did not matter to Allard, nor did it matter to many of their patrons. Although the issue of authenticity—of an object's value being located in it being "original"—was gaining importance in the 1890s, many of the Allard firm's patrons conveniently viewed the newly made simply as a perpetuation of tradition. "We could reproduce," a representative for Allard wrote, "so you couldn't tell the difference."[5] Sometimes the firm even purchased hardware from stock catalogues, then applied a patina to give the appearance of age.

Henry L. Bouche, who studied interiors before coming to the United States in 1877, ran Allard's New York office. In New York he worked as a painter for Tiffany & Co., building a reputation for being highly knowledgeable of French high-style interiors. As an Allard employee he worked on most of Richard Morris Hunt's Vanderbilt commissions and on many of McKim, Mead & White's elite residential jobs. He could take White's drawings, even rough sketches, and transform them into completely outfitted rooms.[6]

The Allard company was known for working quickly, and the firm's work for the Mackays went smoothly—most of the time. By June 1900 they had made and shipped, from Paris to New York, eighty cases of materials for Harbor Hill. But the house's construction was not very advanced at the time, and Allard complained about mounting storage charges.[7] Bouche expressed this impatience to Stanford White: "If we have rushed this order so thoroughly, it was to please Mrs. Mackay, who assured me that the house would be turned over to her the 1st of November, and made me promise to have our work finished by the 1st of November. . . . Unfortunately, it is all for naught."[8]

As the decorative materials awaited installation, concern about the safety of the cases grew, and in February Allard brought to Clarence Mackay's attention the need for an insurance policy.[9]

When installation finally began in mid-1901, the usual problem arose: the work was going too slowly for Katherine. Bouche wrote to White: "Mrs. Mackay called this morning and we had a long conversation about the work. . . . I think she left understanding more fully the cause of the delay.[10] And of course, the usual questions arose over extras in the bills—for instance, the unexpectedly high cost of a dais to support Katherine's bed and chaise longue and her heliotrope carpet (the latter excess resulting from her premature order that White's sketches be delivered to Allard as "finals" [see Chapter Four]). "The order for the platforms was subsequent to the first order," Allard wrote, "therefore we had to have additional carpet made."[11]

Allard decorated the main salon in a Louis XV style with a robust carved wood cornice, and furnished the room with assorted tables and chairs, some purchased from William Baumgarten, a New York decorator and furniture dealer who had worked for Herter and opened his own firm in 1891. A great polar bear skin lay on the Versailles-pattern parquet floor. According to Allard's contract, the paneled walls were painted a luxurious "pure white with light lines of mauve color." The mantel, designed to White's specifications, was of "Pavonazzetto marble, the ornamentation on the same to be in finely chiseled gilt bronze."[12] A life-size full-length portrait of Katherine Mackay by the French painter Edmund Chartran, in a frame designed by White, dominated the wall above the mantel—"a lovely speaking figure," in the opinion of Barr Ferree.

While Allard's work was taking shape, a second design firm was decorating other parts of the mansion. Albert H. Davenport, proprietor of the second interior design firm Katherine chose, was an American native son from the middle-class industrial town of Malden, Massachusetts. He began his working life as an accountant for a furniture-making company, which he eventually purchased. Like the others involved in designing for Harbor Hill, Davenport was a standard bearer for the American Renaissance, and his work met the highest standards of both quality and fidelity to historical precedent. In the mid-1880s Davenport worked with McKim, Mead & White on Henry Villard's mansion in New York City, and after that they continued to employ him. (A specialist in Early American reproductions, Davenport was the primary furniture maker for McKim's remodeling of the White House in 1902–3.[13])

Davenport's chief designer was Francis (Frank) Bacon, brother of Henry Bacon (for many years Charles McKim's right-hand man, whose own designs included the Lincoln Memorial). Like Henry, Frank Bacon had worked for the McKim firm back in the late 1870s and early '80s before joining Davenport. His knowledge of historic interiors—he had assembled the McKim, Mead & White library—made A. H. Davenport a preeminent purveyor of traditional fine furniture and interiors.

In Davenport's five-story factory building in Boston, where his firm made all its products, a crew of cabinetmakers, carvers, seamstresses, and upholsterers worked alongside the design staff under Frank Bacon's supervision. The company purchased hardware and fabrics from other suppliers, some English, some French. Once the furniture and decorative pieces were completed, they were shipped to New York, where the company maintained an office at 351 Fifth Avenue. Victor Twiss was Davenport's New York representative on the Harbor Hill job.

Davenport's responsibility included adapting the elaborately carved antique wood panels (*boiserie*) that White had purchased in Europe for the great hall's great staircase, installing the monumental fireplace, and producing coordinating door surrounds. The firm also supplied two English oak sideboards for the dining room (at a cost of $600 apiece), large oak tables ($400) for the main hall, and an Axminster carpet for the main stairs ($750).[14] Davenport also furnished

Clarence's suite, the stair hall, the billiard room, and the bedrooms for the children and guests—including nightstands, mattresses, and bedspreads.

Allard and Davenport coordinated their work. Both were involved in the décor of the main hall. Allard furnished the salon (that is, the so-called library), and the Stone Room, which opened off the salon; Davenport attended to the elaborate details of the stairway. In general these tasks went smoothly, even with two design firms working, as it were, separately together, and with Stanford White always a supervisory presence. But the occasional need for further clarification could not have been unexpected, as when one of Davenport's designers wrote White's assistant before ordering carpet: "We are beginning work on the doors for the Mackay hall and it is important that we have a section of the doors as Mr. Allard is making his part, so we can determine as to the thickness of the hall side."[15]

The carpet for the main staircase hall, in elaborate Henri II style, was a cause of dispute. On the day before Christmas 1901, two days before the Mackays' planned grand housewarming, Albert Davenport himself wrote to Stanford White. "I can not learn to-day who is in error in regard to color of carpet. I had always understood that the stair carpet was to be red to go with the black oak. I heard last week that Mrs. Mackay was pleased with all that had been delivered and said if Mr. Mackay did not like his room, it was his own fault for she took the sketches to him and tried to get him interested. Failing in that she took the responsibility to place the order."[16] Two days after Christmas, Victor Twiss wrote Katherine to explain that he had been sick and to express his surprise that she "would not permit them to lay [the carpet], as it was red instead of green." Twiss showed admirable restraint when he wrote her: "Now, I have never had green suggested by you for this carpet. Red was the color that I suggested when the order was give [*sic*] by you and the color that I have on memorandum. There were no curtains or wall covers in connection with this stair carpet to call for any special shade; so, I did not submit a sample of colored sketch, as in the case of the principal rooms that we made rugs for. . . . I am quite sure that if you had suggested green, I would have been very particular to have you designate the shade, as I never would, under any circumstances, suggest a green carpet to go with black oak woodwork."[17] Katherine relented—petulantly—and the red Axminster carpet was laid.

Another subject of contention was the color of the *boiserie* panels for the walls in the main hall. Not only did they have to be fitted to the spaces provided; in Katherine's opinion, they were too dark. Davenport found a way to lighten them with an acid that dissolved the old varnish, but Katherine remained dissatisfied. Having admired the staining of *boiseries* White had done for William C. Whitney, she asked if that success could be replicated. In Davenport's view that was impossible: the wood from which old varnish had been removed could not simply be stained again to a color Katherine preferred. He wrote White with some exasperation: "It will be impossible to wash off the stain and refinish according to Mr. Whitney's color." The antique *boiseries* would have to be scraped, planed, and carved all over again. "I had one car load already to ship when you telephoned Mr. Bacon in regard to the color," Davenport wrote. Furthermore, "I had hired about twenty extra men to work at the house to hurry it some. All of these men will have to be discharged if the color of the woodwork is changed."[18] Katherine finally agreed leave the original color of the *boiseries* alone (a year later she again approached Davenport about remodeling the hall and making the *boiseries* grayer, but the subject was dropped).

The Mackays disbursed a total of $182,265.61 to Katherine's handpicked decorators: to Davenport they paid $78,407.25 and to Allard, the astounding amount of $103,858.36.[19] But by no means did expenditures on Harbor Hill's interior stop there. Both Allard and Davenport continued to be asked now and then to meet some incidental decorative need. And Stanford White was always prepared to find new ways to spend the Mackays' money.

To adorn the great hall and the stairway leading up from it, White purchased from a London art dealer an enormous tapestry by François Boucher. The tapestry was hung over the first landing near an antique tall-case clock. From the ceiling over the staircase hall hung what Barr Ferree described as "a great bronze lamp—a late Renaissance masterpiece finding [a] final resting place in this newest of American great houses."[20]

For the intentionally dark dining room White had supplied a fireplace from his cache of scavenged European treasures. The ceiling—said to be antique—caused Frank Bacon something of a headache: the Mackays, he wrote to the McKim office, "would like a full size detail of ornament to go in Centre of panels—as I suppose Mr. White would not want the coat of arms shown on original ceiling! Wanted quick."[21] Davenport also supplied English oak tables and chairs based on sixteenth-century models and upholstered in imitation antique brocade.

Stanford White continued his tireless shopping abroad on behalf of his clients. In 1903, the Paris dealer Germain Seligman wrote him, "I saw the chimney pieces today, and they are so undoubtedly old and genuine that I undertake to guarantee, if you saw them you would not need to ask if they were old." Seligman also offered twenty-two sixteenth-century columns from a castle near Dijon: "Would they interest you?" Seligman spelled out the conditions. The dealer would add 10 percent for the agent, and then resell them, ideally, to the Mackays. But "If Mr. Clarence Mackay does not want one or the other you may be sure we will sell them to somebody else, as they are harder to purchase than to sell." If White were to come to Europe, Seligman wrote, he would accompany White to the castle.[22] White also dealt with one Stefano Bardini in Florence; one cable, addressed to White's pseudonym, "Giddydoll," said, "Senti [*sic*] photographs mantels doors ceilings how many [*sic*] ceilings wanted."[23] While this purchase related to Harbor Hill, obviously White could use the pieces on other jobs if the Mackays did not want them. Bardini later informed White, "Donatello door sold send photographs of new one."[24]

As planned by White and executed by Davenport, the billiard room, to which the men could retire after dinner for cigars, port, and a game of pool, was also dark. To convey the impression that the master of the house came from a long line of great hunters, the walls were hung with antelope heads and great racks of antlers. A capacious men's dressing room opened off the billiard room and was outfitted with four sinks, lockers, a shower, and clothes racks.

Of the mansion's many fireplaces, Barr Ferree noted that, "All the chimney pieces on the main floor are old ones, the spoils of European palaces. . . . The one in the hall is by far the largest of the collection, and is so huge that the wood of a [whole] tree can be burned within it."[25] The work of Davenport and Stanford White, the hall's chimney breast featured a central shield with two lions and roundels on either side; the roundels framed male and female portraits that recalled Italian Renaissance portraits. Soon the hall housed, against one wall, a set of antique choir stalls purchased abroad by White and refitted by William Baumgarten & Company.

Under the aegis of McKim, Mead & White, and the Allard and Davenport companies, many well-known specialty houses contributed to fitting out Harbor Hill. George Glaenzer & Co., "Architectural Decorators/Art Furnishers" with a shop in Paris, supplied some of the lighting and stained glass. Edwd. F. Caldwell & Company of New York, known for specialty lighting, followed White's designs for many of the fixtures. Tiffany Studios provided light fixtures in the service areas. John M. Jones, "Painter and Decorator," with an office at 297 Fifth Avenue, contributed ornamental painting. New York's Tuttle & Bailey Manufacturing Company supplied the decorative bronze registers for the ventilation and heating. Some of the fire backs came from William Jackson Company of Union Square. J. G. Wilson, a firm in New York that boasted six gold medals and seven silver and bronze medals, provided the blinds for the windows.

Letterhead of Wm. H. Jackson Co. *(Private Collection)*

Letterhead of Tuttle & Bailey Mfg. Co. *(Private Collection)*

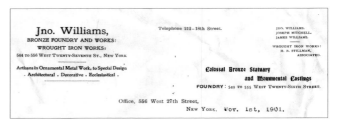

Letterhead of Jno. Williams *(Private Collection)*

Jno. Williams of New York, makers of "ornamental Metal Work Special Design," supplied decorative elements such as the bronze dolphins in the conservatory fountain.

When it came to the kitchen, which had to provide for huge parties and myriad houseguests, White put himself in charge. To outfit it, he turned to Duparquet Huot & Moneuse Company, with offices in New York, Boston, Chicago, and Washington, D.C. Importers of "Imperial French Cooking Ranges," Duparquet acquired a 9-foot-long range; the stove's two fires consumed an estimated eighteen tons of coal every six months (stove coal delivered in Roslyn cost six dollars a ton in 1901).[26] Duparquet also supplied the cooks' table, a "Russia Iron Dish Heater,"

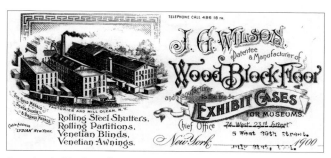

Letterhead of J. G. Wilson (Private Collection)

Letterhead of Edwd F. Caldwell (Private Collection)

Letterhead of Tiffany Studios (Private Collection)

Letterhead of Robert Fisher Co. (Private Collection)

stove hoods and vents, some of the sinks, iron oven doors, marble carving boards, a butcher block, laundry heater, and other materials. The food refrigerator came from Lorillard Refrigerator Company, but an ice house constructed on the property provided more refrigeration.

Wine, of course, was an important commodity at Harbor Hill. Duparquet furnished the basement with wire wine racks for the main wine cellar, which would hold almost twenty thousand bottles, and for the daily wine room, which would hold two thousand bottles.

Regarding work on the interior, Clarence could be as implacable as Katherine. Robert Fisher and Company, a venerable firm on Manhattan's East Houston Street that was well-known to McKim, Mead & White, supplied much of Harbor Hill's specialized marble work, including several floors, the stair hall, and the lions on the terrace. Fisher's letterhead proclaimed its versatility: "Importers of and Workers in Foreign & Domestic Marbles. Venetian & Roman Mosaics. Granite and Marble Monumental Work. Special Attention Given to Architectural & Monumental Work. Lessees of the Royal Irish Green Marble Quarries, Connemara, Ireland." A serious contretemps arose about marble columns for the main hall. At the doors leading off the great hall, four green Connemara marble columns with white marble bases and capitals were to stand before matching wooden pilasters. Fucigna Brothers, sculptors with offices in Carrara, Florence, New York, and Paris, were subcontracted, via R. C. Fisher, to supply them. The Fucigna firm was well known in the trade, and had already provided mantels and mosaic floors in some of the bathrooms at Harbor Hill, including the mosaics and carved marble tub in Katherine's bathroom (cost, $6,055). For the main hall, however, Angelo Fucigna claimed he could not furnish the selected green marble in single shafts: the columns would have to be made in segments. After much back-and-forth, Fucigna contacted Clarence Mackay directly for approval while at the same time producing the columns in pieces of mismatched colors. White was enraged. Fucingna wrote Clarence again, trying to defend himself. "The only fault Mr. White can properly find is that one of the pieces is a trifle dark," adding, "to throw out my columns will ruin me." He continued, "I know the amount involved seems small to you, but to me it means a loss of ALL I have, and more besides." He concluded, "I am a poor struggling artist, trying hard to make a reputation and a living for myself and my family. To make my work satisfactory to you means so much to me. . . . [I] have hoped it would bring me orders from your friends. Let me appeal to your kindness of heart and sympathy."[27]

But Clarence, who recalled the earlier conversation differently, dismissed Fucigna's pleas: "You will have to see Mr. White in regard to these columns." As for the idea that the differing colors were a mere trifle, Clarence strongly objected. "The color of the columns does not match, and never will match, and that's all there is to it."[28] But now the columns were in place, and Katherine rushed into the fray. "[Have] them removed *at once*," she wrote to White. "I wish the four columns removed within one week & I expect you to see it is done."[29]

The case wound up in lawyers' hands, and a settlement was reached.[30] Another marble-cutting firm, Piccirilli Brothers, ultimately supplied Irish green Connemara marble columns in single shafts.

The decoration and outfitting of Harbor Hill had no end date. Repair of constantly emerging problems and modifications to the house got under way almost immediately after building began.[31] In October 1902, White visited to investigate reports of damp and seepage in the service wing. In his hurried scrawl he noted, "Kitchen floor wet. . . . Both Basement and kitchen store wet. Closet outside of kitchen wet, Servants hall wet. All basement floor back to laundry wet. Wet under piazza but not outside. . . ."[32] Nor did the Mackays' desire to achieve ever greater heights ever end: in 1903 Clarence requested a copy of the original source book, Sauvageot's *Palais, Châteaux, Hôtels et Maisons de France du XVe au XVIIIe Siecle.* Many of the initial participants in building and decorating Harbor Hill remained involved with the Mackays long into the owners' occupancy.

Leland Sudlow, the construction chief, complained about the inferior marble of Allard's hearths. The poor stone was causing some of the mantels to crack, and smoke from the laundry was finding its way through adjacent flues into rooms on the second floor. Other malfunctions included the fact that "When the laundry fire is used smoke comes into the Blue Rooms on the second floor, which, however, only occurs when the bedroom fireplaces are not used." The flues in all of these rooms were in a single stack, so that "[t]he smoke seems to curl over and down the bedroom flues." Sudlow believed that most of these problems could be solved by replacing the original hearths with soapstone and installing flu dampers.[33]

The need to solve the smoke problem so it would not make its way to the third-floor room, where the nursery was located, must have increased in urgency: by 1904, two little girls lived there—the Mackays' firstborn, Katherine, and then baby Ellin. Katherine found other problems on the third floor as well, including a leak in the Pink Room. Leland Sudlow was unable to find the source on a clear day. He would have to "make a further examination the next stormy day."[34] Ultimately, the leak was located and sealed.

Drawing (pencil on tracing paper) by Stanford White of frame and painting of Katherine Mackay by John White Alexander (The New-York His-torical Society) (see also painting, pg. 44)

Katherine continued to tyrannize the workmen. During some remodeling in 1905, Leland Sudlow asked White: *Do you not think it would be best to let Mrs. Mackay know that we are doing the work of repairing the columns in the mail hall? If she goes down there, she will surely throw the men out of the house unless she is notified.*"[35] A telephone message from Sudlow to White reported, "Mrs. Mackay gives us until Thursday to have everybody out of the room, including Mr. Finn's men painting the ceiling. The men Mr. Finn now has here, working all day Sunday and Saturday, could with the addition of six more men, finish on time. . . ."[36]

There is no better example of the extent of the design changes that regularly occurred than the library. Every good house must have a library, but in the French-Italian Renaissance-chateau-palazzo that was Harbor Hill, satisfying the clients was problematic. The first version—Stanford White's Stone Room—reflected Katherine's preferences. But Clarence's wishes, which ultimately prevailed, called for relocation and transformation, which occupied a great portion of 1904–5.

As decorated by Allard, according to White's design and Katherine's demands, the Stone Room was hardly a library. When Barr Ferree saw it in 1903 he noted that "Most of the books have been taken elsewhere, but the name [library] remains."[37] The walls, in the Italian Renaissance mode, were entirely of stone. Two huge Renaissance torchères (ill-suited to reading) flanked the fireplace, which, along with the ceiling, was a White import. Clarence hung several paintings,

Italian stone room, photo c. Nov. 1902–June 1903 (Museum of the City of New York, McKim, Mead & White Collection)

Billiard room, photo c. Nov. 1902–June 1903 (Museum of the City of New York, McKim, Mead & White Collection)

but the room's main effect came from the tapestries—an initial passion of both the Mackays. Indeed, Katherine had telegraphed White, "I will not have the tapestry anywhere but in the library hung on the window as I said and," Katherine being Katherine, she added, "I wish it hung this week."[38]

When the Mackays finally confronted the Stone Room's inadequacy as a library, they went to White for new designs. Clarence questioned the cost of the remodeling, and White's reply was characteristically breezy: that he had cut $14,000 off the original $40,000 estimate although he noted that the price did not include the "moveable portieres and curtains, the moveable candelabra, and fireplace fixtures."[39]

Ultimately, the couple decided to remodel the bil-

liard room into a library. T. D. Wadelton & Company installed a high, paneled dado of polished wood below green striped velvet wall covering. Robert Fisher's carvers modified the original, antique mantel and placed on it a bust of Voltaire copied by Piccirilli Brothers from Jean-Antoine Houdon's famous portrait. Above that hung a painting of John William Mackay, Clarence's father, in a boldly contoured gilt frame made by Allard & Sons. Various tapestries, such as one in a Boucher style, depicted Herod's Slaughter of the Innocents, indicating Clarence's religious concerns.

The transformation of the billiard room into a library had its tensions. Katherine inserted in the specifications that the contractor had to "post a notice that no smoking is allowed, and to discharge any workman who is found smoking."[40] This was not a new stricture: three years before, Victor Twiss had reported that "My men were given positive order at their first entrance on this job, that they would be discharged if caught smoking."[41] And Stanford White's final bill came with a note meant to soften the blow: "No charge has been made for Mr. Sudlow's time."[42] Despite the stresses, however, the new library provided a suitable place not only for reading but also for Clarence's burgeoning passion: collecting art.

Clarence Collects

With the completion of the new library, Katherine's interest in art began to wane. Participating with White in purchasing art as interior furnishings—the Boucher tapestry for the stairway hall, for instance—engaged her, but when acquiring art for decoration came to an end, Katherine lost interest. Clarence, in contrast, had developed an avid interest and a connoisseur's eye, complemented both by the depth of his pockets and by Stanford White's creed of eclecticism.

Clarence scrutinized the pre-auction displays in New York at the leading houses, such as the American Art Association, and Anderson Gallery. He would appear with a roll of ten-dollar bills in one pocket and fives in the other: if he liked what he saw he passed out tens to the gallery attendants; if not, they got fives. A gallery visit from Mackay could forecast the success of the auction.[43] The collection he ultimately assembled would be counted, along with those of J. P. Morgan, Henry E. Huntington, and Joseph H. Widener,

Loggia, c. Jan. 1902 (Private Collection)

Dining room, c. Jan. 1902 (Private Collection)

dered works of art from their predecessors. . . . America was taking a leading place among nations and had, therefore, the right to obtain art wherever she could."[46] After White's death, Clarence continued to collect on his own.

Frequenting auctioneers' showrooms, Clarence kept in touch with such dealers as Seligmann, Gimpel, and French & Company. Joseph Duveen, the most famous (and infamous) dealer of the era, schemed to get Clarence into his stable of clients, trying to lure Berenson to Paris to introduce them. (Merchants in other luxury markets, notably piano builders and automobile dealers, like-

among the country's most important.[44] In the heady years before and after World War I, when dealers were offering major European works of art, Clarence Mackay became one of the art market's leading buyers.

Clarence's attitude toward collecting reflected America's eager self-identification with the Italian Renaissance. As a financial power in a country seeking cultural respect (both internally and abroad) Clarence made choices determined by the prevailing reverence for the European past. Indeed, America would surpass the Italian Renaissance. Bernard Berenson, the Boston connoisseur and authority on Italian Renaissance painting, prefaced his 1894 book, *The Venetian Painters*, with the observation, "We ourselves, because of our faith in science and the power of work, are instinctively in sympathy with the Renaissance. . . . the spirit which animates us was anticipated by the spirit of the Renaissance, and more than anticipated. That spirit seems like the small rough model after which ours is being fashioned."[45] White in effect authorized Clarence's acquisitiveness: "In the past, dominant nations had always plun-

Hall, view to north without armor, only tapestries, photo c. Jan. 1902 (wrongly labeled, "Another view of Drawing Room" in Desmond and Croly, Stately Homes in America [New York: D. Appleton, 1903])

Main hall (south side, without armor, but with tapestries), photo c. Nov. 1902 (Museum of the City of New York, McKim, Mead & White Collection)

wise had the Mackays in their sights.) Except for Isabella Stewart ("Mrs. Jack") Gardner, however, Berenson detested American millionaires (whom he referred to as "squillionairres"[47]), and he refused Duveen's request to meet with Clarence.[48]

Clarence's aesthetic interests ranged widely, but he focused his attention mostly on European and English art and antiques from the Middle Ages through the Baroque period. White helped him to fill his house with mantels such as the stone one in the main hall "which Mr. White sold them personally," as Davenport remarked, tapestries purchased in Paris, stone statues for the garden, Chinese bowls and vases, ivory boxes, and more.[49] He covered the floors with Oriental rugs and tables with porcelains from East Asia. On the walls he hung English masterpieces, such as Sir

Thomas Lawrence's 1804 portrait of the great tragic actress, Mrs. Sarah Siddons, and Edwin Austin Abbey's more recent painting of the coronation of Edward VII.

Clarence's interest in sport led him to acquire *Springer Spaniel* by the contemporary English painter of dogs, Maud Earl; a painting of the Mackay dogs by Percival Leonard Rosseau, an American artist living in Paris who came over in late 1913 to paint the portrait, made the news. Rosseau announced to an interviewer that he had "taken up animal painting partly because several years experience had taught him that portraying the nude didn't pay."[50] But these works were rarities for Clarence, and few American pieces entered his collection—certainly none of the modern paintings or sculpture disdained by exponents of the American Renaissance. Although eclectic in medium, period, and subject matter, Clarence had two major passions: armor and religious art. Clarence acquired such pieces to furnish Harbor Hill's great hall, the mansion's centerpiece, and in the early years it was a joint project with Stanford White. "My heart is wrapped up in making a success of that hall," Clarence wrote White. Later he wrote White that he agreed "to your distribution of armor for the hall . . . it certainly sounds very well on paper." And a month later: "I approve of the general scheme of the hall, as set forth in your

Great hall with armor, c. 1918 (Author)

memorandums, and in your colored drawing of the hall itself."[51] White envisioned Harbor Hill's hall much like that of a great English country house, filled with banners, animal heads, and armor. Hunting trophies were easy to come by, but the other elements proved more difficult.

Letters and telegrams went off to White's European agents. From Paris, Franz Schultz replied, "I don't possess any old flags at the present time. This article is very rare. . . ." But armor could be found, and Schultz wrote, "I know very [*sic*] series about 12 pieces, each one making a large panel in red velvet with an armor in the middle. Formerly I wanted to buy them but the owner did not wish to sell."[52] But Clarence and White wanted complete suits. By mid-January 1902, White was ready to scour Europe. He sent Clarence copies of proposed letters, to which Clarence replied, "I think you have covered the ground very thoroughly." But Clarence wondered, "whether you intended to leave out the large stone table and the eight electric standards of stone and bronze in the hall, and the carpets, or whether you intended to take these up with any other dealers."[53]

White also contacted Rutherford Stuyvesant, a wealthy collector of armor and one of the founding trustees of the Metropolitan Museum of Art in New York City, but Stuyvesant replied that he was sorry that White and his wife did not have time to come out to his country place in New Jersey and added, "In regard to armor, it is very hard to find and the only dealer I know is Bachweewau, Rue de Provence, Paris . . . a reliable and a competent judge," but "his prices are high. . . . The Duc de Dino collection is for sale, but only as a whole. It is the best private collection in existence," Stuyvesant ended, "too good to be used for decorative purposes. . . . I am very anxious for the Museum to buy this collection."[54] The Metropolitan Museum trumped Clarence.

White sent British-born Arthur Acton to view the Duc de Dino collection. Described by Bernard Berenson as "a 'bounder,' but he has a flair for good things," Acton served as Florence agent for wealthy Americans; through such dealings, and his marriage to a Chicago heiress, Acton was able to purchase and restore a large fifteenth-century Florentine villa, La Pietra (now the property of New York University).[55] When White vis-

Great hall with armor, c. 1920 (print from Armor collection, Metropolitan Museum of Art)

complete suits of mail and twenty good shields, each surrounded by eight or ten weapons, Renaissance and Moorish, said to be very unusual." The collection reportedly had belonged to a nephew of the late Cardinal of Toledo. Besides the suits of mail, the collection contained jousting spears, helmets, shields with gold inlay, and other items. Platt commended Leopold Schondorff, a middleman who worked out of Toledo's Grand Hotel, informing White that, "If you are sending a man over there, he would be likely to know of other things, as that is his business." The price Platt reported was 40,000 pesetas, or about $6,000, but, according to Schondorff, "if the collection has not been sold, it could probably be got cheaper now."[59]

ited Italy, he and Acton together visited dealers and called at great houses, but things moved slowly at first.[56] The Duc de Dino—like White a bon vivant and womanizer—was known to need money, so White and Acton bided their time. Then, however, Clarence received a cable from a London dealer, Charles Davis, with whom White had done business: "The Duc de Dino has placed his collection in my hands for sale privately, and his price is 80,000 pounds." Davis urged Clarence to come view this prize, but, Davis added, March "would probably be too late to negotiate for the collection as a whole. . . . However if you might be willing to buy a certain number of these fine things. . . . I shall be very pleased to undertake your commission."[57] Clarence did not bite. In the end, Stuyvesant, in collaboration with J. P. Morgan, purchased the collection for the Metropolitan (where it still provides the nucleus of the museum's arms and armor collection).[58]

In February 1903 a friend of White's, Charles Adams Platt, who was developing a landscape and architectural business, wrote White about a collection in Toledo, Spain. Platt had learned that, "There are nine

Prompt action was called for. White persuaded Clarence to finance a scouting expedition through Europe by Arthur Acton. On February 21, Acton headed out from Florence to visit Naples, Palermo, Malta, Marseilles, Barcelona, Madrid, Retiro Cordova, Seville, Lisbon, Opporto, Burgos, Bordeaux, Paris, Turin, Pisa, and other places—in search of armor, tapestries, chairs, paintings, carpets, and more. When Acton cabled White to report on his expedition, the message was many pages long. Two typical entries read:

Naples. Gaetan Pepi
I gilt stucco Renaissance carved ...... 4000 lire
1 Doorway travertine stone good period 15th
    century H 3 met. W.2.50 10000
Palermo no antiquarians of import
Collection of armour as per photographs[60]

In May, Acton embarked on another scouting trip, this time visiting Amsterdam, Berlin, Dresden, London, Munich, Paris, and Vienna. From London he cabled Giddydoll (White) again: "Three complete suits Christies going tomorrow two at two hundred one four hundred pounds."[61] To Duveen in New York, who was also acting as Clarence's agent, he cabled: "nine demi suits with helmets entirely genuine will cost us about two thousand pounds advice [sic] white strongly buy."[62] Acton's list was marked with Xs and Os, including some beside seven "decorative panels by Boucher" and "100 swords and halberds." White's scrawled notes appear on the cablegram: with the swords and halberds, "many of them good," while next to some suits of armor, "too expensive."

In the end, just what Clarence purchased through agents or on his own is unclear, but however it came together, the collection earned high regard. A leading historian of armor declared it "unquestionable [sic] the most important corpus of material ever put together by an individual in modern times."[63] The completed collection encompassed about a dozen full suits dating to the fourteenth and fifteenth centuries from England, France, Germany, and Italy, and a number of swords including one originally belonging to the Electors Palatine, Archbishops of Mayence (i.e., German Mainz) and a half suit of armor once owned by the sixteenth-century Spanish king, Philip II. Clarence purchased the embossed and gilt armor of the Earl of Pembroke and a harness of the Earl of Cumberland; these were widely regarded as the best-preserved Elizabethan armor in existence. To create an appropriate setting for the armor, Clarence also purchased French, English, and German medieval and Renaissance tapestries depicting courtly life.

When the armor collection was mostly complete, Clarence continued to frequent auction houses and stay in touch with dealers. Although he never built a chapel in his mansion as his princely Renaissance predecessors did in their palaces, some of Harbor Hill began to take on a distinctly religious aura—specifically, that of Clarence's Roman Catholic faith.[64] Both with Stanford White and without, he built a collection of religious work by Italian masters of the early

and high Renaissance. Among the paintings he acquired was Duccio di Buoninsegna's *Calling of Saints Peter and Andrew*. He bought eight panels by Sassetta (Stefano di Giovanni); Bernard Berenson himself owned one panel from the same Sassetta altarpiece. Giovanni Bellini's *St. Jerome Reading*, Andrea Mantegna's *Adoration of the Shepherds*, Andrea del Verrocchio's *Madonna and Child*, and Raphael's *The Agony in the Garden* all entered the Mackay collection.[65] (The Berenson stamp of authenticity did not always withstand scholarly scrutiny; Clarence's Verrocchio painting was later demoted to "in the style of.")

Clarence bought Italian Renaissance sculptures on a comparably high plane. As noted by the eminent scholar W. R. Valentiner (founder of *Art in America* and *Art Quarterly*), Clarence's collection included several early Renaissance Madonnas, Verrocchio's bust of Lorenzo da Medici, Donatello's *St. John the Baptist*, Desiderio da Settignano's bust of a Florentine Lady, and several terracotta busts by Benedetto da Majano.[66] Also among Clarence's holdings were four early-fifteenth-century marble mourners from the tomb of the Duke of Burgundy, purchased from the collection of Baron Arthur de Schickler; a fourteenth-century English alabaster relief plaque of the Virgin Mary from Nottingham; and a bust by Agnolo Bronzino. Every day Clarence offered the Bronzino one perfect flower as a tribute.[67]

Besides martial trappings and fine religious art, various other items of historical interest came to Harbor Hill. The Mackays amassed scores of valuable pieces of furniture including a Louis XIV commode with chiseled ormolu mounts and a Louis XV center table with parquetry and ormolu mounts; some of these were signed, others were attributed to leading cabinetmakers. Two large Italian Renaissance bronze andirons with figures of Mars and Venus stood in the hall's fireplace.[68] Somewhat anomalously, Clarence also acquired the silver-plated revolver of Mexico's ill-fated Emperor. Among the myriad tapestries was a medieval "King Arthur" reputed to have cost the Mackays a half-million dollars; three late-fifteenth-century works

Entrance hall stair hung with Boucher tapestry, photo c. Nov. 1902–June 1903 (Museum of the City of New York, McKim, Mead & White Collection)

Katherine's anteroom, second floor, photo c. Nov. 1902–June 1903 (Museum of the City of New York, McKim, Mead & White Collection)

from the Chateau de Chaumont representing Youth, Music, and Sunshine; several Bouchers, and four Beauvais panels from around 1700 woven by Philippe Behangel after designs of Jean Baptiste Berain; and a pair of early-sixteenth-century Flemish panels woven with scenes from the life of Christ.

Royal Cortissoz, who as a young man had worked in the McKim firm, recognized the deep religious devotion reflected in Clarence's choices of paintings and sculpture. He commented on "the cult of the Madonna and other phases of devotional art" and the "religious lyricism" present in the works on display. At the

"Mrs. Mackay's Bathroom," c. *Jan.* 1902 (Private Collection)

Katherine's bedroom, photo c. Nov. 1902–June 1903 (Museum of the City of New York, McKim, Mead & White Collection)

same time, Cortissoz did not fail to note the setting of Harbor Hill or the hand of Stanford White in building the collection. He surveyed the ensemble: "one in which house and garden, gleaming water and episodi-cal statuary, trellised roses and other lovely flowers, blend in an unmistakable unity." The interior and the "hall or chamber of lordly dimensions" had an "atmos-phere of beauty."[69]

SIX

Maintaining Standards in Service at Harbor Hill

❉ ❉

"If there are any unhappy souls here, their unhappiness is not discernible to the outsider."

—Grace A. Fowler, "The Servant Question at Harbor Hill," *Harper's Bazaar*, September 1904

THE MACKAYS' EARLY YEARS in Roslyn saw the town's population rise from 1,378 to 1,876 between 1900 and 1903. Certainly not all that growth can be attributed to Harbor Hill, but at least some can. In the course of constructing the house and grounds, more than one thousand workers were in and out of Roslyn. Once the house and grounds, including the farm, were operating at full capacity, some one-hundred and eighty men and women "in service" worked for Clarence and Katherine. Only after 1910 did the Harbor Hill staff shrink—to a mere one hundred and twenty-five.

Harbor Hill employees thus made up a small community, and Roslyn's other residents welcomed them, not only out of goodwill, but also out of curiosity. When the Mackays were in residence they regularly opened the estate for holiday celebrations; in their ab-

sence, for short periods and long, the staff remained to keep the operation running smoothly. At these times the property was an object of particular interest to Roslyn locals, and the servants allowed surreptitious visits. The servants themselves expressed awe of their surroundings. The assistant postmistress, Mattie Replogle, for instance, left with a vivid memory of the interior. Its sheer size and the lavishness of the furnishings astounded her—especially Katherine's tub, which one "entered by going down steps and [which] was furnished with gold faucets." Replogle also marveled that on the canopied bed, "The sheets were changed every day."[1]

In Service at Harbor Hill

Harbor Hill was typical of large estates in the U.S., and their owners' aspirations to reproduce the class-structured society of England and continental Europe. But in a nation established on the ideal that all men were created equal, the notion of an innate subservient status was anathema. Harvard psychology professor

Footmen in livery at Harbor Hill, c. 1904 (Roslyn Landmark Society)

Silver vault, photo from Grace A. Fowler, "The Servant Question at Harbor Hill," Harper's Bazaar 38 no. 55 (September 1904)

Hugo Munsterberg observed in 1904 that, "It is quite characteristic that the only labour which is really disliked is such as involves immediate personal dependence, such as that of servants. . . . Even the first generation of children born in the country decline to become servants."[2] Another writer observed the upward mobility of American society: "Fifty years ago very few servants read, or cared to read," but that was no longer the case. Now they read novels and did fancy work, and "service can no longer be considered the humble labor of a lower for a superior being."[3] Men and women in household work usually wanted a different and better future for their children.

One popular book advised, "The society woman soon realizes that the personal charge of her house is impossible;"[4] therefore, she needed a talented staff, but too few men and women were willing to work in household service. Another writer complained, "There are not enough competent servants or even competent available housekeepers to make the domestic machinery run smoothly."[5] Employers' attitudes toward their employees, however, could help ease the situation. The wise master and mistress of a house recognized their servants' feelings and needs.[6] To their credit, Katherine and Clarence Mackay treated their servants, if not as equals, at least with consideration for their wants.

A roll call compiled from the memories of Stewart Donaldson, who worked at Harbor Hill off and on for twenty years, reveals the complexity of the estate staff and the longevity of many employees. (As a teenager, Donaldson's father worked in the greenhouses; he was later promoted to chauffeur.) Donaldson's recollection of the division between "inside" and "outside" workers reflects the standard practice of the time.[7] Inside personnel were further subdivided into household servants and personal attendants. Several names appear more than once in Donaldson's remembered roster, because a number of people devoted long years to service at Harbor Hill, some performing different jobs at different times.

INSIDE		OUTSIDE	
Housekeeper	Miss Katherine Thompson	Superintendent	Winslow Clark
Valet	William Mundy		Charles H. Hechler
Butlers	Mr. Twomblin	Estate office employees	Scott Libby
	William Powley		Electa Sniffen
	George "Cheerio" Mercer		Peter Hess
	Arthur Chapman		Charlie Lustig
Chefs	Mr. Ronne		Adolph Hess
	Mr. Adam	General handyman	Mike Bastack
	Ferdinand Coombes	Bricklayer	Dominick Dipalo
Assistant Chef	Gaston La Vanche	Plumber	Dan Dickinson
Nurse	Mary Finnerty	Painters	Ed Mott
Maids	Bella McIntyre		Jud Freeman
	Mary Cunningham	Carpenters	Oscar Wiggins
	Nellie Bayne		Walter Penny
	Martha Jordie	Electricians	Edward K. Pietsch
	Mme. DeMoutier		Angelo Graziosi
	Hilda	Gateman at the lodge	Ed Burke
	Louise	Engineer, water pumping station	Edward Harwood
Waitresses	Hilda		
	Nellie Burke	Blacksmith	Jack Linden
Kitchen Help	Margaret Herd (Chapman)		
	Lizzie Proudfoot	*Farm Workers*	
	Minnie Steed	Farm Superintendent	Frank "Kaffoo" Lupton
Laundresses	Mrs. A.J. McCann	Farm carpenter	Mike Bastak
	Mrs. Linden	Gang foremen (each with five men)	Henry Hendrickson
Handyman	Mike Smith		James Walsh
Girls' Governess	Miss Josephine Noel		Patty Daly
Footmen	Louis Hall	Laborers	"Old" Tim Donahue
	Charles Podevin		Tony Solomito
	John Fraser		Frank Nostrand
	Jack Bremerer		Tony Martino
Armor Collection	Mr. Tachaux		Matt Kennelly
	Mr. Leon Masselin		Pete Hollenzer
Night watchmen	Adam Heis	Team Drivers	Mr. Fitting
	Ambrose McCann		Mr. Tyma
	John McCann		Jim Lyons
	Charley Purick		Ike Eaton
Boiler or fireman	Mr. Rymers		"Old" George Washington
Janitor	George Shepherd	*Farm Stables*	
Housemen	Arthur Chapman	Stable Caretaker	John Kerr
	Billy McAlpin		

Main Stables			Greenhouses and Gardens	
Superintendent	John Theodore Mackie, Sr.		Head gardener	Frank Demak
Cook	Hugo Larsen		Outside garden head	Steve Weyland
Stablemen	Bill Carle		Outside garden workers	Nick Foloky
	John Finn			Barney Feeney
				John Ruggerio
Polo Stables				Dominick Della Ratta
Head	James Canivan			Angelo DiPaolo
Workers	John Tice		Greenhouse workers	William Coyne
	William Donaldson			Adam Whelan
	Walter Mace			Timothy Donohue
	Hubert Gilmartin		Flower Arranger	Frank Miller
			Vegetable man	Charles Purick
Garage			Plower	John Jannotta
Chauffeurs	Herb Ludlum			
	Jim Gillespie		Dog Kennels	
	Mr. Barton		Dog handler	Mr. Ted Armstrong
	James Haregan			
	Gunmar Rockman		Chicken Farm	
	William Pike		Poultryman	Daniel Sullivan
	William Donaldson			
	John Theodore (Jack) Mackie, Jr.		Casino and Outdoor Tennis Courts	
	Matt Powers		Caretaker	Mr. Genova
	Harry Tyson			
	Nat Jacobs		Indoor Tennis Courts and	
Washers	Nat Jacobs		Swimming Pool	
	Gus Noren		Caretaker	John Canary
Auto mechanics	Charles Pontifex		Tennis Instructor	Cecil Fairs
	Edward Andersen		Masseur and rubber	Walter Baldwin
Dairy				
Dairymen	William Sanders			
	Peter Letson			
Milk bottlers/butter	"Old" Mr. Letson			
	Mr. Drake			
Cowmen or herdsmen	Allen King			
	Charley Stevens			
	Fred Grunner			
	Rocco Abbandondola			
	Frank Mackney			

In addition, Katherine and Clarence had a personal staff, including a maid and valet/butler who traveled with them. Katherine had a personal secretary who helped schedule her day, answered mail, and did publicity-related tasks; among them were Isabelle Rowland and S. L. Libby. Clarence's personal secretary, a Mr. Havemeyer, was employed by the Commercial Cable Company and stayed in New York. Havemeyer's job entailed overseeing the bills forwarded to him by the housekeeper and other staff members and assisting with running the Harbor Hill estate.

Arthur Chapman, born in England in 1879, entered service to train as a butler-footman, and around 1908 accompanied his employer on a trip to Canada. He decided he wanted to travel, and in 1910 he accepted an offer to have his way paid if he would work for George Washington Vanderbilt at Biltmore in North Carolina. After a stint as footman-butler in Asheville he accepted a similar position at Harbor Hill. He fought in World War I, and returned to Harbor Hill, where he met and married Margaret Herd, an immigrant from Scotland who worked at the Ogden Mills estate before becoming a housemaid at Harbor Hill. The couple had two girls, Peggy and Grace, before Arthur contracted a pulmonary ailment caused by a poison gas attack during the war. Clarence paid to have Arthur treated for two years in Colorado Springs. What was first diagnosed as severe asthma turned out to be emphysema. By 1930 Arthur was almost too weak to walk, but Clarence kept him on the payroll. In return for Arthur's monthly fifty dollars, Margaret continued to work at Harbor Hill as a cook.[8]

For the successive waves of European immigrants arriving in the U.S., household service offered a significant source of jobs—for 60.5 percent of all the Irish arriving, for 42 percent of German immigrants, and for 62 percent of Scandinavian immigrants.[9] Like America itself, therefore, the composition of a great country house's staff was a rich mix of nationalities.

Although prized, household servants were pressed hard. They commonly reported for duty at six o'clock in the morning and stayed well into the evening; the usual work week was six and a half days. When anyone from the owner's family was in residence, there had to be at least one staff member on call around the clock.

Wages, which varied according to position, rose steeply over the first two decades of the twentieth century. Employees with managerial responsibilities were paid distinctly more than their underlings. A superintendent, head butler, or head housekeeper made roughly $100 a month in 1900 and $250 in 1920; a common housemaid, in contrast, might make $10 a month in 1900, but by the 1920s this had risen to

perhaps $70. Room and board were also offered as compensation. For inside staff, lodgings were provided for the employee only; outside workers, however, were provided quarters for their families, along with garden plots and some provisions.

Working for the Mackays had distinct advantages, leading in many cases to long terms of service, and even the passing down of a father's job to a son. Scottish-born John Theodore Mackie Sr., for instance, worked as a carriage driver and then as a chauffeur; after his death, John Theodore Mackie Jr. took over, working also as superintendent of the stable, where he lived with his wife and children.[10] Such faithfulness spoke well of the working conditions at Harbor Hill.

Like other estate owners, Clarence Mackay provided all his employees with medical care. For a yearly retainer of $10,000, Dr. John Mann of Old Westbury was on call for any medical emergencies. When summoned, he would sit at the patient's bedside and take the patient's pulse while looking at "his watch with his lips puckered up and silently whistling air through his lips."[11]

In the early years, servants' children were forbidden at Harbor Hill, but in time this prohibition relaxed, yielding an abundance of childhood memories. One one-time Harbor Hill child reminisced, "One thing that will always stand out in my mind about Harbor Hill was the quiet and stillness of the woods."[12] Another recalled awakening in the early morning in the stable's quarters to the raking of gravel. To servants' children, Clarence was remote—a distant figure with a great mustache.[13] A gardener's son recalled that, because Mr. Mackay was the boss, "Everybody on the estate was expected to vote Republican; this wasn't a big problem."[14] Others remembered picking strawberries and apples and fleeing from the caretaker—and during parties, sneaking up to the mansion to peek at the celebrities. Stewart Donaldson told of Theodore Roosevelt's visit from nearby Sagamore Hill to play tennis with Clarence. The former president also played baseball with the boys, autographing a ball before throwing it into the air: "How he did laugh as we scrambled for the ball."[15]

Edward K. Pietsch, Harbor Hill's electrician, led the local Boy Scout troop. A large man and very popular, Pietsch played Santa Claus at the annual Harbor Hill Christmas party, springing from the giant fireplace in the main hall.[16] On the Fourth of July, he organized the annual outing in which the village and estate Boy Scouts played games, swam in the Mackays' pool, joined the Mackays' guests on the terraces to watch the fireworks set off from the lower garden, and camped overnight on the estate.

Except on such occasions, however, servants' children were under strict orders never to be seen. When one of the housemaids discovered boys swimming nude in the little mirror pond, she chased the young miscreants away.[17] Peggy Chapman (Grosser) told of being in the kitchen with her mother and hearing Clarence approach; petrified, she hid under the large table. But Clarence "bent down and said 'peek-a-boo' and I thought I was going to die. He was a wonderful man."[18] Peggy's sister remembered going into the library when the Mackays were away and being told "don't touch anything"; the huge tapestry of King Herod's *Slaughter of the Innocents* so frightened Grace Chapman Laundis that she never "looked at it again."[19]

However, sadness tinges some childhood memories of Harbor Hill. Roslyn seemed so far away, some people said. Elsie Letson, the chief dairyman's daughter, recalled, "Because we lived out of town, we missed out on the usual neighborhood pursuits of childhood."[20]

Top-Down Management

The growth of the American millionaire class, and their accompanying enormous households, created not only a need for numerous servants, but also questions about how to manage them. Books and articles offered guidance, especially on dealing with female servants. The duties and treatment of each employee were outlined, along with how to negotiate the occasional complica-

tion such as, "Now and then a romance occurs below stairs." To this problem the solution was simple: "In plain English it is not 'good form' for footmen to have wives and homes."[21] Indeed, the sexes were kept strictly apart in the house; any crossing of this barrier resulted in dismissal (another rule that relaxed with time).

Katherine Mackay embraced the current new ideal of humanitarian household management. In a *Harper's Bazaar* article, "The Servant Question at Harbor Hill," Grace Fowler described a household run by a "queen" and a "gentlewoman" who drew from her staff a "harmonious responsiveness." According to Fowler, Katherine Mackay "inspires in her servants an anxiety to please." The article gave a detailed picture of the staff's quarters, their jobs, and all their advantages, from Katherine's "allowing tea to be served for those who desire it" between three and four in the afternoon, to the provision of a sewing room where housemaids, when off duty, could gather to create "dainty lingerie and pretty aprons. . . ." Fowler concluded: "If there are any unhappy souls here, their unhappiness is not discernible to the outsider."[22] In fact, however, a rigid hierarchy emulating that of the English aristocracy controlled the inside-the-mansion staff, with the housekeeper and butler at the top in command of everybody except the chef and cooks.

The ideal housekeeper, Fowler wrote, was "a woman of intelligence, tact, and refinement, and wonderful executive ability." She supervised who came and went, and knew what everybody was doing at each hour of the day. She was in charge of the housemaids and laundresses, and she shopped for all the supplies. Besides making sure that every bathroom "had dainty soaps and toilet waters, sponges, brushes, and other things," she also controlled the writing of checks for the indoor staff and directed the payment of bills. Her quarters at Harbor Hill were a small suite of rooms on the main floor, directly opposite the kitchen so she could see who was approaching. Her sitting room was well appointed, with a fireplace, pink striped wallpaper, pictures (including several of Katherine), and plants. Her rooms were furnished with a matched set

Linen closet, photo c. Nov. 1902–June 1903 (*Museum of the City of New York, McKim, Mead & White Collection*)

including a desk, bureau, and tables (new, not cast-offs, and with locking drawers), and a sofa, chairs, and a bed. The quarters were made homey by bowls of cut flowers, a song bird in a cage in a window, and "on a fur rug in a sunny corner a fuzzy little ball of a dog." She had her own bathroom and was provided with a surrey for drives on the estate and into town.

The housekeeper also supervised the laundry—the washing, drying, and pressing of household linens and the clothing of the staff as well as that of the Mackay family and their visitors. Harbor Hill was equipped with modern electric dryers and irons of many sizes. The servants' linen was kept in one room, but a major feature was the cedar-lined linen room on the third floor that one writer claimed "looks as if it had been hollowed out of one large block of this fragrant wood." The household linens—every piece "ordered from Paris by the mistress of the house"—was organized and stored on fragrant cedar shelves and tables; most of the linens were hemstitched by hand and embroidered with the Mackay crest. Grace Fowler bowed to Katherine: "One is almost awed by the amount of money the contents of this linenroom represents, the exquisite tastefulness shown in the selection of it is equally impressive."

Upstairs in any grand house the maids were invisible figures who cleaned daily and were otherwise seen only when summoned. Like the housekeeper, they

lived in the house and were unmarried. A maid could be of any age, but younger women were usually preferred. Some were recent immigrants and most likely illiterate. Their rooms and those of their male counterparts were similarly furnished, with white-enameled furniture and muslin curtains. Each room had an outside window as well as electricity and steam heat.

Katherine's personal maid had a room on the second floor, not far from Katherine's, as "she must be

Parlor maid's bedroom, from Grace A. Fowler, "The Servant Question at Harbor Hill," Harper's Bazaar 38 no. 55 (September 1904)

Butler's den, from Grace A. Fowler, "The Servant Question at Harbor Hill," Harper's Bazaar 38 no. 55 (September 1904)

Housekeeper's room, from Grace A. Fowler, "The Servant Question at Harbor Hill," Harper's Bazaar 38 no. 55 (September 1904)

Servants' sewing room, from Grace A. Fowler, "The Servant Question at Harbor Hill," Harper's Bazaar 38 no. 55 (September 1904)

conveniently near her mistress at all hours of the day and night." This room was larger than those of the other maids, but similarly furnished in white with a soft green velvet carpet. On her dresser were silver-colored toilet articles, and plants grown in the windows. Besides a wide closet for her own belongings, Katherine's maid had another one where her mistress's gowns could be hung for brushing or mending.

Another major inside-the-house figure was the head, or first, butler—originally a Mr. Twomblin from England, who was said to be "fond of art"; he was succeeded by William Powley and then by George Mercer. Englishmen were preferred for this job, since they greeted the guests and were the primary conduit to the world beyond the estate. Harbor Hill's butler ordered all the liquor and supplies, such as fruit for the butler's pantry. He supervised at least four footmen and the many handymen, who polished silver, shined shoes, and did other odd jobs. The butler's room (also called a "den") was located on the second floor and comparable to the housekeeper's in furnishings and appointments, except it consisted of only one room.

The butler and footmen were expected to be well groomed and to speak proper

English. The regular footmen answered the door and served at table; for big parties extra footmen were engaged. Facial hair was frowned upon for inside help, though it was acceptable for the grounds staff. An early footman was a musician and "enthusiastic camera fiend" who delighted in taking flash pictures of the staff and the grounds.

The chef lived in his own world. A good chef—especially a sought-after one trained in France—testified to the house's status. The Mackays' head chef shuttled between New York and Roslyn with the family. Harbor Hill had three French chefs in succession: Mr.

Kitchen, from Grace A. Fowler, "The Servant Question at Harbor Hill," Harper's Bazaar 38 no. 55 (September 1904)

Minnie Steed and an unidentified assistant in the kitchen of Harbor Hill, 1909 (Bryant Library
Local History Collection, Roslyn, NY)

One of Clarence's personal valets, William Mundy, was an Englishman who stood about six feet three inches and wore knickers. He was remembered as never taking a day off and going everywhere Mr. Mackay went. Mundy purchased all of Clarence's clothes as well as his shaving supplies and cologne. He married the staff nurse, Miss May Finnerty ("Finny"), who was also on duty all day every day, with aspirin, iodine, and a thermometer at hand. Finny also traveled with the family. When Mundy and Finny married, Clarence gave them a house in the nearby village of Munsey Park and an automobile.[23] (Clarence was more lenient than Katherine about the separation-of-the-sexes rule at Harbor Hill.)

Ronne, Ferdinand Coombes, and Mr. M. Adam, who had worked in England and at several New York hotels. Under the head chef were assistant, or second, chefs, four cooks (some of whom might be women), and kitchen maids who did much of the grunt work. The head chef—who wore a white coat and pants and the high white *toque* of his trade—submitted a menu each day to the mistress (or later, to the master), who would cross out and add dishes. The chef then wrote out the menu on plain white cards engraved with Katherine's crest—a lavender orchid outlined in gold. When the master and mistress dined alone, "a butler and three footmen in livery [were] always present to minister to their needs."

The kitchen maids, or "girls," wore white; the men wore white shirts, blue pants, and white aprons. Perfect order ruled in the spotless, white kitchen. One writer noted the shine of the copper pots and "even the handles of the utensils on the shelves are placed at uniform angles." A fastidious married man, Chef Adam liked to visit the chefs at neighboring mansions on Sunday afternoons after the big midday dinner and imbibe a glass of cognac.

In addition to the housekeeper, butler, chef, personal maid and valet, and nurse, the elite of the house staff included a tutor (by 1907 a new baby boy, John, had joined young Katherine and Ellin). The elite of the house staff—the butler, housekeeper, chef, valet, nurse, tutor, and special maids, along with the maids and valets of guests—ate in the upper servants' dining room on the main floor, and had their own servant (in the 1920s, Nellie Burke). It was furnished with a suite of Colonial Revival furniture, plants, and pictures hung on the walls. The Guastavino vaulted ceiling was fully visible. Their meals were the same as the Mackays, with the exclusion of the "fancy dishes." The housekeeper presided at one end of the table, and the chef carved the meat. Adjacent was a screened–in porch for the servants to use during the warm months, and where the men could smoke.

The rest of the house staff—the second-tier servants—served themselves in a basement dining room. Described as an immense, well-lighted, and airy space, its table could seat seventeen. Their meals were served promptly at seven A.M., noon, and six P.M. The walls were hung with typewritten regulations over Katherine's signature: the head footman was to carve; a parlor maid to pour tea and coffee; and no servant was to sit at table longer than half an hour.[24]

Between indoors and out was the staff retained to tend to Clarence's athletic interests. A masseur gave rubdowns to users of the athletic facilities housed in the Casino, which included a Turkish bath, dressing and lounging rooms, and a kitchen. Clarence employed a tennis instructor, Cecil Fairs, who taught the Mackay children and their friends and played with the guests. Stewart Donaldson remembered that Fairs "always won all the games from Mr. Mackay when they

Dining hall for the second servants, from Grace A. Fowler, "The Servant Question at Harbor Hill," Harper's Bazaar 38 no. 55 (September 1904)

Dining room for the upper servants, from Grace A. Fowler, "The Servant Question at Harbor Hill," Harper's Bazaar 38 no. 55 (September 1904)

were playing for money; Mr. Mackay could never understand this."[25]

Order Outdoors

Management of the estate itself fell to a succession of supervisors. The first, a dairyman named William Sanders, encountered familiar problems with Katherine. He purchased young cattle that could not meet the milk needs of the house; Katherine lost patience with his excuses and fired him. After Sanders came Charles H. Hechler, a farmer from Missouri who was a nephew of Mr. Havermeyer. Hechler took a particular interest in the farm's prize cattle and seems to have had better luck with meeting Katherine's demands.

On the Mackay's model farm, as on the properties of many estates, was a herd of award-winning Guernseys. Peter Letson, who had specialized in dairy studies at Rutgers University's agricultural college, was in charge of building a great herd that eventually reached fifty-five to sixty head, including twenty-five milk cows. The Mackay cows were constantly tested, fed weighed rations, and milked four times a day. A running joke on the estate was that Clarence charged twenty-five cents for a quart of milk that cost two dollars to produce. Masher Galore, a prize bull that loved having its head scratched, was rumored to have set Clarence back $75,000. Mackay Guernseys were entered in the Nassau County Fair each year, and occasionally won.[26]

One goal of an estate's farm was to provide the household's vegetables and fruits, and a wide range of produce was cultivated at Harbor Hill, including potatoes, tomatoes, peppers, radishes, string beans, cabbage, turnips, beets, carrots, spinach, and several types of lettuce. An orchard provided apples. Harbor Hill produce was served in the house while the family was there; during the winter, when the Mackays were in town for the social season, a chauffeur made three trips each week to the city with home-grown supplies.[27]

"Masher Galor," Mackay prize Guernsey bull with Peter Letson and handler at Harbor Hill (Bryant Library Local History Collection, Roslyn, NY)

"Land o'Burns," Mackay prize show horse with handler at Harbor Hill, c. 1910 (Bryant Library Local History Collection, Roslyn, NY)

The same workmen who tended the farm gardens also cleared the brush on the estate, plowed the roads during the winter, tilled and hayed the fields, cut wood, and helped keep the main drives and the garden areas manicured.

Running the Mackay estate could be a challenge, as superintendent Charles Hechler discovered in December 1909, when he received orders to cut the laborers' wages from $1.75 a day to $1.50. The reason

given for the pay cut was to enable the laborers to remain employed all winter on reduced hours. A protest forced Hechler to call the Nassau County sheriffs, who arrived with shotguns and guarded the gates. Excluded from the reduction, however, were the gardeners and the more specialized help. The *New York Times* identified the problem as "chiefly Italians, Poles, and Russians"— code for labor agitators. The fracas lasted two days. With armed deputies on the property, the rebellion fizzled. A few of the insurgents went back to work; the rest moved on.[28]

The duties of the large gardening staff included work on the estate's plantings and in its various greenhouses and conservatories. In the spring the gardeners took the potted bay trees to the terraces; the trees stood twelve to fourteen feet high. For the winter, they took the trees in using a flat wagon drawn by Belgian horses. In the six-sided palm house special plants, including orchids, were grown for the main house. Plants for decoration were raised year-round in the greenhouses, including roses, carnations, gladiolus, dahlias, chrysanthemums, sweet peas, snapdragons, violets, and asparagus ferns.

Frank Demak, who was in charge of the greenhouses and gardens, developed several new species, including a chrysanthemum that he named the "Ellin Mackay" in honor of his employers' second child. Temperatures were held in the rose house between 57 to 62 degrees, and in the orchid house, between 67 to 72 degrees during the winter; at night men came in to oversee the boilers (for which they were not paid extra). The garden staff was also charged with making an enriched potting soil that combined sod, cow manure, and other additives; this would be "set" for three years prior to use.[29]

The maintenance of the horse stables and dog

Harbor Hill servants in buggy with driver, c. 1910 (Bryant Library Local History Collection, Roslyn, NY)

William Donaldson, coachman for the Mackays, in front of Trinity Church, March 22, 1907 (Bryant Library Local History Collection, Roslyn, NY)

Grooms and horsemen in front of stables, c. 1912 (Bryant Library Local History Collection, Roslyn, NY)

Harbor Hill servants in auto with chauffeur, c. 1920 (Bryant Library Local History Collection, Roslyn, NY)

kennels occupied still more workers. Some lived with their jobs, as for instance in the polo stables, which housed the head handler. On the second floor of the main stable was a large apartment for the superintendent and an ample kitchen—with a chef who cooked for the estate's unmarried workers living on the grounds.

The chicken farm was never very successful and was gradually phased out. Likewise the dog kennels fell into disuse, as interest in hunting declined. The capacious quarters that for a while housed dog handlers were converted into housing for Chef Adam and the head butler, George Mercer.

Technological breakthroughs in transportation did not lessen the need for staff. Horse-powered mobility initially dominated the estate, but as early as 1902 Katherine Mackay acquired an automobile—the first in Roslyn—which necessitated a driver. The first chauffeur was Jim Havigan. Mattie Replogle recalled watching from the post office as Katherine came into the village ringing the car's bell: "people would run out into the streets to see this modern marvel."[30]

Clarence eventually surpassed Katherine as a car enthusiast. By the 1920s, the garages at Harbor Hill housed a Rolls Royce, a Chandler, a Packard, two Buicks, a Metz, and two White trucks. These required not only chauffeurs but also a staff of auto mechanics. Horses still provided much of the muscle for farming activities into the early 1930s, but Stewart Donaldson's remembered roster indicates that car and garage personnel eventually outnumbered stable hands as automobiles replaced horses as the most prestigious form of transportation.

In summarizing conditions at Harbor Hill, Grace Fowler noted in *Harper's Bazaar*, "The home life of the servants here stands out in most favorable contrast to that of servants in similar homes in England and France."[31] As employers, Katherine and Clarence inadvertently outshone the European aristocrats they aspired to emulate. The long tenure of many Harbor Hill workers can be attributed, at least in part, to the Mackays' democratic—and uniquely American—awareness that employees will stay only if treated to a measure of comfort and respect.

Portrait of Katherine Mackay, inscribed: "Only what is real endures. Katherine, January 16, 1909" (Private Collection)

SEVEN

At the Top, Together and Apart

❧ ❧

"I am very happy to marry the man I love."

—Katherine Mackay quoted in C. F. Bertelli, "Dr. Blake,

Free 24 Hours, weds Mrs. Mackay."

THE MACKAYS regarded Harbor Hill as their permanent residence, but they were there only part of the time. In the summers they often visited in Newport or Saratoga (when they traveled within the United States, they did so in a private railroad car), or they went to Europe. They spent the winter social season in New York City. For a while they had a house at 99 Madison Avenue; they next took suites at fashionable hotels such as the Waldorf-Astoria, the Ritz-Carlton, and the Plaza. Sometimes they leased houses, such as the Havemeyers' at 244 Madison Avenue. Finally, Clarence purchased a house on East Seventy-fifth Street. However, whether present at Harbor Hill or absent, the Mackays were effectively the lord and lady of Roslyn.

The chill that had met the Mackays' arrival in Roslyn turned quickly into a warm embrace, as they drew widespread attention to the town and showed themselves to be good citizens. By November 1900, the hostility reported earlier in the *Roslyn News* had given way to adoration. "Mr. & Mrs. Clarence Mackay take such an interest in our city and its welfare," one columnist wrote, "as well as the happiness of its habitants. We would mention many instances of the kindness of their Hearts, in their distribution of gifts and remembrances, but it is not necessary. . . . On Thanksgiving Day 26 families, the majority of which would have had to go without such meals, will receive them through the bountiful generosity of Mr. & Mrs. Mackay."[1]

Whether in the city or the country, the Mackays never rested. The power that came from being incredibly rich and, in Katherine's case, surpassingly beautiful, demanded constant activity. A magazine article, "Busy Women of the Idle Rich," described Katherine's days as being "scheduled as systematically as those of a railroad magnate."[2] Besides hosting grand social events, the Mackays opened their doors and their purses to the benefit of concerns both local and national. Beginning around 1905 they made the estate the site of Fourth of July celebrations, and together they welcomed all of Roslyn. But beyond that, the causes they espoused reflected their differences.[3]

Guests arriving for party, Harbor Hill, c. 1906 (Society for the Preservation of Long Island Antiquities)

Guests and footmen, Harbor Hill, c. 1907 (Bryant Library, Local History Collection, Roslyn, NY)

Noblesse Oblige

Even before work on the house was complete, Katherine found "distressed and forlorn" Roslyn's public William Cullen Bryant Library, which was located in the Town Hall and named for the town's earliest distinguished resident. She ordered new carpeting and engaged two librarians to sort and reclassify the books, at a cost of $1,500. Some four hundred books were discarded and replaced (in the process the librarians found a sizable trove of old books in Bryant's house, Cedarmere). Complaints arose when word spread that

Katherine had removed lithographic portraits of Longfellow and Bryant, and that they would "no longer appear on the walls." But when it was learned that the pictures were being cleaned and re-framed for rehanging, the *Roslyn News* claimed the entire community would be grateful that "Mrs. Mackay has shown a most generous and kindly spirit in her work of re-habilitating the library and has the approval and gratitude of all its patrons."[4]

Harbor Hill provided a splendid setting for Katherine's charity bazaars. In September 1904 she organized a benefit for the Nassau County hospital. The initial intention was to disregard social barriers, so admission started at only twenty-five cents. But as ticket sales for the event quickly rose, the price of admission doubled. Katherine gave over the first floor to the fête, and in Clarence's beloved main hall straw thatched sales booths were erected. Katherine asked Stanford White to contribute a graphic design for the event; she planned to use the designs for the invitation card and to have an edition of 1,500 posters printed to sell for the hospital's benefit.[5] As usual Katherine found White laggardly and took her familiar imperious tone:

"Games at Annual Picnic, Harbor Hill," c. 1907 *(Bryant Library, Local History Collection, Roslyn, NY)*

Sunday school party, Harbor Hill, c. 1910 (Bryant Library Local History Collection, Roslyn, NY)

"I am very disappointed that you have not sent me sketch of poster as I must [have] them delivered to me not later than August 24, please hurry."[6]

The Mackays' acquaintances pitched in. Oliver

H. P. Belmont, Foxhall Keene, and Senator William Cox tended bar. Mrs. Belmont came dressed as Longfellow's Evangeline, and other ladies wore "mouse gray frocks with aprons of bolting cloth and coquettish Puritan caps."[7] Katherine herself was clad in a nurse's uniform consisting of a pale blue gown with a striped white-and-blue muslin apron and a "fluff of white lace on her head . . . caught by a single large shaded pink rose." Her co-hostesses wore "beautiful white Louis XVI costumes." An orchestra on the balcony played all afternoon, and in the salon a fortune teller told society women what lay ahead for them. Thirty-five hundred guests attended; the party yielded $8,000 for the hospital.[8]

Katherine's friendship with the Duchess of Marlborough, *née* Consuelo Vanderbilt, always stood her in good stead, as photos of the two attest.[9] A party at Harbor Hill usually greeted Consuelo's return visits to the United Sates. A charity bazaar that Katherine hosted in 1906 offered the attraction of the duchess as a helper.[10]

Roslyn's houses of worship stood to gain especially well from the Mackays' benevolence. Instead of the household chapel many European nobles possessed, Katherine and Clarence became actively engaged in Roslyn's churches: Clarence at the Roman Catholic St. Mary's, Katherine at the Episcopalian Trinity.

As early as 1898, when the Mackays still occupied temporary quarters on the property, Clarence attended St. Mary's, a small church of recent creation. In 1867, a handful of Catholics had begun to worship in their wooden "shanty"; a clergymen sent out weekly from Brooklyn celebrated Mass. By the early 1870s St. Mary's laid a foundation for a permanent brick building. Consecrated in 1878, it was built in the round-arched Italianate idiom favored by the American Catholic hierarchy in the post-Civil War years.

Clarence gave St. Mary's a pipe organ in memory of his late father and donated funds to cover an organist's salary; the organ was dedicated on January 21, 1902. Other gifts followed, including funds for a rectory and electric lighting (provided by the firm Clarence established with E. D. Morgan) and stall seating in the gallery. Clarence also helped finance a local chapter of the Knights of Columbus, dubbed the John W. Mackay Council.[11]

Katherine looked to the needs of Trinity Church. Trinity's beginnings were much like St. Mary's, with a small board-and-batten building erected in 1862. The first of Katherine's many gifts was a new baptismal fount commemorating the christening of baby Katherine in 1900. Then, taking a cue from Clarence, she donated an organ, and then a large opalescent window depicting the Creation produced by New York's Church Glass and Decorating Company. She also hosted church fundraisers, which culminated in an of-

St. Mary's Church, Roslyn, NY (*Bryant Library Local History Collection, Roslyn, NY*)

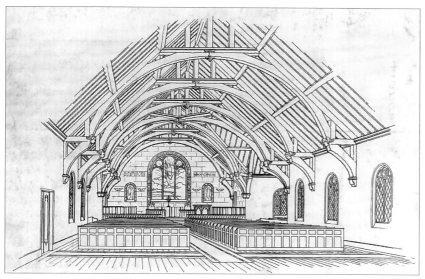

Trinity Church, Roslyn, McKim, Mead & White, architects, interior rendering by Jules Crow, c. 1906 (Avery Architectural and Fine Arts Library, Columbia University, McKim, Mead & White collection)

Trinity Church, construction photograph, 1906 (Bryant Library Local History Collection, Roslyn, NY)

structure. But Katherine's gift—a sort of challenge grant—was contingent on the church's launching a fundraising program for a new main building. She grew impatient with the church's efforts, however, and instead of retracting her offer, in April 1906 she simply gave the vestry $40,000 to erect a new building, plus $5,000 for landscaping in memory of her mother. The Roslyn newspaper took note: "Mrs. Clarence H. Mackay is having built a fine new church and parish house as memorials to her parents."[12]

In the protracted construction process, however, Katherine managed to antagonize nearly everybody. The usual problems with Stanford White cropped up, and her letters to him—many undated and with her familiar coy apologies—grew more and more shrill: "Listen and *think*! I do not like the altar and window arrangement. . . . Don't think me a bore."[13] Surprisingly, Katherine still did not understand how buildings were paid for; she inquired, "You must be bored to death with me and the church. . . . Is it customary to give a percent to the builder?"[14] In another letter she explained, "I find the 3 horrible picture windows over the pre-existing altar are memorial windows so they will have to remain in the church."[15] She found the plans for the interior excellent, but, "I do not like the exterior: it is not only high and ugly but it is unfriendly. . . . [P]lease do not think me a nuisance." Then she ordered him to come to Roslyn: "As far as the altar trimmings are concerned . . . make me three designs: one very simple, one moderately so and an elaborate one (cross, 2 vases and two candlesticks)."[16]

More hauteur followed: "I do not like the altar

fer, on Christmas Day 1905, of a new parish house in memory of her father, William Alexander Duer, who lived at Harbor Hill after he was widowed in 1903.

Once again Katherine turned to Stanford White—this time to design a parish house of four rooms for Sunday school and social functions, with a caretaker's apartment. It was in fact Walter R. Wilder, a White assistant, who designed the modest new

Trinity Church, Roslyn, NY (Bryant Library Local History Collection, Roslyn, NY)

Trinity Church, photo of Sunday School interior with Duer/Mackay memorial windows and labels by Church Glass and Decorating Company (Bryant Library Local History Collection, Roslyn, NY)

mauve stationery kept the McKim office busy, as she sought to keep the costs down and get what she wanted. Although White died in June 1906, all evidence indicates that the church as built closely followed his design. Trinity Episcopal Church, Roslyn, is an unusual design in Stanford White's oeuvre. Although not normally known as a church architect, White worked on several while he was with Richardson in the 1870s, and then with McKim and Mead he had designed a number of churches, including the Judson Memorial Baptist Church (1888–93) and Madison Square Presbyterian Church (1903–6), both in New York. White attempted something different with Trinity, Roslyn. As completed, it was a variation on mid-thirteenth-century English parish churches. The most immediate model for the main facade was a series of Episcopal churches done by Richard Upjohn in the 1840s and 1850s which drew upon Saint Michael's, Long Stanton (c. 1230), Cambridgeshire. This later church had been a favorite of the Anglo-Catholic (or High Anglican) Cambridge Camden Society in the 1840s, and they exported its basic form around the world. White essentially adopted the buttressed end gable with small belfry and the longitudinal hall plan of the St. Michael's model, added transepts and changed the traditional pointed arched windows to round-headed openings. In a sense he married the English Gothic with the Romanesque; the consequence is an awkward exterior with unlikely contrasts of parts. The other notable exterior feature is the Harvard bond clinker brick laid up with only headers exposed, and the tall cross-gabled roof laid with Vermont slate shingles.

and window arrangement. Can't we marry the altars to the window by connecting them with flat columns or some frame?" She specified that the interior wood finish either be "grey oak (like our hall) or . . . 'mission' green as we planned for the pews, wood trim and rafters."[17] Numerous letters on Katherine's hallmark

The *Roslyn News* reported that the church "will not be delayed by the *murder of Stanford White*"[18] [emphasis in original]. Leland Sudlow, who had supervised the construction of Harbor Hill for the firm, now oversaw the church project, and White's former assistant William S. Richardson took over for the office. Jules Crow, the office renderer, provided presentation drawings of the final design.

White had always put up with Katherine's demands, but the problems worsened after his death. In mid-November 1906, George Varney, the main builder-contractor, wrote to the subcontractor for brick laying, James McNeill, that while the work was fine, "It is common gossip throughout the village that the job is more a joke than reality—that the men do as they please, take their own time, start when they please and quit when they please. In addition to these shortcomings we have found you have a very disagreeable habit of drinking during working hours, especially your leaving the work and men to run themselves, and find it necessary to visit the gin mill on the corner."[19]

Varney himself was on shaky financial ground, and the numerous design changes Katherine ordered introduced into the design led him to notify her in February 1907 that he would file for bankruptcy unless he were paid more. Katherine stood her ground, and in March Varney went out of business. The suppliers of the building materials then sued her, upon which she responded that the supplies firm had recommended Varney, and she would never employ them again.

When the rafters were painted a color she found inappropriate, Katherine directed the firm to "correct their error in the color of those rafters and trim at their own expense. . . . I want samples submitted to me and I want to see that this work is started by Monday next."[20] To Sudlow she wrote, "When I call at the church late Thursday I shall expect to see most of that dreadful stuff redone properly."[21]

The church's eighty-foot-tall interior is dominated by the massive king truss at the crossing and the stained glass. The trussed wooden hammer beams have carved heads of cherubim at the knees and similar delicate carving is used on pew ends, the organ case, and in other areas. All the wooden and carved interior furnishings, including the chancel stalls, screens, pulpit, and pews were done by T. D. Wadelton. Indicating this was a low Episcopal church rather than a "high" Anglo-Catholic parish, the marble altar table was relatively restrained and lacked a reredos. Instead, dominating the altar is a large opalescent window entitled *The Creation*, Katherine's gift to the earlier church done by the Church Glass and Decorating Company of New York. God is in the center with his hand raised allowing in the light, and surrounded by billowing clouds. On either side are two smaller celestial windows made by M. T. Lamb's "Art Stained Glass" studios of Brooklyn. Lamb also repaired and reinstalled along the south side the older memorial windows from the earlier church and provided the windows for the parish house. In the west transept are several memorial windows dating to 1906–7 by the Church Glass and Decorating Company of New York. The central window, *Moses Viewing the Promised Land*, is a memorial window to Harbor Hill's Long Island neighbor, William Collins Whitney, who died in 1904. The rose window overhead and the window to the *Jacob's Dream*, are also by the same firm. The last window in the west transept on the south side, the Hooper Memorial, is signed by Louis C. Tiffany and dates to 1927. The Church Glass and Decorating Company provided the small chapel windows on the east side which were a memorial to Katherine's late uncle, her father, and Clarence's older brother John William Mackay. Splendid in their coloration and treatment of the robes, these windows contained the faces of Katherine and Clarence's children, Katherine, Ellin and John. E. F. Caldwell provided the lighting fixtures and W & J Sloane provided the kneelers. Guy Lowell provided some advice on the church's grounds.

The church was finally consecrated on March 22, 1907, and Reverend Norman O. Hutton was installed as the new minister. Clarence and the children attended, along with many other members of New York

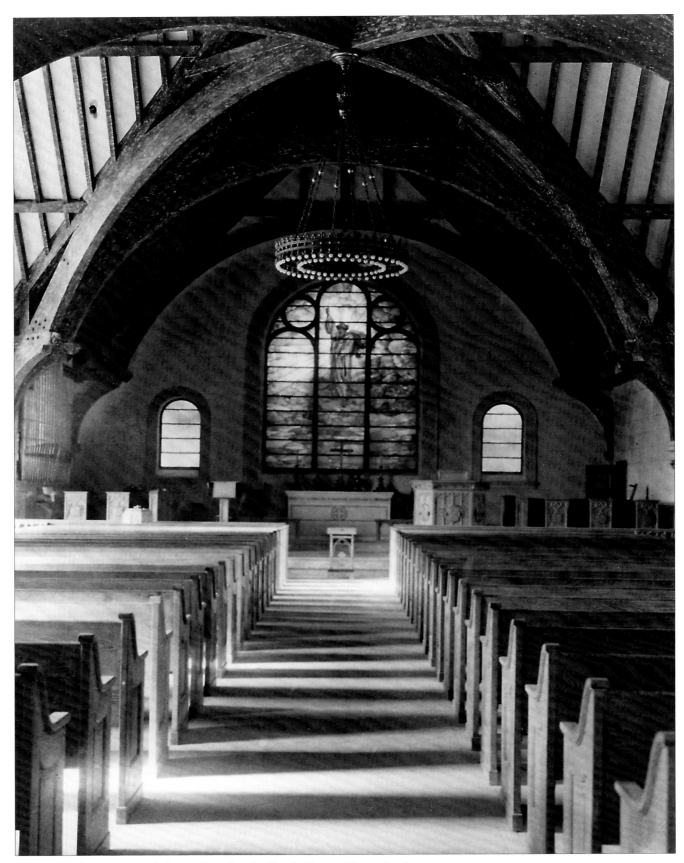

Trinity Church, main nave and altar with windows by Church Glass and Decorating Company (Bryant Library Local History Collection, Roslyn, NY)

Clarence Mackay and daughter Ellin arriving at dedication of Trinity Church, March 22, 1907 (Bryant Library Local History Collection, Roslyn, NY)

society. Following the procession of clergymen, Katherine entered and walked quickly down the aisle. Although she reportedly requested "no ostentation" in the service, her black attire found its way into the press: "a large picture hat and bird of paradise plumes. . . . Pearls and diamonds were her ornaments."[22] That the accounts focused mainly on Katherine's raiment from the neck up may reflect a certain discretion about her state: she was pregnant at the time. The Mackays' third child—a third John William—arrived later that year.

The *New York World* characteristically exaggerated the church's cost and sneered, "Mackay's $500,000 Club Nearly Ready."[23] The actual cost was $58,196.21 for the church and parish house, plus the architect's five percent commission.[24]

Katherine was deeply involved with Trinity Church. She took over the annual autumn church fair, putting Consuelo Vanderbilt in charge of the candy table. (In town, too, Katherine and the duchess teamed up in acts of charity. The ladies inspected conditions in New York's main prison, the Tombs, in lower Manhattan; Katherine expressed delight at the cleanliness of the Tombs.[25]) She persuaded other society ladies, such as her neighbor Mrs. E. D. Morgan, to

participate as well. Church literary meetings concluded with tea at Harbor Hill.[26]

Not everybody associated with Trinity Church appreciated Katherine. In an annual election held two weeks after the consecration, her handpicked team of vestrymen lost to a group sponsored by E. D. Morgan. Following this defeat of "the Mackay regime," a vestryman sued her over the sale of the old church building.[27] The new rector—"Mrs. Mackay's rector"—left what the *New York Times* called "Mrs. Clarence Mackay's church" after only two years, for Chicago.[28]

Katherine's community interests extended to education and politics as well. She donated costumes to the high school for dramatic productions and helped coach rehearsals. She donated funds to decorate the teachers' lounge. In 1904 she started an annual party at Harbor Hill for the school children of Roslyn: the elegant Delmonico's restaurant of New York catered.[29] At one party the children marched four abreast up the hill behind three bands. The newspaper noted that "Mrs. Mackay and her children . . . [were] dressed as simply as their simplest guests. . . ."[30] Young Katherine and Ellin took positions atop pillars and parapets as statue-like greeters. In 1906, Katherine contributed money for the establishment in nearby Mineola of a state "normal school," or teacher's college.[31]

When the school board rejected some of Katherine's suggestions, she decided to run for a seat; during the campaign her opponent, Dr. J. H. Bogart, claimed "petticoat rule," implying that women had no place in politics.[32] Clarence came from Saratoga to vote alongside more than one hundred Harbor Hill employees. "Mrs. Mackay was unable to come herself, but sent words of encouragement to her lieutenants."[33] She won the seat on the board.

At the next school board election, Katherine urged her former opponent to run for a newly open seat. At the first meeting of the newly elected board, Katherine joked with the doctor "about her generosity in letting bygones be bygones. . . . Why, we're the scandal of the school," she told Dr. Bogart, adding, "I've come all the way down from Lenox [Massachusetts] to vote for you and heap coals of fire on your head. Aren't you grateful?'"[34] A *New York Herald* article noted, "His attitude toward the proposals that come from the woman who read him out of the school board and then read him back in again is now said to be as distinctly respectful and considerate as that clever woman could wish."[35]

The Roslyn schools provided an outlet for Katherine's humanitarian concerns. She led the movement to abolish corporal punishment of pupils, to which grateful schoolboys responded by scrawling "MRS. MACKAY IS ALL RIGHT" on fences, sidewalks, and barns.[36] She sponsored an essay contest on the subject of women's right to vote and caused a commotion by bringing suffragettes to address the students. "It's coming, sure as fate," she declared.[37] At graduation she wore the cap and gown acquired in 1908 along with an honorary Master of Arts from the State University of Nevada, where Clarence and Louise had endowed the Mackay School of Mines (later the School of Earth Sciences and Engineering).

In 1910, she resigned. "I feel that it is not fair for me to hold this office," she explained, "when my absences from Harbor Hill compel me to miss meetings which, as a school trustee, I should always attend."[38] Indeed, Katherine was now missing from Roslyn much of the time.

Katherine's advocacy of women's rights went beyond Roslyn. She founded the Equal Franchise Society in New York City. Along with ladies from high society, the organization's board included the publishing tycoon Colonel George Harvey, and the progressive education reformer John Dewey.[39] The organization sponsored lectures at Columbia University; Dewey, the first speaker, addressed an audience of several hundred.[40] Katherine's flair for publicity elicited much media attention. She was quoted as saying that "a feminine mastery of detail and thorough understanding of children" would improve the school boards and educational systems nationwide, and she demanded, "Why shouldn't women who pay taxes have a vote . . .?"[41] She denounced militant suffragists and pinned her hopes on educating the public.[42] She invited leading speakers to gatherings at her New York house.

Katherine addressed the Interurban Suffrage Council. She believed, as a pamphlet documented, that mankind was slowly changing the nature of government from brute force to thought and morality. The male, she said, "has always persistently kept the good moral element in the race, mainly woman, from having any place in government at all." Men, she allowed, with their "selfishness" will continue to develop "the commercial instinct," but the "mother-instinct" enabled women "to analyze, to discriminate; to feed upon the good, passing by the evil."[43]

At the first Woman's Suffrage Convention, held at Carnegie Hall in 1909, Katherine's address stressed the equal rights of women and their place in education. She was breathless and flushed at the end, and the great applause brought an unfamiliar, almost shy Katherine back to the podium. Blowing two-handed kisses, she exclaimed, "You don't know really what this means to me. . . . I have never spoken before in a place like this and I am really frightened to death."[44] Even when the topic was women's rights, Katherine's glamour stole the show. One article, headlined "WINS SUFFRAGISTS BY HER GOOD LOOKS," noted that she wore a "beautiful décolleté gown of turquoise blue, with a little coat of gold lace."[45]

Katherine gave frequent interviews and she set up a large meeting in Albany to speak to the New York State legislature and the governor.[46] She held fundraisers featuring *tableaux vivants*, with participants costumed and posed as characters from historical events and famous works of art (Katherine sometimes appeared as Lady Kitty Duer; once she was Florence Nightingale on a battlefield).[47] She recruited her friends to join the women's movement.[48] In Newport, she got Mrs. O. H. P. Belmont (the former Mrs. W. K. Vanderbilt) to open Marble House to suffragist activities.

But in April 1911, Katherine resigned from the Equal Franchise Society. The reasons were unclear. Rumors spread that she was dissatisfied with how the suffrage movement was being managed. The only explanation she gave was that she was "not entirely certain of her plans for the near future."[49] Nobody knew what this meant.

Like much else about the Mackays, Katherine and Clarence pursued their interests separately. Clarence usually took a month-long trip to Europe in the late spring or summer; sometimes Katherine went with him, sometimes not. In the fall, without her, he went on shooting trips of several weeks to Scotland or North Carolina, or both. The charities he supported reflected his strong and largely unshared passions for art, culture, the nation's patrimony, and sports.

Clarence served as secretary of the Lincoln Farm Association, which purchased Abraham Lincoln's rural Kentucky birthplace; on its board, he and Boston Brahmin lawyer-reformer Joseph H. Choate rubbed elbows with artistic patriots such as Augustus Saint-Gaudens and Samuel L. Clemens (Mark Twain).[50] Clarence was treasurer of the Dickens Centenary Fund in England, which raised money to support the granddaughters of Charles Dickens. Clarence became an underwriter of the Society of Beaux-Arts Architects' Van Alen prize, given to promising young architects to study in Paris.[51] He became a director of New York's Metropolitan Opera in 1908. And three years later, he established the Mackay Trophy, administered by the National Aeronautic Association and awarded for "the most meritorious flight of the year."[52]

Not all of Clarence's community involvement could be called charitable. Sports occupied much of his spare time, and he won numerous racquet trophies.[53] In addition to raising and racing horses, he instituted the Harbor Hill Cup for jumpers at Belmont Park.[54] His horses appeared annually at major shows both at home and abroad. At the Mineola Fair on Long Island, Katherine attended and served several times as a judge.[55] She also promoted her education agenda by awarding prizes to students.[56]

In 1912, Clarence teamed up with several other landowners to refurbish and enlarge the old Piping Rock Club in nearby Locust Valley, where his horses regularly appeared. Known as one of America's most exclusive country clubs, Piping Rock hosted both golf and horse shows. As vice president, Clarence helped negotiate for Guy Lowell the commission to build Piping Rock's clubhouse: a series of linked houses resembling Long Island's older summer residences, unified with a shingled exterior offset by several large temple porticos and a long veranda. The result prompted a writer for *Country Life* magazine to characterize Piping Rock as "the sort of thing that George Washington would have built if he had the money." Clarence paid for a giant fireplace in the main room and the plantings on the grounds.[57]

Whether motivated by charity, conviction, vanity, or plain pleasure, Katherine's and Clarence's largesse made them the leading figures of Roslyn; their comings and goings were always news. Clarence came home to a "large welcome to our popular townsman . . . on his return from abroad." A group of local politicians and businessmen presented him with a loving cup and "a set of resolutions, properly bound and embellished, setting forth the high esteem in which he is held."[58]

Clarence as Architectural Patron

In addition to the buildings in Roslyn, McKim, Mead & White were involved in other work for Clarence Mackay, such as a casino in Saratoga which was never built, and a hunting lodge in North Carolina. Clarence owned a large hunting preserve in Guilford County, near Jamestown, North Carolina, where he and friends would retire in the fall and spring to hunt. Stanford White and his assistant Frederick Adams produced several designs for Deep River Lodge, as it was known; the one erected by 1905 had stout Doric columns holding up the gambrel roofs of an H-shaped building. Stylistically it recalled Colonial American buildings, with its Palladian windows and widow's walk.

Far more important and impressive were the

Mackay School of Mines buildings at the University of Nevada at Reno, where Clarence and his mother Louise began making donations in 1903, in the name of the late John William Mackay. The initial donation was $1,500 although later donations were greater. The funding was not just for buildings but to attract faculty and provide operating expenses.

White was the architect for the School, and his scheme grew out of his University of Virginia project of the late 1890s. After White's death in June 1906, William S. Richardson took over the job and guided it to completion. Arranged in a rough quadrangle, Richardson proposed adding several buildings, including a domed library; however, only the School of

McKim, Mead & White, Mackay Deep River Lodge, Guilford County, near Jamestown, North Carolina, 1905 (Private Collection)

Dedication of Gutzon Borglum's John W. Mackay statue, University of Nevada, Reno, June 10, 1908. Clarence Mackay is standing to the left of the stage, and Lieutenant and Acting Governor Dickerson is addressing the gathering. (University of Nevada, Reno)

Aerial rendering of Mackay Hall and quadrangle, University of Nevada, McKim, Mead & White, architects, Jules Crow, renderer, c. 1906 (Avery Architectural and Fine Arts Library, Columbia University, McKim, Mead & White collection)

"Mackay on Top," Clarence Mackay being carried on the shoulders of students at the University of Nevada, October 23, 1909: students are Claude Teel; Dudley Homer; Ernest Folsom; Kenneth Tillotson; Neil McVicar; Cecil Creel; Walter Harris; Frank Hobbins; Leon Long (University of Nevada, Reno)

Mines was constructed. A large, blocky, red brick structure, its entrance was a large Tuscan portico. The Mackay School of Mines cost $72,323 when completed in 1908. Clarence and Louise also commissioned Gutzon Borglum to create a statue of John Mackay with a hand resting on a pick and dressed in miner's garb and boots. Borglum's bronze statue stood in the middle of the courtyard at Reno and a copy was placed in Harbor Hill. Katherine and Clarence journeyed west for the building and statue's dedication, and Katherine was presented with an honorary M.A.

Clarence was so pleased with the building and statue, and the reception he received, that he funded more projects, including athletic facilities designed by two former McKim, Mead & White office men with a practice in San Francisco, Walter D. Bliss and William B. Faville. At the dedication of the Mackay Field and Training Quarters in October 1909, students kidnapped Clarence from the president of the university's dinner, paraded him through town, and took him into the hills where he was entertained with a barbecue dinner. He was late for the president's event, but said 'he was glad he had the experience.' At the game the next day Clarence donned the garb of a university senior—sombrero, flannel shirt and corduroys—and ran

onto the field with the football team. He had promised the team $5,000 if they won, and he cheered and threw his sombrero in the air when the Nevada team kicked the final winning field goal. Well into the later 1920s Clarence continued to make donations to the university in the names of his father and older brother.[59]

Basking Under Scrutiny

With all the money in the world, and Harbor Hill with which to display it, the Mackays reached the pinnacle of society in New York City as well as in Roslyn. They acquired their own box at the Metropolitan Opera and were invited from time to time to sit in Mrs. John Jacob Astor's box.[59] André Brouillet, a French portrait painter, attributed his success in America to having letters of introduction to Mrs. Astor and Mrs. Mackay, which "were sufficient to open all doors." The Astor and Mackay salons were "the places of reunion for the elite, and . . . to be received in either is equivalent to a patent of nobility."[60]

The press's fascination with the Mackays was

Katherine's boudoir, with Katherine on dais, photo c. Nov. 1902–June 1903 (Museum of the City of New York, McKim, Mead & White Collection, #90.44.1.950)

much abetted by Katherine's appetite for publicity. She threw Harbor Hill's doors open to photographers. When journalists came, they toured not just the grounds and the public rooms but Katherine's private apartment as well. An unpublished photograph showed Katherine reclining on the dais in her boudoir. Photos of her ermine rugs and the sunken marble bathtub were published in magazines.

Inevitably, one gossip sheet remarked that money poured into the estate, "so thick and fast that you can almost see it lying on the ground." Harbor Hill, the writer proclaimed, was built "for future generations as well as for the present time."[61] It was so well suited to "one of the most delightfully extravagant young women of the day. . . . a perfect specimen of willful, wistful beauty." Another columnist commented on Katherine's penchant for mauve and its use in her

clothes, boudoir, stationery, and even the postage stamps she used.[62]

Like her mother-in-law a keeper of scrapbooks, Katherine filled albums with countless articles on and mentions of both the house and herself. In 1901 alone, the name Mackay appeared in the *New York Times* 189 times. Not all these references were to Katherine, but she made up the lion's share, with about three-fourths of all the 1,181 *Times* references between 1900 and 1910. With coverage in all the other New York dailies combined, the Mackays appeared in print an average of once a day throughout the decade.[63] So keen were they on exposure that they allowed piano and car dealers to cite them in ads as satisfied customers.[64] Katherine's love of publicity was especially well remembered: Mattie Replogle, Roslyn's assistant postmistress, recalled that Katherine "often called on Mr. Crandall,

Boy Scout troop at Harbor Hill, July 4, 1911, Clarence with son John William *(Bryant Library Local History Collection, Roslyn, NY)*

Party, July 4, 1911, at Harbor Hill, left to right: Ellin, Clarence, John William (in front), and Katherine, or Kay *(Bryant Library Local History Collection, Roslyn, NY)*

Katherine Mackay with chauffeur Jim Havigan, c. 1902 *(Bryant Library Local History Collection, Roslyn, NY)*

Clarence Mackay at racetrack with E. R. Thomas , c. 1912 (Library of Congress)

Clarence Mackay with J. W. Gerard at Mineola Country Fair (Library of Congress)

Mrs. Clarence Mackay at Mineola (Fair), c. 1905 (Library of Congress)

the editor of the *Roslyn News* to inform him personally of her plans."[65]

Clarence made news in 1903 when he refused to pay a personal assessment of $150,000 on Harbor Hill. He claimed that the house and its contents were the property of his wife—a gift to her from his father.[66] Indeed, the taxes on Harbor Hill often made news, such as when Clarence failed to avoid personal property taxes on the art. A rare press appearance of both Mackays together occurred on July 4, 1903, when Katherine and Clarence attended the historic first launch of an around-the-world telegraphic message via Clarence's Commercial Pacific Cable company from President Theodore Roosevelt's Sagamore Hill at Oyster Bay.

The press's Mackay fascination was not limited to the Northeast, nor was it always accurate. A St. Louis newspaper reported that Harbor Hill "was built from designs by Mrs. Mackay" and published a photograph of her along with the claim that the mansion had twenty-six marble Pompeian rooms with the baths sunk in the middle of the floor."[67]

And of course, newspapers reported on Katherine's dresses and those of little Katherine: "She worships her

little girl, and whenever the little one is in particularly good form there is a pilgrimage to the photographer's."[68] Much attention focused on Katherine's jewelry, especially a crown similar to that of the Queen of England.[69]

Katherine's attire made good copy. Of an appearance at the opera a writer reported, "She wore a black chiffon gown and her dark hair showed a filet-like tiara in Greek key pattern of diamonds, the band not being over an inch and a half wide, the diamonds being of the same size. . . ." The article described Katherine's black velvet coat, the shape of her collar, and her corsage.[70] When Katherine rode in Clarence's four-in-hand coach wearing a long black coat embroidered in white, a large black hat with a flat crown "entirely of white convolvuli" and a "black fox boa," it made the papers.[71] Though Katherine was often reported to be wearing black, she favored other colors, too; her gowns of silver, yellow, blue, dark green, pink, and gold, with plumes, furs, and jewels, all received notice.[72] (Katherine knew what flattered her. One of her granddaughters observed that Katherine always wore her dresses longer than was fashionable, because "The famous beauty had piano legs."[73])

Sending the first around-the-world cable, July 4, 1903, Sagamore Hill, Oyster Bay. Katherine Mackay seated with hat; standing to her left is Clarence Mackay (Tribune Photo, 1903)
(Private Collection)

Artists, too, could not resist Katherine's good looks and sense of style. In addition to the Edmund Chartran portrait that initially hung in Harbor Hill's salon, Howard Chandler Christy, John White Alexander, and Giovanni Boldini painted her. André Brouillet, who pronounced "American women . . . the most beautiful in the world," placed Katherine at the top of his list. While Brouillet noted American women's reputation for coquettishness and fondness of dress, he still found in them a youthfulness of face and figure, a "new type superior."[74]

Katherine and Clarence of course entertained on a grand scale, holding several major dinner parties and dances

Katherine with Ellin and Katherine (Kay) in Harbor Hill boudoir, c. 1905 (Private Collection)

every year. About thirty favored guests would be invited for dinner, followed by a dance reception attended by more than one hundred; the evening concluded with a light supper. The house was elaborately decorated, and Carl Haupt's orchestra played. More than one hundred electric lights lined Harbor Hill's drive and gardens and hung from trees. An electric star "visible for miles" blazed atop the mansion.[75]

Katherine the Romantic

Katherine harbored literary ambitions, as is evident from the book plate she commissioned for Harbor Hill's library. Against the background of a magical city, the tree of literature grows out of three volumes labeled Carlisle, Voltaire, and Goethe. Like many other women of privileged upbringing, Katherine had written some sentimental poetry in her youth. Her literary aspirations might have been inspired by Edith Wharton, who, though considerably older than Katherine, was born into the same elite New York social stratum and whose work was well-known in the 1900s. Both Wharton's and Katherine's writings might be described as making critical judgments of individuals' actions, but the two differed fundamentally: Wharton was a naturalist, while Katherine was a romantic melodramatist.

Her first major literary effort, *Gabrielle. A Dream from the Treasures Contained in the Letters of Abelard and Heloise*, was a play; it was published in 1903 in *North American Review*. Modeled on the medieval French tale of Abelard and Heloise, Katherine created a beautiful French maiden, Gabrielle, who falls in love with her tutor, Theophile, a monk of aristocratic birth. The medieval settings included a great library hall with a blazing fireplace, tall candlesticks, and wide windows through which "one sees the city of Paris and the country beyond."[76]

Gabrielle garnered some minor recognition, but mainly on society pages. One report noted the author's

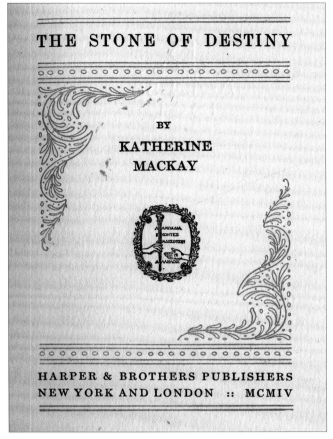

Title page of The Stone of Destiny by Katherine Mackay, 1904 (Author)

Katherine Mackay book plate designed by Frances W. Delehenly, c. 1901 (Private Collection)

intellectual inclinations rather than her social life, but then went on to observe that Katherine Mackay was "a leader in New York society by reason of her birth, beauty and fortune. . . ."[77]

Katherine's other major literary effort, a 112-page novella titled *The Stone of Destiny* (1904), is similarly melodramatic. Like *Gabrielle*, it is set in France, mostly in "a fine old house" filled with distinguished tapestries and furniture. The story revolves around unfilled expectations: those of Theodore, who becomes a great artist and attempts to serve humanity, and his wife, who is "indolent in the luxury about her," and unfaithful. The melodramatic finale includes a deathbed scene in which the wife, recognizing her failures, receives redemption.[78]

The Stone of Destiny received modest reviews, most of them noting that the author lived at Harbor Hill and focusing on her social life and the Mackay fortune.

Katherine Mackay's fiction must be interpreted cautiously, but if one acknowledges even a hint of autobiography in a writer's tales, then Katherine's writings revealed a frustrated melodramatic imagination. Her fiction suggests a person less than entirely happy in her marriage.

How much did Katherine's early literary effort reflect a growing dissatisfaction with her marriage to Clarence? Later accounts in gossip sheets implied that the marriage had been unstable from the start, and Roslyn locals noticed that "Mrs. Mackay has been at the Harbor Hill estate not more than two weeks at the outside since early last summer, and that during most of this time she was in Paris while Mr. Mackay was in this country." "Gossip is rife," the paper observed, but neither Katherine nor Clarence offered any explana-

Clarence Mackay with children Ellin and Katherine (Kay) in Harbor Hill library, c. 1905 (Private Collection)

tion. Rumors also circulated that many Harbor Hill staff members would be laid off, though this was denied.[79] Not until 1913 did a widening schism between Clarence and his wife hit the newspapers, and Katherine's quest for publicity turned it into a nightmarish media event.

The society columnists had a field day. It had not been a love match, they said. One observed cynically that the marriage suited the Mackays' social ambitions and the Duers' need for wealth. Clarence lacked Katherine's artistic temperament, and she cared little for his business or philanthropy. "She wants to found a salon, to surround herself with artists and literary geniuses," one reporter claimed, while he "wants amusement."[80] Clearly, the reporter did not know his subjects well.

Clarence went into seclusion for a while at his North Carolina hunting preserve. Then he rented a cottage at Spring Lake on the New Jersey shore. The gossip intensified when, later that month, he sailed with the three children to Europe on the *S.S. Imperator*, traveling under an assumed name and guarded by detectives—and with what the newspapers claimed was a staff of thirty. (Actually, the retinue was somewhat smaller; it included two Canadian nurses, a Danish governess, an American tutor, a French courier, and a German maid, plus the regular valets). Katherine voiced surprise at Clarence's actions and denied that she had threatened divorce.[81]

Then, in September 1913, another, even larger, bombshell hit. Catherine Ketchum (Mrs. Joseph A.) Blake, the wife of a prominent New York surgeon, filed a $1 million suit against Katherine for "alienation of affections."[82]

Dr. Blake had operated on Clarence's throat in 1910, and in the course of the treatment had noticed the charms of his patient's wife. Described as having a "long, bony pirate's face and easy, genial manner," Dr. Blake was known to have an eye for the ladies.[83] He and Katherine began meeting for private dinners. As Clarence recuperated in town, the wheels of the gossip mills started to crank. When Clarence was away from

Clarence Mackay and children on ship to Europe, 1913 (Library of Congress)

Harbor Hill, Dr. Blake paid a visit, which "became a town scandal."[84]

Mrs. Blake charged Katherine with having "willfully, wickedly, and maliciously enticed her husband from her."[85] She withdrew her suit a month later, however, and instead filed a suit against her husband for desertion. The Blakes separated in January 1914 and divorced in November of that year.

The Mackays, meanwhile, picked Paris as the site of their divorce. They had kept a house there for many years, and now Katherine purchased another house nearby. On February 11, 1914, a mutual divorce was granted, on the grounds of desertion on both sides. The divorce proceedings were held *in camera* (in private, probably in a judge's chambers), but within a week the press was trumpeting the news. On the front page of the *New York Times* the headline read:

Portrait of Katherine Mackay, Paris, c.1914 (Private Collection)

"MACKAYS OBTAIN DIVORCE IN PARIS," followed the next day by "MRS. C. H. MACKAY SILENT."[86]

Along with access to Clarence's millions, rights to which she turned over to her husband and young son, Katherine gave up custody of all three children. Dr.

Blake joined her in Paris, where one newspaper reported, "She has lived very boldly . . . running an auto over the boulevard and carrying Blake with her."[87] Katherine was thirty-three and Clarence thirty-nine when their fourteen-year marriage imploded.

By that autumn, Europe was at war. Katherine volunteered for the Red Cross in Paris, and Blake worked as a surgeon. The day after his divorce came through, after a morning of service at a military hospital, Blake washed his hands, discarded his coveralls, and he and Katherine proceeded with a few friends in a Red Cross automobile to the district mayor's office to marry. When the fateful question was asked, Blake responded in an "emotional voice." Katherine's voice was a "clear [and] warm tone." She wore "a dark blue tailor-made suit, extremely simple, but very smart with a marquise hat." After the ceremony Katherine took the wheel and drove Dr. Blake to the hospital to resume surgery. That night "costly flowers arrived and Dr. Blake came home to dinner."[88]

One newspaper account moralized: "The end is what was expected. And it justifies every thing of Mr. Mackay in ridding himself of her." Dr. Blake's former wife chimed in: "I can only wish her all the unhappiness that is her just due."[89] Katherine's response was disarmingly simple: "I am very happy to marry the man I love."[90]

Clarence's Triumph and Defeat

❋❋

Clarence Mackay on ship, c. 1916 (Library of Congress)

KATHERINE'S BETRAYAL SHATTERED Clarence, but he was determined to maintain a brave face. Of course he had to follow the dictates of his faith; as one newspaper noted, "Mr. Mackay is a Roman Catholic, and his church does not allow divorce."[1] But instead of sequestering himself, Clarence plunged back into New York society, and in the next few years emerged as one of America's leading Catholic laymen. Harbor Hill played a central role, as it was where Mackay entertained the elite of society, business tycoons, nobles, a king-to-be, and a future Pope, Cardinal Pacelli, who in 1939 became Pope Pius XII.

Clarence in Charge

Clarence took responsibility for his family. To assert himself as the parent in charge, he had himself pho-

Portrait of Clarence Mackay with children, Katherine (Kay), John William, and Ellin, c. 1914 (oval format) (Private Collection)

tographed with his three newly motherless children. Nobody smiles in the pictures—not thirteen-year-old Katherine, ten-year-old Ellin, six-year-old John William, nor their father. Perhaps their blank faces can be ascribed to the time, when camera shutter speeds were slow and convention equated rigid expressionless with dignity. But hurt surely is discernible in the four Mackays.

Clarence tried to protect the children by drawing them closer and limiting their contact with outsiders, but the effect was just the opposite. There was no escaping the fact: their mother had given them up for a man not their father. The memory wounded them permanently.

Their Irish Catholic heritage could have deepened the children's sense of estrangement and loss. Prejudice against Irish immigrants had not diminished in the decades since Mrs. Paran Stevens admonished their grandmother Louise about the obstacles she faced. But high society—the realm of white Anglo-Saxon Protestants—was the world in which the Mackay children lived, where they went to school and socialized. Clarence's wealth kept the doors of high society open to his half-Irish children. He himself was invulnerable to prejudice: rich as he was, he wore his Catholicism proudly. Two years after his divorce from Katherine, Clarence was made a Knight of St. Gregory; he was later accorded the highest papal honor as a Knight of Malta.

Clarence kept his children's several homes on an even keel. He stayed in the city house on East Seventy-fifth Street and maintained his vigorous pace in society, business, and philanthropy. The popular Cubist caricaturist Marius DeZayas portrayed him in evening dress with a cigarette, deep in thought over more good works.[2] Approaching middle age, Clarence cut a figure, for as a granddaughter remembered, he had a pompous air with his "mouth a tight, thick line under his brush mustache, blue eyes blazing, indignant in every portion of his small, tidy, imperious frame."[3]

Harbor Hill continued to run like a well-oiled clock and remained Roslyn's centerpiece, with Clarence and the children in residence on weekends and during the summer, and bands playing on the mansion's steps as fundraising efforts for the local schools. Even during the war, the Fourth of July parties for Roslyn's residents proceeded. When the war ended, Clarence fêted the Allied victory at Harbor Hill.[4]

Harbor Hill changed little during the sixteen years after Katherine's departure. Her portraits disappeared from the salon, replaced by Renaissance works of art, most with religious themes. Clarence also added valuable papal robes and other religious items to the salon's decorative scheme. Of these, one grounds worker sniffed, "Mackay being an Irish Catholic went in for this sort of thing."[5]

"Mr. Clarence H. Mackay deep in the problem of . . . charitable work . . . for the Allied Cause." (Marius DeZayas, Puck, Feb. 5, 1918)

Here we have **Mr. Clarence H. Mackay**, deep in the problem of finding some additional avenue through which he can increase the sum total of the charitable work he is doing for the Allied cause.

View of house with trees in bloom, c. 1920 (Private Collection)

Marine Corps Band on garden steps, Harbor Hill, c. 1920 (Bryant Library Local History Collection, Roslyn, NY)

A distinct change occurred in 1919, when Clarence's mother joined the household. Widowed in 1902, Louise had stayed in London, sometimes crossing to the Continent until the war prevented such travels. A year after the war ended, Clarence's half-sister Eva, who had been living in Italy after her marriage ended, died, and nothing more kept Louise in Europe. Once settled at Harbor Hill, Louise managed her son's social schedule and served as hostess when he entertained. Some years after her arrival, Clarence commissioned a prominent English society painter, John Lavery, to do two

Photo of Louise, Mrs. John W. Mackay, inscribed "To Darling Clarie, from Loving Mammey, 1921" (Private Collection)

interior views. One is set in the library and shows Louise pouring tea for Clarence and young John William; a dog lounges on the floor. Lavery's second interior (see jacket) depicts Clarence's granddaughter standing in the great hall, dwarfed by the scale of the presentation.

The grounds remained immaculate. In the formal garden, a contemporary sculpture by Paul Manship replaced the neoclassical Triton fountain Clarence and Katherine had acquired from Stanford White in 1902. (The old fountain wound up in the possession of Ohio's Severance family, major supporters of Western Reserve University and the Cleveland Orchestra.)

Photo albums of the estate at the time show both the architectural features and recreation on the grounds, including John William learning to box and run a lathe in the stable machine shop. Clarence's love of sports never flagged. With the advance of technology and increasing electrification of the United States,

he ordered the installation of a small electric deer track. Now he and his marksman guests had stuffed deer to shoot. Clarence still strolled over his twenty-five-plus miles of road, his Rolls Royce following.

A 1921 list published by the leading social arbiter Maury Paul—known as "Cholly Knickerbocker"—named Clarence one of the fifty "Old Guard."[6] He was invited onto the boards of several of New York's loftiest institutions, including the Metropolitan Museum of Art, the Metropolitan Opera, and the New York Philharmonic Society, which he chaired until his death. Clarence helped persuade the great Italian conductor Arturo Toscanini to come to the Philharmonic and had a hand in founding the Chicago Grand Opera Company. (Years later, these activities resulted not only in a medal from the National Institute of Social Sciences for his contributions to the musical arts, but also an honorary master's degree in music from New York University). For his philanthropy he also was made an officer of the French Legion of Honor and a knight commander of the Belgian Order of the Crown, and won special recognition from the crowns of Italy and the Netherlands.

Through his involvement with the Metropolitan Opera, he became acquainted with a diva, Anna Case. A native of South Branch, New Jersey, Case was at the time the Metropolitan's only singer not trained in Europe. She had caught his eye while performing in Massenet's *Werther*, and at some unrecorded point the two began a clandestine liaison; for as long as Katherine lived, Clarence remained a married man in the eyes of the Church. Case eventually pursued a career on the concert stage rather than in opera.

Entertaining at Harbor Hill continued in high style—higher, indeed, than ever. Clarence gave several memorable parties, the kind of festivities depicted by F. Scott Fitzgerald. The Prince of Wales, the future King Edward VIII, visited the Old Westbury-Roslyn area in September 1924 for the International Polo Matches at the Meadow Brook Club. Clarence planned a dinner for seventy-five at Harbor Hill, to be followed by a ball for twelve hundred; most of New York soci-

Clarence Mackay with the Prince of Wales, 1924 (Private Collection)

Clarence Mackay and His Royal Highness the Prince of Wales and others at Piping Rock Club, 1924 (Piping Rock Club and Society for the Preservation of Long Island Antiquities)

the formal garden. The head gardener, Frank Demak, and Mr. Smythe of Wadley & Smythe created arrangements of American Beauty roses, including on the north terrace a "pavilion of flowers" that formed a large marquee. Some of the armor displayed in the main hall was removed so the ball could be held there. Paul Whiteman's orchestra, in two sections, played throughout the evening.[7]

As usual, Louise was the hostess; as the newspapers reminded their readers, she had "become a close friend of the Prince's grandfather, King Edward VI" while in London.[8] When His Highness was introduced to Louise, she produced a photograph of him as a baby given to her by the Princess of Wales.[9] The dinner table was set with the famous Mackay silver, and Clarence's two daughters were seated on either side of the guest of honor. The Prince did not stay at Harbor Hill, but he spent time viewing the estate and described it:

A copy of a French chateau, it stood on top of a wooded rise overlooking Long Island Sound. I spent the day going through the place, marveling at all it contained. The art treasures alone would have sufficed the needs of an ordinary museum, and I particularly remembered the vast hall lined with figures in armor that had been obtained from various old European collections. Now paintings, tapestries, old china, and armor would have been commonplace enough in a British country house: what was surprising was to find on the same property a squash-rackets court, a gymnasium, an indoor swimming pool, and a Turkish bath.

It was only as I prepared to leave that I

ety appeared on the guest list. The grounds were lighted as for a spectacle, with thousands of colored lanterns hung along the main driveway and "as far as you could see into the woods" to evoke "a natural autumn bloom." Harbor Hill's electrician, Mr. Pietsch, concealed great floodlights to shine on the house and outlined its architectural features with tiny orange light bulbs. He also illuminated the potted trees and statuary on the terraces and the fountain in noticed in the entrance hall an object strangely different from all the rest; a small statue of what appeared to be a workman with a pick in his hand.

"What is that?" I asked Mr. Mackay.

"A replica of a statue of my father I have erected on the campus of the University of Nevada at Reno," he answered proudly. I admired Mr. Mackay for that.[10]

Another of Clarence's grand parties, on June 13, 1927, honored Charles Lindbergh's solo flight across the Atlantic after the great ticker-tape parade in Manhattan. Clarence's promotion of aviation with the National Aeronautic Association's Mackay Trophy made Harbor Hill the ideal venue. But the event almost did not happen: Lindbergh complained of fatigue but did put in an appearance. The guest list included New York City's Major Jimmy Walker and his wife. This time the estate was festooned with seven thousand red, white, and blue illuminated Japanese lanterns, and floodlights buried in the shrubbery and at the summit of the roof cast a soft gray light over "Mr. Mackay's famous Versailles garden."[11] The dining room, with places set for eighty,

again featured the Mackay silver. Lindbergh, at the head table, was flanked by Clarence's elder daughter, Katherine, and his mother. Louise found the handsome young aviator courteous but withdrawn, as though he were wearing armor "as he warily felt his way along an unfamiliar path."[12]

The Trouble with Ellin

Young Katherine, an apple-cheeked brunette, married at age twenty-two on September 21, 1922, in St. Mary's Church, Roslyn. Like her father, her groom, Kenneth O'Brien, was of Irish extraction. Although not of New York's elite 400, the O'Briens were among the city's top Catholic laity. Kenneth's father Morgan was a justice on the New York Supreme Court. The newlyweds received a blessing via cable from Pope Pius XI. The bride's mother was not invited to the wedding. Kenneth O'Brien pursued a career in law and politics, and the couple had three children.

Seven years later, on February 2, 1929, John William married a Catholic, J. Gwendolyn Rose, a

Illumination for Charles Lindbergh party, June 13, 1927 (Private Collection)

granddaughter of New York's William M. "Boss" Tweed. Their wedding took place at St. Brigid's in Westbury. Again, the pope sent his blessing.[13] Clarence was pleased with the marriage, since the Roses were not only Catholic but also well-to-do. The groom's mother did attend this wedding—but came unaccompanied.

Ellin, the middle child, took a different path from that of her sister and brother. Between her and her mother there was special bond, and despite Clarence's admonitions, Ellin visited Katherine Blake in Paris (though reportedly, she never spoke to Dr. Blake). Ellin's early education had been with governesses and in private schools; she attended Barnard College to study English but left after one term. By age twenty-one, in 1924, she was known to be beautiful, outspoken, and cosmopolitan. Photos and accounts of Ellin depict a willowy young woman with a keen sense of fashion who drove a sporty red roadster. She became engaged to an English diplomat in Washington, not because she was in love with him, but because her father thought the time was right.[14]

Ellin's desires lay elsewhere, however. The accounts of how the love of her life began differ: some say it was at a dinner party, others that it was at Jimmy Kelly's speakeasy on Sullivan Street in Greenwich Village, where

Wedding party, from left to right: Clarence Mackay, Katherine Mackay, Louise Mackay, and Kenneth O'Brien, Harbor Hill garden, September 21, 1922 (Bryant Library Local History Collection, Roslyn, NY)

Wedding of Katherine Mackay and Kenneth O'Brien at St. Mary's, Roslyn, September 21, 1922 (Bryant Library Local History Collection, Roslyn, NY)

Ellin Mackay met the man born Israel (Izzy) Beilin in 1888 in a shtetl in Czarist Russia. His father, Moses Beilin, was a cantor in a small synagogue. The family—Moses, his wife Leah, and their six children—escaped a pogrom in 1893 that incinerated their village. The Beilins made their way across Europe to Antwerp, Belgium, where they boarded the *SS Rhynland* to New York City. Their fare was fifteen dollars per adult and half that for each child. They arrived on September 13, and the authorities at Ellis Island entered the family's name as Baline.

Like countless other Jews, the Balines settled in

Ellin Mackay, c. 1925 (Private Collection)

for songs such as "Sadie Salome, Go Home" sold more than three hundred thousand copies. In 1911 came "Alexander's Ragtime Band," and Berlin's success was ensured. By the 1920s Berlin was America's most popular songwriter, creating show music for Florenz Ziegfeld's Follies, the Marx Brothers, and Broadway musicals. New York society hostesses eager to display their awareness of popular culture sought Irving Berlin's presence at fashionable affairs.[15]

How Ellin and Irving were introduced no one knows for sure, but the two hit it off. He was fifteen years her senior. Romance bloomed, and although they tried to keep their relationship quiet, the newspapers and gossip sheets were soon in hot pursuit of a new Mackay scandal.

Ellin Mackay's romance with Irving Berlin displeased her father, and he ordered her to break it off. The widespread prejudice against the Irish failed to open Clarence's mind, and in his view a ghetto Jew was unfit com-

a tenement on Manhattan's Lower East Side—a beginning not unlike that of Ellin's paternal grandmother. Israel dropped out of school to work the streets, first as a newspaper boy and then serving beer in dance halls, where he acquired a reputation as a singing waiter downtown on the Bowery and in the hub of popular music on East Twenty-eighth Street, Tin Pan Alley.

Small successes followed as he began to compose his own songs, and he changed his name, becoming Irving Berlin. He could play the piano in only one key, and could not read music, but Irving Berlin became a composer of vaudeville songs and shows of all types, from the profane to the very popular. The sheet music

pany for a high-society Catholic girl. He hired detectives to shadow Berlin in search of misbehavior. Little about Irving Berlin came to light besides burgeoning fame, and that he had been involved with Governor Al Smith's ill-fated attempt to secure the Democratic presidential nomination; Clarence, needless to say, was a Republican. The newspapers had a field day with the Berlin-Mackay romance; at least one noted a certain rags-to-riches parallel between the Mackays and Balines. Clarence was not amused.[16] He worried that Berlin might crash his gala for the Prince of Wales and ordered the staff to bar the songwriter from the premises. Berlin was not interested in attending, although in a sense he was there anyway: Paul Whiteman's band played many of his songs including, "What'll I Do?" to which Ellin danced with the Prince.

Clarence whisked Ellin away to Europe, and when they returned he shipped her out West. But Ellin's mother met Berlin and encouraged her daughter to stand her ground.

In September 1925, the editor Harold Ross invited Ellin to join the staff of his new magazine, *The New Yorker*. Ellin's first piece, titled "Why We Go to Cabarets—A Post-Debutante Explains," revealed the "picturesquely depraved" younger generation who sought new experiences with different types of people. Openly defiant, Ellin took aim at the debutante's "exclusive party" with its stag line of "extremely unalluring specimens." She described and a cartoon depicted, "hundreds of pale-faced youths, exactly alike . . . with whom, if they so choose, she must continue to dance at every party." *The New Yorker* released Ellin's article to the press several days before publication; the *New York Times* published a front-page story headlined "SOCIETY GIRLS SEEK ESCAPE" and another advising "DODGE 'POISONOUS' TYPES." Both of Ellin's parents were amply mentioned. The article even made headlines in Paris, where an aspiring writer named James Thurber read about it and immediately decided to contact Ross for a job.[17]

Ellin followed with a second shocking *New Yorker* article, this one titled "The Declining Function, A Post-Debutante Rejoices." In it she asserted that, "A party should be a group of congenial people," and not the "bore" that most society events had become. Pointedly referring to her father and his set, she deplored the "rush . . . to Long Island for the week-end . . . [and] the Piping Rock Horse Show." And then a personal note: "Modern girls are conscious of their identity and they marry who they choose, satisfied to satisfy themselves."[18]

Not a month later Ellin Mackay took the first ride of her life on a New York City subway: on January 4, 1926, she and Irving Berlin went to City Hall for a civil marriage ceremony. A few days later they sailed for Europe on the *S.S. Leviathan*.

Clarence Mackay broke off all communication with his daughter and disinherited her. He issued statements bemoaning the marriage, although he denied any estrangement. Ellin and Irving's first child, Mary Ellin, was born in 1926; Clarence ignored her. Two years later, Ellin sat with her father, sister, and brother in the front row at St. Mary's for her grandmother Louise's funeral; Irving did not attend. Toward the end of that same year the Berlins' second child, Irving Jr., was born on December 1, 1928 but died on Christmas; Clarence Mackay and Irving Berlin met then for the first time and reconciled.[19] The Berlins had two more daughters, Linda, born in 1933, and Elizabeth, born in 1937.

Clarence's grandchildren enjoyed a "grandfatherly" grandfather. When he commissioned John Lavery to paint interior views, one depicted little Katherine O'Brien standing in the great hall among the tapestries and armor. One grandchild described him as

Ellin and Irving Berlin in Atlantic City, 1927 (Photo by Novelty Photo Studio, Atlantic City) (Private Collection)

"a nice old gentleman . . . [and] a wonderful grandfather. . . . He would pull a five dollar bill out of a curtain." He loved to tease his grandchildren with his mustache, pretending it was false and "asking you to pull it to check, then giving off a yulp!"[20]

Irreversible Losses

Clarence apparently believed that the good times would last forever for his Postal Telegraph and Commercial Cable Company. The firm continued to lay cables and open offices around the world. During the Great War—much to his outrage—the federal government requisitioned Postal Telegraph, but returned it to his control in 1919. Profits remained good, but the company started to fall behind its main competitor, Western Union. By 1927, Postal Telegraph claimed only 17 percent of the market.[21] Without explanation, Clarence refused offers to invest in either the rapidly expanding telephone business or in radio, except for a local Long Island company. Some opportunities he turned down for "religious reasons": reportedly he would not work with Jews.[22]

Aware in 1928 of impending trouble, Clarence agreed to a merger with Sothenes Behn of the Behn Brothers, owners of the International Telephone and Telegraph Company. He became chairman of the board of the American division. Unfortunately, he took his nearly $300 million payment in the form of ITT stock, and on October 24, 1929—Black Thursday—Clarence saw his fortune decimated. This turn of fate earned for him the dubious distinction of incurring one of the greatest losses of the Wall Street crash.

Katherine and Joseph Blake had stayed in Paris throughout the war, both serving in the Red Cross. With a son and three daughters, they returned to the United States in 1923, and Katherine attempted to reclaim her social position. A society chronicler of Newport and New York recounted, "Social leaders insisted neither would be 'taken up'—and they weren't." After an unsuccessful campaign to win a place in Newport society, they took a house at Tarrytown, New York, and another in the city.[23]

Katherine developed a tumor in her right eye, and an operation left her somewhat disfigured. As one reporter put it, "She no longer had the great chic that made her an outstanding figure. . . ." The union with Dr. Blake appeared to endure—that is, until the summer of 1929, when Blake, in Maine where he always kept a house, announced that he and Katherine had been divorced and he had remarried. His new wife, a nurse from Toronto, was said to be forty years his junior.[24]

Now an invalid, Katherine received Clarence when he came to call, and a reunion briefly seemed possible. But Clarence did not pursue it. In a last, ironic act, Katherine converted to Catholicism. Less than a year after her second divorce and just before her fifty-first birthday, Katherine Blake contracted pneumonia and died at home at 12 East Eighty-seventh Street. Her funeral service was held at St. Vincent Ferrer, a new Catholic church on the Upper East Side designed by Bertram Goodhue and his partners. During the service Clarence Mackay sat "with stern imperiousness" in a front pew beside their children. Dr. Blake sat "inconspicuously, far in the rear of the edifice."[25]

Time Overcomes Harbor Hill

The era of the great American estate was drawing to a close. Harbor Hill—the house and its contents, the casino, the stables, the gardens, and the rest of the grounds—was becoming a dinosaur. Though the estate still looked palatial, it was tottering toward extinction. Apparently oblivious to the vast changes occurring around him, Clarence Mackay nevertheless kept Harbor Hill going.

The death of Katherine freed him from his Catholic marital vows, and on July 18, 1931, he mar-

Clarence Mackay and Anna Case Mackay at Harbor Hill, c. 1932
(*Bryant Library Local History Collection, Roslyn, NY*)

ried Anna Case. The ceremony was held very early on a Sunday morning at St. Mary's in Roslyn. Two priests and only seven members of the immediate Mackay family—including Ellin and Irving Berlin—were present.[26]

Clarence and Anna Case Mackay took up residence at Harbor Hill, but not for long. Just weeks after the wedding, nearly all the estate's staff was let go, except for a few gardeners to keep the roads open. Anna dismissed William Donaldson, the chauffeur who had worked there since 1902, and she fired the longtime gardener, Frank Demak. For Arthur Chapman, the former footman who had been gassed during the war, the arrangement of $50 a month was continued, but only on condition that his wife clean and cook.[27] The families of a few dismissed personnel were allowed to stay in their Harbor Hill houses, but only until they found other employment.

In June of the next year, Anna Case and Clarence moved into the house he and Katherine had occupied while the mansion was under construction, and the great house was shuttered. Before the estate's final closing, visitors were allowed in, but they found the greenhouses and many other buildings already closed.

The Depression hit Clarence Mackay hard. The merger with ITT had brought together two firms with weak financial bases, and by 1935 the company was in receivership.[28] The ITT holdings that in 1928 were valued at $149 per share by 1934 were worth a mere $2.64. Then in late 1937, Clarence and his company faced an anti-trust suit. Six years later, the former Postal Telegraph finally became part of Western Union.

Clarence continued to buy art and lend to exhibitions, but in reality his collection was on the market. He was deep in debt.[29] By 1933 he had already begun to dispose of his collection through auction houses. The Metropolitan Museum of Art purchased some tapestries, including the *King Arthur*. The museum also bought the Mantegna *Adoration* and the Raphael *Agony in the Garden* (see Chapter Five).[30] Two years later, the National Gallery in London acquired all the Sassetta panels. And after that, the Kress Collection acquired his Duccio (for an alleged $250,000); this, along with the Verrocchio, the Botticelli, and the Giovanni Bellini, went to the National Gallery of Art in Washington, D.C.[31]

Clarence was able to rent out the farmhouse he was living in and to reopen part of the mansion 1935, but none of the staff was rehired.[32] Then he announced, through a broker, that he would subdivide a hundred-acre section of the estate into lots for sale, although nothing came of this.

Clarence's death at age 64 on November 12, 1938, made front-page headlines. He had suffered from various ailments, including a recurrence of the throat cancer on which Dr. Blake had operated nearly three decades before. News reports eulogized him and his many accomplishments, noting also his father's wealth, the scandal with Katherine, the problems with

View of Roslyn and Roslyn Heights showing Mackay estate and Roslyn High School, 1936 (Bryant Library Local History Collection, Roslyn, NY)

Ellin and Irving Berlin, and the glories of Harbor Hill. His funeral took place at St. Patrick's Cathedral in New York City. John Barbirolli conducted the orchestra and choir. That night at Carnegie Hall, the maestro made an addition to the program in Clarence's memory, inserting at the beginning the "Liebestod" from Richard Wagner's *Tristan und Isolde*.[33]

Harbor Hill went on the real estate market in 1939, to be sold either as a unit or subdivided. Clarence had left some money to his wife, children, grandchildren, and St. Mary's church, but the estate's debts were colossal. In the promotion for the property, attention dwelled on the estate's history and Stanford White's role. Photos and sketches were published along with commentary such as "Dark Mansions for Sale" and the "dismal job" of the six employees on the skeleton staff hired to patrol the vast acres.[34]

The arms and armor collection went up for auction in New York and London. At the Metropolitan Museum of Art, curator Stephen V. Grancsay, who had advised Clarence on his acquisitions, now attempted to buy the Mackay armor for the museum. But the Metropolitan too was feeling the bite of the Depression. (Grancsay on his own bought some pieces and later donated them to the museum.) Some of Clarence's full suits of armor were purchased by a Massachusetts steel executive "to inspire steel workers, to attract superior recruits to the industry, to stimulate art in industry, to extol steel craftsmanship and to inform the public."[35]

Aerial view of development on site of Harbor Hill (Society for the Preservation of Long Island Antiquities)

Mackay Way, street sign (Author's Collection)

Some of the art was sold privately through dealers and auction houses in New York and London.[36] Other pieces, from antique furniture to copper cookware, went on the block at other auctions.[37] Yet more remained: as executor of the estate, John William made an agreement with Gimbel Brothers department store to dispose of the rest in an over-the-counter sale. Prices ranged from $19,500 for a Persian rug to $1.95 for a sword.[38]

The house sat empty. Twenty-eight acres were purchased in 1941 for a development of new "American Colonial style" houses. During World War II, the six-foot-high, three-thousand-foot-long iron fence and other items were recycled for the war effort.[39] The house served briefly as a submarine-spotting station. After the war it fell prey to vandals.

Still in the news, a headline read, "MACKAY'S MONEY, MANSION, MISERY"; and "HOUSE FOR SALE: 50 rooms, 15 baths, 100 acres. Greenhouse, formal gardens. Equipment and outbuildings suitable for experimental farming. Original cost $2,000,000 but owner satisfied to get back 10% of investment."[40]

In 1947 John William directed a wrecking crew from the Mar-Gus Company to begin stripping the house. Some portions of the interior were removed, and one hundred tons of cast iron and fifty thousand cubic feet of granite were extracted for resale.[41] When the demolition was complete, one reporter summed it up: "A pile of Junk. A mass of weeds, That is all that's left now of once magnificent Harbor Hill, the $6,000,000 French Gothic chateau. . . ."[42] Some outbuildings still stood, but in 1949 Clarence's Casino went up in flames, cause unknown.[43] In 1955, with almost all buildings leveled, 368 acres were subdivided into more than four hundred sites for ranch, split-level, and two-story Colonial-style houses. One road was named Mackay Way.

Today little remains of the original grand estate besides the gate house, a servant's house, and one farm building.[44] One of the two life-size, pink marble, rearing Marly horses Clarence acquired still crowns a hilltop; the other was moved to the Roslyn school.

This lifespan of Harbor Hill—less than three generations—was about normal for most of the great estates and mansions erected around the turn of the last century. A few have been preserved as historic houses or museums. Some have been converted into inns and spas, others to institutional buildings. Scarcely a handful of the great country houses—and of these, mostly the smaller ones—still serve their original purposes: to display and enjoy wealth, and to define and present oneself with all that money can buy.

Notes

❋ ❋

1. HARBOR HILL AND ITS WORLD

1. Letter, Stanford White to Clarence Mackay, April 18, 1900, McKim, Mead & White Collection, The New-York Historical Society (henceforth, NYHI); *Roslyn News*, Nov. 21, 1899, typescript, Mackay collection Bryant Library, Roslyn, New York (henceforth, Bryant Library); *New York Times*, August 16, 1899, 7. Period treatments of Harbor Hill will be noted below. More recent treatments include: Wayne Craven, *Stanford White: Decorator in Opulence and Dealer in Antiquities* (New York: Columbia University Press, 2005); M. Christine Klim Doell, *Gardens of the Gilded Age: Nineteenth-century Gardens and Homegrounds of New York State* (Syracuse: Syracuse University Press, 1986) 31–34; Roy Moger, *Roslyn Then and Now* (Roslyn: Roslyn Public Schools, 1964), 113–129; Lisa and Donald Sclare, *Beaux-Arts Estates: A Guide to the Architecture of Long Island* (New York: Viking Press, 1980), 30–31, and passim; Lawrence Wodhouse, "Stanford White and the Mackays," *Winterthur Portfolio* 11 (1976), 213–233; Monica Randall, *The Mansions of Long Island's Gold Coast* (New York: Hastings House, 1979) 165–68; and my essays in *Long Island Country Houses and Their Architects, 1860–1940*, ed. R. B. MacKay, et al. (New York: W. W. Norton Co., for the Society for Preservation of Long Island Antiquities, 1997), 273–280 and 291–297.

2. Computing the relative value of currency is controversial. I have chosen the most conservative conversion or the consumer price index. Information can be found at http://www.measuring-worth.com/.

3. "The Poor Taste of the Rich, . . . the Clarence H. Mackay House," *House Beautiful*, 17 (January 1905), 14–16.

4. "The Modern American Residence," *The Architectural Record*, 16 (October 1904), 301. The article, while on "Dwellings of the Middle West," included Harbor Hill as a comparison, with illustrations.

5. "Clarence Mackay Dies . . ." *New York Times*, November 13, 1938, 1, 46.

6. Henry James, *The American Scene* (New York: Horizon Press, 1967 [1904–1905]), 192.

7. Mark Twain (Samuel L. Clemens) and Charles D. Warner, *The Gilded Age: A Tale of Today* (New York, 1873); Matthew Josephson, *The Robber Barons: The Great American Capitalists* (New York: Harcout, Brace & World, 1934); Ray W. Ginger, *Age of Excess: The United States from 1877 to 1914* (New York: 1965).

8. Thorstein Veblen, *Theory of the Leisure Class* (New York: Macmillan, 1908).

9. Peter Ross, *A History of Long Island* (New York and Chicago: Lewis Pub. Co. 1902), 914.

10. Among the many treatments see: Clive Aslet, *The American Country House* (New Haven: Yale University Press, 1990); Mark Alan Hewitt, *The Architect & the American Country House* (New Haven: Yale University Press, 1990); Roger W. Moss, *The American Country House* (New York: Holt, 1990); Richard Guy Wilson and Steven Bedford, *The Long Island Country House* exh. cat. (Southampton: Parrish Art Museum, 1988); Robert B. MacKay, Anthony Baker and Carol A. Traynor, Eds. *Long Island Country Houses and Their Architects, 1860–1940* (New York: Norton, 1997).

11. Croly, "The Lay-out of a Large Estate, 'Harbor Hill', the Country-Seat of Mr. Clarence Mackay at Roslyn, L. I.," *The Architectural Record*, 16 (December 1904), Ferree, "On Architecture," *Scientific American Building Monthly*, (September 1903), 47, 60.

12. *Sturgis' Illustrated Dictionary of Architecture and Building* (New York: McMillan, 1901–1902), vol. 1, 696–697.

13. Many books deal with Newport; the classic study is Antoinette F. Downing and Vincent Scully, Jr., *The Architectural Heritage of Newport, Rhode Island*, 2nd ed. (New York: Potter, 1967).

14. Craig Gilborn, *Adirondack Camps* (Adirondack Museum and Syracuse University Press, 2000).

15. John M. Bryan, *Biltmore Estate: The Most Distinguished Private Place* (New York: Rizzoli, 1994).

16. Jay Nixon, *Stewards of a Vision (A History of the King Ranch)* (King Ranch, 1986); and other materials supplied by King Ranch.

17. Clive Aslet, *The Last Country Houses* (New Haven: Yale University Press, 1982), 190–206.

18. "Clarence Mackay's 'Harbor Hill,'" (August 1, 1902), Bryant Library.

19. Mark Girouard, *Life in the English Country House* (New Haven: Yale University Press, 1978), 2. See also Girouard, *The Victorian Country House* (Oxford: Clarendon Press, 1971).

20. Croly, "The Lay-out of a Large Estate, 'Harbor Hill,'" 535.

21. Washington Irving, "Rural Life in England," [1818] in *Sketch Book* (New York: Educational Pub. Co., 1903), 73.

22. [Henry James] "An English New Year," *The Nation*, 28 (January 23, 1879), 65–66, republished in his *Portraits of Places* (1883; reprint ed., New York, 1948), 325.

23. The survey published by the *New York Tribune* in its supplement, *The Tribune Monthly*, June 1892, is republished with commentary in Sidney Ratner, ed. *New Light on the History of Great American Fortunes* (New York: Augustus M. Kelley, Inc. 1953), Mackay's entry is on page 6.

24. On this background see: Peter J. Schmitt, *Back to Nature: The Arcadian Myth in Urban America* (New York: Oxford, 1969); Leo Marx, *The Machine in the Garden* (New York: Oxford, 1964); Morton and Lucia White, *The Intellectual Versus the City* (New York: New American Library, 1962).

25. Andrew Jackson Downing, *The Architecture of Country Houses* (New York: D. Appleton & Co., 1850), 257–258; see also, Marianna Griswold Van Rensselaer, "American Country Dwellings I", *Century, 32* (May 1886), 3.

26. Desmond and Croly, *Stately Homes in America, From the Colonial Times to the Present Day* (New York: D. Appleton & Co., 1903), 3. See also, Herbert Croly, "Rich Men and their Houses," *Architectural Record*, 12 (May 1902), 27–32.

27. Herbert Croly, "The American Country Estate," *The Architectural Record*, 18 (July 1905), 2.

28. Wilhelm Miller, "Successful American Gardens II, The Breese Estate . . ." *Country Life in America* 18 (May 1910), 45–56.

29. *Brooklyn Daily Eagle Almanac 1901* (Brooklyn, Brooklyn Daily Eagle, 1901), 90. On Roslyn's Architectural History see: Catherine B Fahnestock, *The Story of Sycamore Lodge* (Port Washington: C. B. Fahnestock, 1964); C. Genovese, E. F. Rosebrock and C. D. York. *Historic Roslyn—A Book to Walk With* (Roslyn: Roslyn Savings Bank, 1975); Peggy and Roger Gerry, *Old Roslyn I* and *II* (Roslyn: Bryant Library, 1953, 1954); Roger Gerry "The Roslyn Historic District" *The Nassau County Historical Society Quarterly*, 28, No. 1 (Winter–Spring 1967); Roger Gerry, *Roslyn Saved*, (Roslyn: Roslyn Landmark Society, 1980, 1989); Conrad G. Goddard, *The Early History of Roslyn Harbor* (Roslyn: C. G. Goddard, 1972); Roy W. Moger, *Roslyn—Then and Now* (Roslyn: Roslyn Public Schools, 1964; Rev. ed. Bryant Library, 1990); Robert B. Mackay, Stanley Lindvall and Carol Traynor, eds. *AIA Architectural Guide to Nassau and Suffolk counties, Long Island* (New York: Dover, 1992); Ellen Fletcher Russell, *Roslyn Restored: The legacy of Roger and Peggy Gerry* (Albany: Mt. Ida Press, 2004).

30. Robert B. Mackay, "Introduction," in *Long Island Country Houses* 26 cites, Prominent *Residents of Long Island and Their Pleasure Clubs* (1916).

31. Frank Milburn, *Polo: The Emperor of Games* (New York: Knopf, 1994), 36, 40; and Newell Bent, *American Polo* (New York: 1929).

32. Mackay, "Introduction," 33.

33. Clipping, *New York Herald* 1902, Bryant Library.

34. *Dictionary of American Biography* (New York: Scribner's, 1946), vol. 20, 165–166; and *National Cyclopedia of American Biography* (New York: James T. White, 1897) vol. 2 407–408.

35. Edwin D. Morgan, *Reflections for My Family* (New York: Charles Scribner's Sons, 1938), 174–175.

36. "Huge Estates Near New York Make it Rival London," *New York Times* (October 13, 1912), SM11.

37. "Scene at the Charity Fete Given Mr. Mrs. Clarence Mackay at Her Long Island Home, Where She entertained 3,500 Guests. *The World*, Sept. 25, 1904, clipping, Bryant Library.

38. Grace A. Fowler, "The Servant Question at Harbor Hill," *Harper's Bazaar 38*, no. 55 (September 1904), 857–865.

39. Ferree, "On Architecture", 4.

40. Edith Wharton, *The House of Mirth* (New York: Scribner's: 1905), 233.

41. Henry James, *The Outcry* (London: Penguin, 2001 [1911]), 56, 57.

42. Clippings of stories at Bryant Library include: Madeline Ryttenberg, "Mackays-Money, Mansion, Misery;" John Gardner, "6 Million Bought Dream House, But Clarence Mackay's Dreams Were Nightmares;" Nancy Randolph "Mackay's 'Heartbreak House' Follows '90s into Oblivion."

2. THE PATRONS

1. Van Rensselaer, *The Social Ladder* 166; Patterson, *The First Four Hundred*, 13–14.

2. Sources on J. W. Mackay's life include: Oscar Lewis, *Silver Kings: The Lives and Times of Mackay, Fair, Flood, and O'Brien, Lord of the Nevada Comstock Lode* (New York: Knopf, 1947); Ellin Mackay Berlin, *Silver Platter* (London: Hammond, Hammond & Co., 1957); James W. Hulse, *The Nevada Adventure: A History* 5th ed. (Reno: University of Nevada Press, 1981); Ronald M. James, *The Roar and the Silence: A History of Virginia City and the Comstock Load* (Reno: University of Nevada Press, 1998); also Robert L. Duffus, "Richer than Solomon's Mines," *Collier's 78* (October 30, 1926), 19, 33.

3. Kenneth T. Jackson, ed. *The Encyclopedia of New York City* (New Haven, Ct.: Yale University Press; New York: New-York Historical Society, 1995) 191–192. Stephen Birmingham, *Real Lace: America's Irish Rich* (New York: Harper & Row, 1973), treats the Mackays briefly along with the issue of Irish acceptance.

4. Berlin, *Silver Platter*, 171.

5. Berlin, *Silver Platter*, 162.

6. Louise Mackay's life was lovingly documented by her granddaughter, Ellin Mackay Berlin, in the book *Silver Platter* (London: Hammond, Hammond & Co., 1957, New York: Doubleday, 1957).

7. Lewis, *Silver Kings*, 75.

8. Quoted from "Unidentified Sister," n.d, n.p., in Anne M. Butler, "Mission in the Mountains" in, *Comstock Women: The Making of a Mining Community*, ed. R. M. James and C. E. Raymond (Reno: University of Nevada Press, 1998), 160, 161, 351; also see Anita

Ernst Watson, Jean E. Ford, and Linda White, "'The Advantages of Ladies's Society,' the Public Sphere of Women on the Comstock," p. 189–190.

9. Harriet Lane Levy quoted in Oscar Lewis, *This Was San Francisco* (New York: David McKay, 1949), 223.

10. Illustrated in Birmingham, *Real Lace*, between 130–131.

11. Lewis, *Silver Kings*, 77.

12. On background see: Eric Hornberger, *Mrs. Astor's New York: Money and Social Power in a Gilded Age* (New Haven: Yale University Press, 2002); Cleveland Amory, *Who Killed Society?* (New York: Harper & Brothers, 1960); Dixon Wecter, *The Saga of American Society: A Record of Social Aspiration* (New York: Charles Scribner's, 1937).

13. Mrs. John King Van Rensselaer with Frederic Van de Water, *The Social Ladder* (New York: Henry Holt and Company, 1924), 136.

14. Ibid.

15. Ibid.

16. Stevens quoted Berlin, *Silver Platter*, 223, 226.

17. Berlin, *Silver Platter*, 231, 242–43.

18. Illustration.

19. Berlin, *Silver Platter*, 238, 256–258.

20. "The Bonanza King Fighting," *New York Times* August 13, 1879, 13.

21. Berlin, *Silver Platter*, 360–378.

22. Lewis Coe, *The Telegraph* (Jefferson, NC: McFarland & Co, 1993); 91; also on background see: James D. Reid, *The Telegraph in America and Morse Memorial*, 2 ed. (New York: John Polhemus, 1886).

23. Unidentified quote from clipping in Tiffany & Company files, and *New York Daily Tribune*, May 30, 1878, both quoted in Charles H. Carpenter Jr. "The Mackay service made by Tiffany and Company," *Antiques* 114 no. 4 (October 1978), 797, 798. See also Berlin, *Silver Platter*, 238.

24. Leon Dabo quoted in Rene Gimpel, *Diary of an Art Dealer* (New York: Farrar, Straus and Giroux, 1966), 326–327.

25. Newspaper report February 1, 1882 quoted in Jerry E. Patterson, *The best families: the Town & country social directory, 1846–1996* (New York: Harry N. Abrams, in association with Hearst Magazines, 1996), 113.

26. Berlin, *Silver Platter*, 288.

27. Lewis, *Silver Kings*, 51–52.

28. Patterson *Best Families*, 112.

29. This is how their granddaughter Ellin summarized their success in Berlin, *Silver Platter*, 342.

30. "Mr. Van Alen's Domino Party, *Newport Journal*, August 31, 1899, 3.

31. *Social Register, New York IV*, no. 1. (New York: Social Register Association, November 1889), 122, their address is listed a 9 rue de Tilsitt, Paris.

32. Oscar Lewis and Carroll D. Hall, *Bonanza Inn: America's First Luxury Hotel* (New York, Knopf, 1945), 251; and Lewis, *Silver Kings*, 58–59, 99, 101.

33. Richard O'Connor, *The Golden Summers* (New York: Putnam, 1974) 179. Berlin, *Silver Platter*, 13, 302. 307–308, 395, 397, 408.

34. "John W. Mackay, Jr.'s Body Here," *New York Times*, Feb. 3, 1896, 1. See also, *New York Times*, Oct. 21, 1895, 5 Oct. 26, 1895, 1.

35. "Mackay Mausoleum at Greenwood," *New York Tribune*, July 22, 1902, 2. Jeffrey I. Richmond, *Brooklyn's Green-Wood Cemetery* (Brooklyn: The Green-Wood Cemetery, 1998), 214–215.

36. Letter John W. Mackay to Corporation of Greenwood Cemetery April 2, 1897, and advertisement "The Muldon Mausoleum Company," August 27, 1901, supplied by Jeffrey Richmond, Historian of Green-Wood Cemetery.

37. Berlin, *Silver Platter*, 255, 408, 404.

38. *Social Register, New York* (New York: Social Register Association, 1887), 25.

39. "William A. Duer Dies," *New York Times*, October 28, 1905, 9. Newspaper quoted Nov. 4, 1905, Patterson, *Best Families*, 61; Berlin, *Silver Platter*, 415–419.

40. Patterson, *Best Families*, 61.

41. Cholly Knickerbocker [Maury Paul], "Tragedies of Society, Katherine Mackay Blake Sacrificed all in her Forlorn Search for Love," c. 1939 clipping Bryant Library.

42. Clipping, *Town Topics*, 46 (Nov. 21, 1901) 5, Bryant Library.

43. Berlin, *Silver Platter*, 412.

44. Consuelo Vanderbilt Balsan, *The Glitter and the Gold* (New York: Harper, 1952) 15; see also Amanda Mackenzie Stuart, *Consuelo and Alva Vanderbilt: the Story of a Daughter and a Mother in the Gilded Age* (New York: HarperCollins, 2005).

45. Berlin, *Silver Platter*, 408, 412.

46. "The Week in the Art World," *New York Times*, March 12, 1898, SRB17.

47. The house no longer exists. Correspondence, Monsignor Thomas J. Shelley (Fordham University) with Author, July 28, 2004.

48. *Illustrated American* vol. XXIII, no. 20, whole number 431, cover picture "A Beautiful Bride of the Week-Miss Katherine Alexander Duer—who becomes Mrs. Clarence Mackay."

49. *New York Times*, May 22, 1898, 15; *Newport Journal*, May 21, 1898, 3.

50. Marie Jonreau, "Skeletons on Society Closets" *Chicago Tribune*, May 15, 1898, 46.

51. Clipping, *New York Evening Journal*, May 17, 1898, Bryant Library.

3. STANFORD WHITE AND McKIM MEAD & WHITE

1. Mead, quoted in Lawrence Grant White, *Sketches and Designs by Stanford White* (New York: Architectural Book Publishing Company, 1920), 17. For treatments of the firm see: Leland Roth, *McKim, Mead & White, Architects* (New York: Harper & Row, 1983); Richard Guy Wilson, *McKim, Mead & White, Architects* (New York: Rizzoli, 1983); Samuel G. White, *The Houses of McKim, Mead & White* (New York: Rizzoli, 1998); Samuel G. White and Elizabeth White, *McKim, Mead & White: The Masterworks* (New York: Rizzoli, 2003).

2. On White see: Charles Baldwin, *Stanford White* (New York: Dodd, Mead, 1931); Paul Baker, *Stanny: The Gilded Life of Stanford White* (New York: Free Press, 1989); David Garrard Lowe, *Stanford White's New York* (New York: Doubleday, 1992); Craven, *Stanford White*; White, *Stanford White*.

3. Letter, McKim to "Judge" Samuel A. B. Abbott, Dec. 1, 1893, McKim Collection, Library of Congress (henceforth LC).

4. Baker, *Stanny:* chp. 19.

5. Among the accounts are: Gerald Langford, *The Murder of Stanford*

White (Indianapolis: Bobbs-Merrill, 1962); Michael Macdonald Mooney, *Evelyn Nesbit and Stanford White: love and death in the gilded age* (New York: Morrow, 1976); E. L. Doctorow, *Ragtime* (New York: Random House, 1975); Suzannah Lessard, *The architect of desire: beauty and danger in the Stanford White family* (New York: Dial Press, 1996); and two movies: *The Girl in the Red Velvet Swing* (1958), and *Ragtime* (1986).

6. Philip Sawyer, *Edward Palmer York: Personal Reminiscences* (Stonington, Ct.: Privately Printed, 1951), 17.

7. F. G. Swales, "Charles F. McKim," *Architectural Review* (London) 26 (October 1909), 186.

8. White, *Stanford White*, 15.

9. Edith Wharton, *A Backward Glance* (New York: D. Appleton & Co, 1934), 149.

10. McKim, "Memoranda" and "To Mrs. Wharton" c. February 3, 1897, LC. See, Wilson, "Edith and Ogden: Writing, Decoration, and Architecture," in, Pauline Metcalf, *Ogden Codman and the Decoration of Houses* (Boston: Boston Athenaeum and David R. Godine, 1988), 152–153.

11. H. Van Buren Magonigle, "A Half Century of Architecture 3," *Pencil Points* 15 (March 1934), 116.

12. Henry Bacon, "Charles Follen McKim, . . "*Brickbuilder 19* (February 1910), 38.

13. Magonigle, 117.

14. McKim quoted in Charles Moore, *The Life and Times of Charles Follen McKim* and (Boston: Houghton Mifflin Co, 1929) 46.

15. Magonigle, 117.

16. A. Apolloni to Charles Coleman, October 13, 1900, White collection, New York Historical Society.

17. Letter, Whitelaw Reid to White, August 19, 1890, Reid Papers, Library of Congress; and Mowbray quoting Morgan, in Moore, *McKim*, 262.

18. White, *Stanford White*, 17.

19. Mead to White, January 28, 1904, copy in Aline Saarinen papers, Archives of American Art.

20. Vincent J. Scully, Jr. *The Shingle Style* (New Haven: Yale University Press, 1955).

21. Mead quoted in Moore, *McKim*, 41.

22. Craven, *Stanford White*.

4. DESIGNING AND BUILDING HARBOR HILL

1. Quoted in Roy Moger, *Roslyn Then and Now* (Roslyn: Roslyn Public Schools, 1963), 120; also clippings, *Roslyn News*, August 23, 1899, Aug. 31, 1899, and November 21, 1899, and Phoebe Goodman, "Harbor Hill: A History of the Mackay Property" nd. Bryant Library.

2. "Saunterings," *Town Topics* 46 (November 21, 1901), 5 also "Saunterings," *Town Topics* 53 (January 19, 1905) 5.

3. K. Mackay to White, July 24 [1899], NYHS.

4. Wharton and Codman, *Decoration of Houses*, 6, 8.

5. K. Mackay to White, July 27 [1899], NYHS.

6. K. Mackay to McKim, Mead & White, Sept. 17 [1899], NYHS.

7. K. Mackay to White, nd. Sunday, c. 1900, , NYHS.

8. K. Mackay to White nd [c. November 1901], NYHS.

9. Cablegrams K. Mackay to White, August 7 and August 9, 1899, NYHS.

10. K. Mackay to White, Thursday nd. [August 10, 1899], NYHS.

11. K. Mackay to White, Oct. 25th [1901], NYHS.

12. K. Mackay to White, Dec. 2 [1901], NYHS.

13. White to K. Mackay, February 14, 1902, Avery Architectural Library.

14. K. Mackay to White, August 20, 1899, NYHS.

15. Cablegram, K. Mackay to White, November 7, 1899, NYHS.

16. Memo, White to Richardson, December 18, 1899, NYHS.

17. Cablegram K. Mackay to White, October 20, 1899, NYHS.

18. K. Mackay to White, nd [c. 1899], NYHS.

19. White to C. Mackay, January 31, 1900, NYHS.

20. C. Mackay to White, March 18, 1901, NYHS.

21. C. Mackay to White, May 9, 1901, NYHS.

22. C. Mackay to White, January 22, 1901, NYHS.

23. C. Mackay to White, May 9, 1901 NYHS.

24. C. Mackay to White, February 24, 1903, NYHS.

25. C. Mackay to White, November 2, 1902, NYHS.

26. White to C. Mackay, April 18, 1900., NYHS.

27. C. Mackay to White, April 15, 1901, NYHS.

28. White to C. Mackay, March 19, 1904; also November 14, 1904, Avery Architectural Library.

29. Winston Churchill, *The Celebrity* (New York: The American News Company, 1898), 53–54.

30. See Johan Cederlund, *Classical Swedish Architecture and Interiors 1650–1830* (New York: W.W. Norton & Company, 2006), Chapter Four.

31. Montgomery Schuyler, "The Works of the Late Richard Morris Hunt," *Architectural Record* October-December 1895, reprinted in Schuyler, *American Architecture and Other Writings* Ed. W. Jordy and R. Coe (Cambridge: Harvard University Press, 1961), II, 550.

32. McKim, "Memoranda" and "To Mrs. Wharton" c. February 3, 1897, LC. See, Wilson, "Edith and Ogden: Writing, Decoration, and Architecture," in, Pauline Metcalf, *Ogden Codman and the Decoration of Houses* (Boston: Boston Athenaeum and David R. Godine, 1988), 152–153.

33. Katherine herself specified these dimensions. K. Mackay to White, July 27, 1899, NYHS.

34. Amelia Barr, "The Servant-Girl's Point of View," *North American Review* 154, issue 427 (1892), 731; Mary Elizabeth Carter, *Millionaire Households* (1903), and Carter, *House and Home a Practical Handbook* (1904).

35. J. S. Haley & Co to MMW, Nov. 21, 1900, NYHS.

36. Baker, *Stanny*, 209.

37. George Collins, "The Transfer of Thin Masonry Vaulting from Spain to America." *Journal of the Society of Architectural Historian* 27 (issue 3, 1968): 176–201. The Guastavino archives are at the Avery Architectural Library and contain drawings for Harbor Hill.

38. *Historical Statistics of the United States Colonial Times to 1970* (Washington, D. C.: U. S. Department of Commerce, 1976), 2 vols. Vol. 1, 91.

39. Figures are excerpted from bills, invoices and statements in the NYHS.

40. Lee [Leland Sudlow] Memorandum for Mr. White, October 17, 1900, NYHS

41. White memos, October 20, 1902, and undated, NYHS

42. Milliken Brothers to W. A. & F. E. Conover, Feb. 14, 1901 NYHS.

43. Milliken Brothers to McKim, Mead & White, April 2, 1901 NYHS.

44. Milliken Brothers to McKim, Mead & White, September 4, 1901 NYHS.

45. Milliken Brothers to W. A. & F. E. Conover, Feb. 14, 1901 NYHS.

46. Milliken Brothers to McKim, Mead & White, July 24, 1901 NYHS. NYHS.

47. K. Mackay to White, Feb. 9 [1900], NYHS.

48. Telegram K. Mackay to White, November 5, 1900, NYHS.

49. K. Mackay to White, Oct. 25th [1901], NYHS.

50. Sudlow to Adams, June 12, 1901, NYHS.

51. Sudlow to Adams, September 27, 1901, NYHS.

52. Sudow to Adams, September 11, 1901, NYHS.

53. Clippings, *Boston Post*, December 26, 1901, and *Baltimore Sun* December 26, 1901, Bryant Library and "What is Society" *New York Times* December 27, 1901, 7.

54. McKim, Mead & White statement, February 12, 1902. NYHS

55. White to C. Mackay, April 18, 1900, NYHS.

56. Guy Lowell's architecture was as significant as his landscape design. His buildings, erected after his involvement with Harbor Hill, included many educational and other cultural structures, such as academic buildings at Phillips Academy Andover, Simmons College, and Brown University, Boston's Museum of Fine Arts, the New York Supreme Court building in lower Manhattan, and the New Hampshire Historical Society Headquarters in Concord. Lowell also designed many private houses.

57. "What is Doing in Society," *New York Times*, July 8, 1902, 7. Marjorie Pearson, "Guy Lowell, 1870–1927" in *Long Island Country Houses*, ed. R. B. Mackay, 262–267.

58. Guy Lowell, ed., "Introduction" *American Gardens*, (Boston: Bates & Guild Company, 1902), n.p.

59. K. Mackay to White, April 7, 1900, NYHS.

60. K. Mackay to White, nd [April 1900] NYHS.

61. Croly, The Layout" 554.

62. Ferree, "On Architecture," 60.

63. Peter Ross, *A History of Long Island* (New York and Chicago: Lewis Pub. Co. 1902), 914.

64. Ferree, "On Architecture," 47.

65. Baker, *Stanny*, 278.

66. Pennoyer, Peter and Anne Walker. *The Architecture of Warren & Wetmore*. New York: W. W. Norton, 2006.

67. White, memo, May 19, 1902, NYHS.

68. M. Christine Klim Doell, *Gardens of the Gilded Age: Nineteenth-century Gardens and Homegrounds of New York State* (Syracuse: Syracuse University Press, 1986) 31–34; Dana Rice, "American Masters the Lore of Gardens" *New York Times Magazine* August 9, 1925.

69. C. Mackay to White, January 30, 1903, NYHS.

70. C. Mackay to White, July 3, 1903, NYHS.

71. White to C. Mackay, October 27, 1904, NYHS.

72. C. Mackay to White, January 24, 1903, NYHS.

73. K. Mackay to White, October 27, 1904, NYHS.

74. K. Mackay to S. White, May 23 [1903]. NYHS.

75. White to Bess White, February 7, 1905, in *Stanford White: Letters to his Family* Ed. by Claire Nicolas White (New York: Rizzoli, 1997), 144–145.

76. "Mackay Casino Opened," *Times* (Brooklyn), June 20, 1907, clipping, Bryant Library.

5. OVERNIGHT RENAISSANCE PALACE

1. K. Mackay to White, April 6 [1900], NYHS.

2. Allard & Sons, "Contracts for the decoration and furniture for the residence of Mrs. Clarence Mackay, Westbury, L.I." November 25, 1899, NYHS.

3. Royal Cortissoz, "The Clarence H. Mackay Collection," *International Studio* 94 (December 1929) 28–34.

4. I am greatly indebted to Paul Miller, Curator of the Preservation Society of Newport County for sharing information with me. He has in preparation a book on Allard.

5. Letter Allard to White, August 1, 1900, Avery Library.

6. "Obituary, Henry L. Bouche," *New York Times*, December 4, 1908, 11; and communication with Paul Miller.

7. Allard to MM&W Sept 19, 1900. NYHS.

8. Allard to White, October 5, 1900 NYHS.

9. Allard to Clarence Mackay, February 11, 1901 NYHS.

10. H. L. Bouche to Stanford White, August 11, 1901. NYHS.

11. Allard to White, April 9, 1902 NYHS.

12. Allard and Sons to Fred Adams, March 13, 1902, NYHI

13. Richard Guy Wilson, "McKim's Renovations: American Renaissance and Imperial Presidency," in *Our Changing White House*, ed. W. Garrett (Boston: Northeastern University Press, 1995), 182–200; Anne Farnham, "A. H. Davenport and Company, Boston Furniture Makers," *Antiques* 109 (May 1976), 1048–1055.

14. Bill A. H. Davenport to Mackay, Feb. 20, 1902 NYHS.

15. Davenport to Adams (McKim, Mead & White), July 11, 1901, NYHS.

16. let AH Davenport to White December 24, 1901, NYHS.

17. Twist to Katherine Mackay, December 27, 1901, NYHS.

18. A. H. Davenport to White, August 14, 1901, NYHS.

19. McKim, Mead & White Bill Books, vol. 8, 23–26, NYHS.

20. Ferree, "On Architecture," 60.

21. Francis Bacon to Ives, (McKim, Mead & White office) June 14, 1901 NYHI.

22. Seligman to White, April 11, 1903, NYHS.

23. Telegram Bardini to Giddydoll, Feb 2, 1903, NYHS.

24. Telegram Bardini to Giddydoll, January 22, 1903, NYHS.

25. Ferree, "On Architecture," 60.

26. Duparquet Huot & Moneuse Co. to White, Nov. 17 1900 NYHS.

27. Fucigna to C. Mackay, Oct. 18, 1901 NYHS.

28. C. Mackay to Fucigna, Oct. 23, 1901 NYHS.

29. K. Mackay to White, nd [c. Oct. 1901] NYHS.

30. Cook to White, October 30, 1901, NYHS.

31. Clippings *Boston Post*, Dec. 26, 1901, *Baltimore Sun*, Dec. 26, 1901, Bryant Library.

32. White, "Mackay House" notes, October 20, 1902, NYHS.

33. Sudlow to White, January 15, 1904, NYHS.

34. Sudlow to White, January 15, 1904, NYHS.

35. "Memorandum for Mr. White from L.S. Sudlow," March 16, 1905, NYHS.

36. "Telephone memo for Mr. White," April 7, 1905, NYHS.

37. Ferree, "On Architecture," 60.

38. Telegram, Katherine Mackay to S. White, February 26, 1903.

39. White to Clarence Mackay, October 27, 1904, NYHS. Some of the designs exist at the NYHS.

40. "Specifications," NYHS.

41. 41 A. H. Davenport [Twiss] to McKim, Mead & White, November 22, 1901, NYHS.

42. McKim, Mead & White Bill books, vol. 8, 368, NYHS.

43. Wesley Towner, *The Elegant Auctioneers*, (New York: Hill & Wang, 1970). 386.

44. "Where Beauty Lies," *Collier's* 81 (April 21, 1929), 12–13. After Clarence Mackay's death in 1938, the art critic Alfred M. Frankfurter eulogized that his was "one of the most distinguished art collections ever formed in America." Alfred M. Frankfurter, "The Mackay Objects on View," *Art News* May 10, 1939, 10.

45. Bernard Berenson, *The Venetian Painters* (1894), reprinted in *The Italian Painters of the Renaissance* (Cleveland: Meridian, 1957), iii.

46. Quoted in Lawrence G. White, *Sketches and Designs by Stanford White* (New York: Architectural Book Publishing Co, 1920), 24–25. Such views of Americans' entitlement to Europe's historical treasures were not universally applauded by White's contemporaries. Edith Wharton, in her novel *The Custom of the Country* (1913), used the character of a French nobleman to unleash a tirade against a rapacious American social climber—a character designed along the lines of the Mackays who would acquire a Boucher tapestry: "You come among us from a country we don't know, and can't imagine, a country you care for so little that before you've been a day in ours you've forgotten the very house you were born in—if it wasn't torn down before you knew it! You come among us speaking our language and not knowing what we mean, wanting the things we want, and not knowing why we want them; aping our weaknesses, exaggerating our follies, ignoring or ridiculing all we care about—you come from hotels as big as towns, and from towns as flimsy as paper, where the streets haven't had time to be named, and the buildings are demolished before they are dry, and the people are as proud of changing as we are of holding to what we have—and we're fools enough to imagine that because you copy our ways and pick up our slang you understand anything about the things that make life decent and honorable for us!" (Edith Wharton, *The Custom of the Country* [New York: Charles Scribner's Sons, 1913], 545.)

47. Linda Wolk-Simon, *Raphael at the Metropolitan: The Colonna Altarpiece* (New York: The Metropolitan Museum of Art, 2006), p. 40.

48. Ernest Samuels, *Bernard Berenson, The Making of a Legend* (Cambridge: Belknap Press of Harvard University Press, 1987), 314.

49. Let A. H. Davenport to Geo. F. Martin (McKim, Mead & White) June 8, 1900; "Final Balance due on [Mackay] House," typescript, nd [c.1906 NYHS]; also "File Mackay House," typescript nd [c.1906 NYHS]; see also Craven, *Stanford White*.

50. "Rousseau Here To Paint Mackay Dogs," *New York Times*, December 14, 1913, 11.

51. C. Mackay to White, October 21, 1902, December 2 1902 January 2, 1903, NYHS.

52. F. Schultz to White, December 11, 1902, cited in Craven, *Stanford White*.

53. C. Mackay to White, January 16, 1903, NYHS.

54. Cablegram Rutherford Stuyvesant to White, nd [ca. December. 1902], NYHS.

55. Letter, Bernard Berenson to Isabella Stewart Gardner, July 16, 1921, in *Letters of Isabella Stewart Gardner and Bernard Berenson*, ed. Roland van N. Hadley (Boston: Northeastern University Press, 1987), 633.

56. Arthur Action to White, May 7, 1903, NYHS.

57. Charles Davis to Clarence Mackay, February 9, 1904, cited in Craven, *Stanford White*.

58. Calvin Tompkins, *Merchants and Masterpieces: The Story of the Metropolitan Museum of Art* (New York: Dutton, 1970), 151–152.

59. Charles A. Platt to White, Feb 6, 1903, NYHS.

60. "Journey Started February 21st, 1903," Typescript, 4-page copy, NYHS.

61. Cablegram Action to Giddydoll, May 7, 1903, NYHS.

62. Cablegram Action to Duveen New York, May 21, 1903, NYHS.

63. Tompkins, *Merchants and Masterpieces*, 237; Carl Otto Kretzschmar von Kienbusch quoted in "Kienbusch Centennial," *Bulletin Philadelphia Museum of Art* 8 no. 345 (Winter 1985), 11.

64. "Famous Clarence Mackay Collection to be Dispersed in New York," *The Art Digest* 7 (May 15, 1939), 7.

65. Clarence Mackay was generous in lending these and other works in his collection for special museum exhibitions. See, for example, B. D., "Notes" *Bulletin of the Metropolitan Museum of Art* 4 (February 1909), 28–29. See also, "Two New Exhibits in the Art Museum," *New York Times* February 6, 1911, 8.

66. W. R. Valentiner, "The Clarence H. Mackay Collection of Italian Renaissance Sculptures," *Art In America* 13, (August 1925), 238–265.

67. Tompkins, *Merchants and Masterpieces*, 237.

68. W. R. Valentiner, "the Clarence H. Mackay Collection of Italian Renaissance. Sculptures," *Art In America* 13, (August 1925), 250.

69. Royal Cortissoz, "The Clarence H. Mackay Collection," *International Studio* 94 (December 1929), 28–29.

6. MAINTAINING STANDARDS IN SERVICE AT HARBOR HILL

1. Helen Glannon, "Recollections of Mrs. Clarence Mackay by Mattie Replogle," June 19, 1960, Bryant Library.

2. Hugo Munsterberg, *The Americans* (New York: McClure, Phillips & Co, 1904), 540, and chp. 1, 21.

3. Amelia E. Barr, "The Servant-Girl's Point of View," *North American Review*, 154 (1892), 729, 730.

4. Mary Elizabeth Carter, *Millionaire Households and their Domestic Economy* (New York: D. Appleton, 1903), 11.

5. David Graham Phillips, *The Reign of Gilt* (New York: J. Pott & Co., 1905), 47.

6. Amelia E. Barr, "The Servant-Girl's Point of View," *North American Review*, 154 (1892), 729, 730.

7. Stewart Donaldson "Harbor Hill, May 1962," and his "C.H. Mackay's Estate Employees" are at the Bryant Library. I have made a few additions and changes, but the list is based upon Donaldson and that published in Elly Shodell, ed., *In the Service: Workers on the Grand Estates of Long Island 1890's–1940's* (Port Washington: Port Washington Public Library, 1991), 18–23. Several individuals appear twice since their jobs changed and also not all those listed worked at Harbor Hill at the same time.

8. Grace Chapman Laundis interview, January 2, 2005; and Peggy Chapman Grosser quoted in "Bill Bleyer, "'It was home'", *Newsday*, December 5, 2004, G 6–11.

9. *Historical Statistics of the United States, Colonial Times to 1970* (Washington, D. C.: U. S. Department of Commerce, 1976), 2 vols. Vol. 1, 111; Vol. 2, 1169.

10. Jean Mackie Chase, interview, January 16, 2005.

11. Stewart Donaldson, "Harbor Hill, May 1962," 48.

12. Donaldson, "Harbor Hill, May 1962," 3, 7.

13. Jean Mackie Chase, interview, January 16, 2005.

14. Fred Letson, as told to Karen Leahy-Barbaro *From Good Beginnings* (Northport: The Story Weaver, nd), 7.

15. Donaldson, "4th of July at Harbor Hill," transcription Myrna Sloam, Bryant Library.

16. Donaldson, "Harbor Hill, May 1962," 19.

17. Donaldson, "Harbor Hill, May 1962," 3, 6, and Elsie Letson.

18. Peggy Chapman Grosser quoted in "Bill Bleyer, "'It was home,'" *Newsday* December 5, 2004, G 6–11.

19. Grace Chapman Laundis interview, January 2, 2005.

20. Elsie Letson, nd, typescript, Bryant Library, 9.

21. Mary Elizabeth Carter, *Millionaire Households and their Domestic Economy* (New York: D. Appelton, 1903), 11, 215. Also see, Harriet Prescott Spofford, *The Servant Girl Question* (Boston: Houghton, Mifflin, 1881); Lucy Maynard Salmon, *Domestic Service* (New York: Macmillan, 1897); and Lillian Pettengill, *Toilers of the Home: The Record of a College Woman's Experience as Domestic Servant* (New York: Doubleday, Page, 1903). For scholarship see: Hasia Diner, *Erin's Daughters in America: Irish Immigrant Women in the Nineteenth Century* (Baltimore: Johns Hopkins Press, 1983); Faye E Dudden, *Serving Women: Household Service in Nineteenth-Century America.* (Hanover, NH: Wesleyan University Press, 1983); David Katzman, *Seven Days a Week: Women and Domestic Service in Industrializing America* (New York: Oxford University Press, 1978); Elizabeth L O'Leary, *At Beck and Call: The Representation of Domestic Servants in Nineteenth-Century American Painting* (Washington, D. C.: Smithsonian Institution Press, 1996).

22. Grace A. Fowler, "The Servant Question at Harbor Hill," *Harper's Bazaar*, 38 no. 55 (September 1904), 857–867. Unless noted, all subsequent citations on the servants are from Fowler.

23. Donaldson, "C. H. Mackays Estate-Employees" np, Bryant Library.

24. Fowler, "The Servant Question at Harbor Hill," 862–863.

25. Donaldson, "Harbor Hill, May 1962," 10.

26. Letson *From Good*, 3, 6; Donaldson, "Harbor Hill, May 1962," 14, 28; and "Nassau Co. Cattle Show," Clipping, August 13, 1913, Bryant Library.

27. Donaldson, "Harbor Hill, May 1962," 46.

28. "Mackay Laborers on Strike," *New York Times*, December 3, 1909, 13.

29. Donaldson "Harbor Hill, May 1962," 11–12, 29, 31.

30. Helen Glannon, "Recollections of Mrs. Clarence Mackay by Mattie Replogle," June 19, 1960, Bryant Library.

31. Fowler, "The Servant Question at Harbor Hill," 867.

7. AT THE TOP, TOGETHER AND APART

1. Clipping, *Roslyn News*, November 1900, Bryant Library.

2. "Busy Women of the Idle Rich," *New York Times*, October 15, 1911, SM8.

3. Clippings, nd. [1905, 1906, etc], Bryant Library.

4. "Mrs. Mackay and the Library," *Roslyn News*, Nov. 22, 1901, clipping; also clippings, *New York Journal*, November 18, 1901, *New York Times*, November 18, 1901, *New York Herald*, November 18, 1901, *New York World*, November 18, 1901, Bryant Library.

5. A photo of a drawing by White labeled: (Mrs. C. H. Mackay, Minneola Hospi, Benefit," is in McKim, Mead & White photo album vol. 12, 72, Avery Architectural Library.

6. K. Mackay to White, nd. [August 1904], NYHS.

7. "Mrs. Mackay's Fete Draws 3,500 Guests." [Sept 1904] clipping Bryant Library; and "Scene at the Charity Fete Given Mr. Mrs. Clarence Mackay at Her Long Island Home, Where She entertained 3,500 Guests. *The World*, Sept. 25, 1904, 3; "What is Doing in Society, *New York Times*, August 25, 1904, 7.

8. "Mrs. Mackay's Fete Unqualified Success," *New York Times*, September 25, 1904, 7.

9. "The Duchess of Marlborough and Mrs. Clarence H. Mackay," *New York Times*, Sunday, April 12, 1902, Picture Section, pt. 1, cover; "Duchess Visits President," *New York Times*, September 21, 1905, 1.

10. *New York Times*, April 12, 1908, Picture Section pt. 1, cover, "the Duchess of Marlborough and Mrs. Clarence H. Mackay."

11. John J. Radigan, "Personal Notebooks on St. Mary's and Roslyn," c. 1950–1962, 5 vols., in possession of Beverly Royce Aulman; "St. Mary's Church Dedication," *Roslyn News*, June 29, 1878; "Historic Roslyn," *Roslyn News*, September 20, 1946, clipping: Letter John J. Radigan, *Roslyn News*, November 1, 1946, clipping, all Radigan collection.

12. *Roslyn News*, Clipping, July 2 [1906], Bryant Library.

13. K. Mackay to White, May 2, 1906, NYHS.

14. K. Mackay to White, April 8, 1906, NYHS.

15. K. Mackay to White, May 1, 1906, NYHS.

16. K. Mackay to White, undated, NYHS.

17. K. Mackay to White, undated, NYHS.

18. *Roslyn News*, Clipping, July 2 [1906], Bryant Library.

19. George A. Varney and Co. to James McNeill, November 16, 1906, NYHS.

20. K. Mackay to McKim, Mead & White undated, NYHS.

21. K. Mackay to Sudlow. "Sunday" [March 1907], NYHS.

22. "Church, Mrs. Mackay's Gift, Dedicated," *New York Herald*, March 23, 1907, 7; see also "Dedicate New Church, *New York Daily Tribune*, March 23, 1907, 4.

23. *New York World*, June 1907, clipping Bryant Library.

24. McKim, Mead & White Billhooks, vol. 9, 68, 184.

25. "Duchess see Thaw at Play," *New York Times*, November 13, 1907, 4.

26. *Roslyn News*, Typescript of clippings Oct 30 [1906], Bryant Library.

27. "E. T. Morgan's Ticket Wins," *New York Times*, April 2, 1907, 1; "Sold the Church for $25." *New York Times*, April 12, 1907, 1.

28. "Mrs. Mackay May Lose Her Rector," *New York Times*, March 3, 1909, 16; "Not Called to Rival Church," *New York Times*, February 9, 1909, 1; "The Rev. Mr. Hutton Leaves Roslyn," *New York Times*, March 13, 1909, 7.

29. "What is Doing in Society," *New York Times*, June 4, 1904, 9; "What is Doing in Society," *New York Times*, June 17, 1905, 9.

30. Clipping, 1905, Bryant Library.

31. "Subscriptions and Contributions to the Minneola Fund," [January 12, 1906], clipping, Bryant Library.

32. *New York Herald*, Typescript, October 28, 1906, Bryant Library.

33. Clipping, 1905, Bryant Library; "What is Doing in Society," *New York Times*, August 2, 1905, 7.

34. "Mrs. Mackay's Coals of Fire," *New York Times*, August 8, 1906,

1, also, "Mrs. Mackay's Good Will," *New York Times*, August 9, 1906, 1.

35. *New York Herald*, Typescript, October 28, 1906, Bryant Library

36. "'Mrs. Mackay Is All Right,'" *New York Times*, August 16, 1906, 7.

37. "Mrs. Mackay pleads for Equal Suffrage," *New York Times*, September 19, 1908, 7; "Mrs. Mackay Gives Out School Prizes, *New York Times*, June 24, 1908, 7.

38. Quoted in Moger, *Roslyn*, 126.

39. "New Suffrage Society," *New York Times*, December 24, 1908, 6.

40. "Suffrage Campaign Opens at Columbia," *New York Times*, July 27, 1909, 14.

41. "A Divided Jury on a . . . ." And "Why I do Want to Vote" Mrs. Clarence H. Mackay, clipping Bryan Lib. Also, *Current Literature*, December 1909, clipping, Bryant Library. On the Suffrage movement see: Alfred Allan Lewis, *Ladies and Not-So-Gentle Women* (New York: Viking, 2001), but it contains some errors.

42. "Militant Suffrage not for Mrs. Mackay," *New York Times*, October 14, 1909, 9.

43. Mrs. Mackay, "An Address on Suffrage," January 15, 1909, pamphlet (NP, ND).

44. "Suffragists Hold City Convention," *New York Times*, October 30, 1909, 1, 3.

45. "Wins Suffragists by Her Good Looks" *New York Times*, April 9, 1909, 11.

46. "Mrs. Mackay Sees Governor," *New York Times*, March 10, 1909, 14.

47. "Society in Tableaux Aid Suffrage Cause," *New York Times*, January 16, 1911, 11. "Historical Tableaux, *New York Times*, December 30, 1909, 9.

48. "Glories of Marble House Attrack Many," *New York Times*, August 20, 1909, 7.

49. "Mrs. Mackay Quits." *New York Times*, April 13, 1911, 13.

50. "Lincoln Memorial Dedicated by Taft," *New York Times*, November 10, 1911, 10.

51. "Prize for Young Architect," *New York Times*, July 31, 1908, 5.

52. "Metropolitan Now Under New Officers," *New York Times*, April 4, 1908, 9 http://www.nasm.edu/nasm/aero/trophy/mackay.htm.

53. "Court Tennis at Tuxedo, *New York Times*, Jan. 15, 1907, 11, and Feb. 3, 1907, 11.

54. "Virginia Jumper won the Harbor Hill Cup," *New York Times*, October 19, 1906, 11.

55. "Saddle Day at Minneola Show," *New York Times*, September 26, 1908, 7; "Mackay's Team First at Piping Rock Show, *New York Times*, October 6, 1906, 6; "Piping Rock Show Closes the Season," *New York Times*, October 4, 1908, S2.

56. "Mrs. C. H. Mackay was Judge," *New York Times*, September 26, 1906, 10.

57. Charles Phelps Cushing, "Country Clubs of America, II-The Piping Rock Club, Locust Valley, Long Island," *Country Life in America* 37 (February 1920), 49. See also, *American Architect* 102 (December 25, 1912), five pages of illustrations; "Piping Rock's Growing Colony and Club," *New York Times*, July 28, 1912, X2; also "Piping Rock's Millionaire Colony Open" *New York Times*, May 26, 1912, SM14; "Piping Rock Club Lights its Hearth," *New York Times*, May 31, 1912, 15.

58. Clipping, August 20, 1911, Bryant Library; "Welcome Home for Clarence Mackay," *New York Times*, September 3, 1911, 2; and "Mackay Stops $5 Dinner," *New York Times*, September 22, 1911, 1.

59. Letter, Mead to Richardson, June 25, 1908, NYHS; McKim, Mead & White, *Billbooks*, vol. 9, 101, 237; Leland M. Roth, *McKim, Mead & White: Architects* (New Yoirk: Harper & Row, 1983), 285, 409; Julie Nicoletta, *Buildings of Nevada* (New York: Oxford University Press, 2000), 66–67; Samuel Bradford Doten, *An Illustrated History of the University of Nevada* (Reno: University of Nevade, 1924), chp. IX; James W. Hulse, *The University of Nevada: A Centennial History* (Reno: University of Nevada, 1974); "Mackay a Prisoner of Nevada Students," *New York Times*, October 24, 1909, 5.

60. "Most Beautiful Women Here," *New York Times*, June 7, 1908, 7.

61. "Personal and Otherwise," *New York Times*, January 8, 1905, X7.

62. "Saunterings," *Town Topics* 46 (November 21, 1901) and 53 (January 14, 1905), 5.

63. ProQuest makes a search of the *New York Times* easy, unfortunately this is not available for other papers, however the scrapbooks at the Bryant Library indicates the huge number of references.

64. "C.G. V." and "Pianola Piano," advertisements, *New York Times*, December 30, 1906, 17; February 7, 1907, PS8; December 16, 1907, 2.

65. Helen Glannon, "Recollections of Mrs. Clarence Mackay by Mattie Replogle," June 19, 1960, Bryant Library.

66. "C. H. Mackay Swears off Taxes, *New York Times*, August 25, 1903, 5

67. "Designing Her Own Home," *St. Louis Republic*, November 12, 1901, clipping, Bryant Library.

68. *New York World*, August 23, 1903, clipping, Bryant Library.

69. "American Women Order Fine Crowns," *Philadelphia North American*, Nov. 17, 1901, clipping, Bryant Library.

70. "Modes of the Moment," *New York Times*, March 10, 1907, X7.

71. "Gowns Worn by Last of April Brides," *New York Times*, May 5, 1907, X6.

72. "A Potpourri of Fashion," *New York Times*, March 17, 1907, X7; "A Potpourri of Fashion," *New York Times*, March 22, 1908, X6; "A Potpourri of Fashion," *New York Times*, October 25, 1908, X3; "Large Muffs as Pet Dog Protectors," *New York Times*, December 29, 1907, X6.

73. Mary Ellin Barrett, *Irving Berlin: A Daughter's Memoir*, (New York: Limelight Editions, 1996), 38.

74. "Most Beautiful Women Here," *New York Times*, June 7, 1908, 7.

75. "Mrs. Mackay Entertains," *New York Times* October 25, 1908, 13.

76. Katherine Mackay, "Gabrielle. A Dream from the Treasures Contained in the Lettes of Abelard and Heloise," *North American Review*, 176 (April 1903), 610.

77. "What is Doing In Society," *New York Times*, March 31, 1903, 9; "Women Here and There," *New York Times, Magazine*, August 23, 1903, 11.

78. Katherine Mackay, *The Stone of Destiny* (New York, Harper and Brothers, 1904), 1.

79. Clipping, *The Eagle*, Feb. 20, [1913], Bryant Library; "Mackay Property Placed in Trust," *New York Herald*, Paris Edition, March 3, 1913, clipping, Bryant Library; *New York Times*, March 2, 1913; *Standard Union*, Brooklyn, March 2, 1913, clippings Bryant Library.

80. "Club Fellow, New York City," February 26, 1913, clipping Bryant Library.

81. Ellin Mackay Berlin, *Silver Platter*, 432, "Sailing With Three Children, Mackay Didn't tell Wife," June 25, 1913, clipping Bryant Library; "Detectives Guard Mackay's Sailing," [June 1913] clipping Bryant Library.

82. "Mackays Obtain Divorce in Paris" *New York Times,* Feb. 19, 1914, 1–2.

83. Mary Ellin Barrett, *Irving Berlin: A Daughter's Memoir* (New York: Limelight Editions, 1996), 38.

84. "And Now They're Married," clipping c. November 28, 1914, clipping, Bryant Library.

85. *New York Times,* Feb. 19, 1914, 1, 2.

86. "Mrs. C. H. Mackay Silent." *New York Times,* Feb. 20, 1914, 1.

87. "And Now They're Married," c. November 28, 1914, clipping, Bryant Library.

88. C. F. Bertelli, "Dr. Blake, Free 24 Hours, Weds Mrs. Mackay," *New York America,* [c. Nov. 28, 1914], clipping, Bryant Library.

89. "And Now They're Married," c. November 28, 1914, clipping, Bryant Library.

90. C. F. Bertelli, "Dr. Blake, Free 24 Hours, Weds Mrs. Mackay," *New York America,* c. Nov. 28, 1914, clipping, Bryant Library.

8. CLARENCE'S TRIUMPH AND DEFEAT

1. "And Now They're Married," c. November 28, 1914, clipping, Bryant Library.

2. Marius DeZayas, "Passing Portraits," *Puck,* February 5, 1918, 6.

3. Mary Ellin Barrett, *Irving Berlin, A Daughter's Memoir* (New York: Limelight Editions, 1996), 26–27.

4. "Clarence H. Mackay Host," c. 1918, clipping, Bryant Library.

5. Donaldson, "Harbor Hill, May 1962," 20, 4.

6. Cleveland Amory, *Who Killed Society?* (New York: Harper, 1960), 132.

7. Typescript of newspaper, nd (September 7, 1924) Bryant Library.

8. "Clarence H. Mackay Is Host to 75 at Dinner for the Prince of Wales," *New York World,* September 7, 1924; also "Dinner and Reception for . . ." *New York Times,* September 7, 1924, 19.

9. Berlin, *Silver Platter,* 437.

10. Edward, the Duke of Windsor, *A King's Story* (New York: G. P. Putnam's Sons, 1951), 200.

11. "Air Hero Lionized at Social Function," *New York Times,* June 14, 1927, 1; see also, "Son's Glory Bring Homage to Mother, *New York Times,* June 14, 1927, 1, 12.

12. Berlin, *Silver Platter,* 439.

13. *New York Times,* February 3, 1929, II, 6.

14. Barrett, *Irving Berlin,* 21.

15. Treatments of Berlin and Ellin are in Edward Jablonski, *Irving Berlin: American Troubadour* (New York: Henry Holt, 1999); Laurence Bergreen, *As Thousands Cheer: The Life of Irving Berlin* (New York: Viking, 1990), which contains numerous errors; and Barrett, *Irving Berlin.*

16. Quoted in Jablonski, *Irving Berlin,* 108.

17. Ellin Mackay, "Why We Go to Cabarets—A Post Debutante Explains," *New Yorker,* 1 (November 28, 1925), 7–8; "Ellin Mackay Calls Cabarets a Refuge," *New York Times,* November 26, 1925, 1; "Miss Mackay looks to Writing Career" *New York Times,* November 27, 1925, 3. James Thurber, "The Years with Ross," *Atlantic Monthly,* Jan. 1958, 66–67.

18. Ellin Mackay, "The Declining Function: A Post-Debutante Rejoices," *New Yorker,* December 12, 1925, 15–16; "Miss Mackay Tells How Society Plays, *New York Times,* December 11, 1925, 3.

19. Jablonski, *Irving Berlin,* 140; "Reunion of Mackays Denied at his

20. Coe, *The Telegraph,* 94.

21. Bergreen, *As Thousands Cheer,* 237.

22. Cholly Knickerbocker, "Tragedies of Society, Katherine Mackay

23. Blake Sacrificed all in her Forlorn Search for Love," c. 1939 clipping Bryant Library; Doris Fleeson, "Mackay at Bier Forgives Estranged Wife," April 23, 1930, clipping Bryant Library; "Mrs. K. Duer Blake dies of Pneumonia," *New York Times,* April 20, 1930, 25. Also, *New York Times* April 22, 1930, 29.

24. Cholly Knickerbocker, "Tragedies of Society, Katherine Mackay Blake Sacrificed all in her Forlorn Search for Love," c. 1939, clipping, Bryant Library.

25. Ibid.

26. "Clarence H. Mackay and Anna Case Wed," *New York Times,* July 19, 1931, 1, 3; and clippings, c. July 19, 1931, Bryant Library.

27. Grace Chapman Laundis interview, January 2, 2005.

28. "Postal Down," Business and Finance, *Time,* nd [c. 1936], Bryant Library.

29. "Fine Display of Rare Armor Held at Metropolitan," *Art News* 29 (august 15, 1931), 3–4. Letter Clarence Mackay to Stephen Granscay, July 8, 1930; and Grancsay to Mackay, February 19, 1931, Metropolitan Museum of Art, Arms and Armor Collection archives.

30. *Bulletin of the Metropolitan Museum of Art,* 28 (March 1933), 48–62. "Metropolitan Acquires Masterpieces from the Mackay Collection," *Art Digest* 7 (April 1, 1933), 12–13.

31. "Clarence Mackay Dies at Home Here After Long Illness," *New York Times,* November 13, 1938, 1, 46.

32. "Mackay to Reopen Country Mansion, *New York Times,* May 15, 1935.

33. Olin Downes, "Mackay Memorial Features Concert," *New York Times,* Nov. 17, 1938, 28.

34. "Dark Mansions for Sale: The Mackay Estate at Roslyn," *New York World Telegram,* December 27, 1939, 21; "Mackay's Estate is Put on Market," *New York Times,* March 26, 1939, sec. 12, 1.

35. Thomas C. Linn, "Rare Armor Sold by Mackay Estate," *New York Times,* April 8, 1940, 12.

36. "Famous Clarence Mackay Collection to be Dispersed in New York," *Art Digest* 7 (May 15, 1939), 7.

37. "Mackay Estate to Auction Art," *New York Times,* August 27, 1939, 2.

38. "Mackay Art in Sale," *Art Digest* 15 (May 1, 1941), 18; "Museum over the Counter: Mackay Collection Joins Sale . . ." *Newsweek,* 17 (May 12, 1941), 17.

39. "Mackay Fence to Aid War," *New York Times,* August 21, 1942, 16.

40. Madeline Ryttenberg, "Mackays-Money, Mansion, Misery," clipping. C. 1946, Bryant Library.

41. "Demolition Crew Beats Vandals In Wrecking Mackay Chateau," clipping, Bryant Library. "Once Proud Homes now Island Ghosts," *New York Times,* February 23, 1952.

42. Nancy Randolph, "Mackay's 'Heartbreak House' Follows '90s into Oblivion." Clipping, Bryant Library.

43. "Fire Razes Famous Court Tennis Building" *New York Times,* January 1, 1949, 16.

44. Robert L. Zion and Beatrice L. Zion, "How our Half Lives: A Stanford White Gatehouse is Restored and Redesigned," *Landscape Architecture* 44 (April 1954), 127–131.

Index

✺ ✺